Internal Combustion

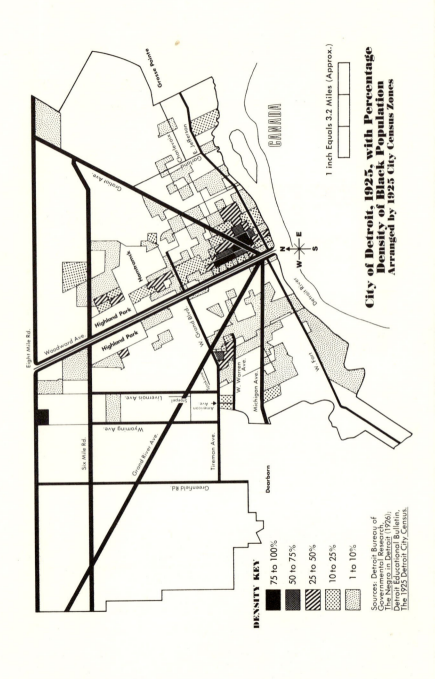

**City of Detroit, 1925, with Percentage
Density of Black Population
Arranged by 1925 City Census Zones**

1 inch Equals 3.2 Miles (Approx.)

DENSITY KEY

- 75 to 100%
- 50 to 75%
- 25 to 50%
- 10 to 25%
- 1 to 10%

Sources: Detroit Bureau of
Governmental Research,
The Negro in Detroit (1926);
Detroit Educational Bulletin,
The 1925 Detroit City Census.

David Allan Levine

Internal Combustion

The races in Detroit 1915–1926

Contributions in Afro-American and African Studies, Number 24

GREENWOOD PRESS
WESTPORT, CONNECTICUT ● LONDON, ENGLAND

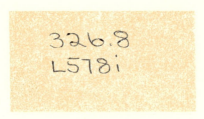

Library of Congress Cataloging in Publication Data

Levine, David Allan.
    Internal combustion.

    (Contributions in Afro-American and African studies ; no. 24)
    Includes bibliographical references and index.
        1. Detroit—Riot, 1925. 2. Detroit—Race question. 3. Afro-Americans—
Michigan—Detroit. I. Title. II. Series.
    F574.D4L45   977.4'34'04   75-35347
    ISBN:08371-8588-2

Library of Congress Catalog Card Number: 75-35347
ISBN:0-8371-8588-2

First published in 1976

Greenwood Press, a division of Williamhouse-Regency Inc.
51 Riverside Avenue, Westport, Connecticut 06880

Printed in the United States of America

To the Memory of My Father

contents

acknowledgments

There are several people for whose aid, encouragement, and advice I am more grateful than I can say. They are Harald Bakken, Stanley Elkins, Rosalyn Foster, and Forrest McDonald. My principal debt is to the late Ray Ginger, who taught me that for a scholar to aspire to competence he must begin by being skeptical.

list of abbreviations

For convenience and brevity, the following abbreviations for manuscript collections and depositories have been used in the notes:

BHC	Burton Historical Collection of the Detroit Public Library
DPL	Detroit Public Library
FA	Ford Archives
LC	Library of Congress
MHC	Michigan Historical Collections, The University of Michigan

chapter
ONE

Presuppositions

I

On September 8, 1925, a black doctor named Ossian Sweet and his family and some friends, armed with ten weapons and 400 rounds of ammunition, moved into a house in a white, working-class neighborhood on Detroit's east side. The summer had been a violent one in Detroit. For a number of years the city had been experiencing a serious housing shortage, with tensions of overcrowding and high rents compounded by a grim racial situation. By 1925 Detroit's black population had grown to 80,000 from some 7000 ten years before. Ghetto neighborhoods were full to bursting, and blacks were actively seeking housing over a wider and wider area, thus establishing open competition between the races for available living space. During the summer, whites in various parts of the city had successfully used the threat of violence to keep blacks from moving in. Now, with the news that the Sweet family was occupying the house at 2905 Garland, the effort at eviction would be made again; and the neighborhood organized for the purpose. On the evening of September 9, 1925, a black man from within the house shot and killed a white man, one of a crowd, standing outside.

The Sweets were arrested and charged with first-degree murder. What happened after that brought Detroit and its racial problems into national prominence. The National Association for the Advancement of Colored People, realizing that a significant legal question—does the black man have the white man's right to defend his home?—was here to be resolved, sought the best legal counsel it could find for the Sweets and hired the famous criminal lawyer Clarence Darrow to head the defense.

A Detroit racial incident involving white crowds and blacks with guns and culminating in killing was likely to attract some national interest in the autumn of 1925, even without Darrow. Like Detroit, every major northern city had experienced a great increase in its black population in the years around the First World War and into the 1920s, as blacks in large numbers left the rural south and sought, like white foreigners before them, the promise of a new world. Racial tension thus character-ized many places, with only the extent and detail differing with the locale. Also, for years there had been clearly discernible a new militance among black men—expressed, for example, in episodes of reciprocal racial violence in Chicago and Washington, D.C.; by the literature of the Harlem Renaissance, proclaiming the emergence of a "New Negro"; and in the regalia and separatist ideology of the Marcus Garvey "Back to Africa" movement. So, many cities shared Detroit's apprehensions and might have paused to pay attention to the outcome of the Sweet case tried by local people. But Darrow's presence guaranteed limelight. Could the man who just that summer had posed science against funda-mentalism in Dayton, Tennessee, and who several years before had rationalized the murder of Robert Franks in Chicago and saved Loeb and Leopold from execution, now also justify what the Sweets had done in Detroit?

What Darrow would bring to Detroit was his gift for biography, his appreciation for the intimate detail that makes a place special, and his sense of force and process that makes it representative of something larger. This dual perspective is also what the historian must bring to the study of local history, the responsibility to explain how Detroit, in this instance, is at once distinctive and yet a model for transformations occurring at the time throughout urban America. It is an inquiry which runs all through the present study.

For example, a number of cities wanted to be the locus of the new automobile industry and had what would seem to have been the eco-nomic prerequisites: experience in manufacturing carriages and marine engines; a skilled, largely nonunionized labor pool; ready capital; and the like. Yet Detroit won the prize almost completely, probably because men with enormous capability happened to live there.

Many cities were developing their economic bases and attracting, as a consequence, larger and larger populations. A major component of this population increase was foreign immigration, so that many cities felt it necessary to do Americanization work to fit foreigners to the new way of life they would find here.[1] Detroit not only participated in the Americanization movement, it was in its vanguard.

Many northern cities experienced a great influx of blacks from the South as part of their general population increase. No major city, however, took in more blacks (as a percentage of its total population) faster than did Detroit.

Many cities experienced housing shortages, and probably no large city has ever been totally successful in housing all of its workers satisfactorily at a given time during its growth spurt. What distinguishes Detroit here was the magnitude of the shortage and the potential for violence, especially given the racial dimension. Homebuilding was, in most instances, the responsibility of the city's real-estate speculators and developers, who were late in recognizing the market need and then could not satisfy it quickly enough.

The crucial facts of Detroit history in these years were the economic growth and shift of population to the city because of great migrations originating elsewhere. Prior to these events Detroit was not very important. An old city by American standards, founded in 1701 as a post to protect and encourage the French fur trade, it did not come into its modernity until the twentieth century and the development of the automobile industry. As a result of this time lag between inception and modern function—a lag much greater than Chicago's, or Kansas City's, or Minneapolis-St. Paul's—Detroit escaped some classic problems but also guaranteed itself a number of others.

For one thing, because Detroit was small for so long, in the memory of the people who grew up there and became its leaders in the first part of the twentieth century, the city was always comprehensible in size. Nothing in their experience had ever suggested that civic problems could be insoluble. New York and Philadelphia had been unwieldy for as long as anyone could remember. But in 1900, when Detroit contained only about 285,000 people, compared to Chicago's 1.7 million, a Detroiter could start walking from the river downtown and be at the northern fringe of settlement in an hour, or at the eastern or western edges in a little more. Consequently the men and women who would set and execute public policy after 1900 were confident that situations could be confronted and problems solved by interested citizens possessing business sense and firm moral principals. Their watchword was "efficiency." As a personal attribute it carried a predisposition to hard work and discipline. In business it meant maximum output through controlled, rational behavior. Logically extended to society it provided a valid motive for progressive reorganization and implementation of programs for social uplift.[2]

Most Americans in these years would have agreed that efficiency in human affairs constituted a total, unambiguous, incontrovertible good. Detroit progressives were not unusual in sharing this set of beliefs. They are special because they acted on them to the point of caricature. There was scarcely an aspect of social organization for profit, uplift, and control practiced in any large city that the leadership class in Detroit did not either pioneer or soon join. There were programs for immigrant education and transformation through the Americanization Committee of the Detroit Board of Commerce and the Ford Motor Company English School. There was black education under the auspices of the Urban League and, to a lesser extent in terms of effectiveness and scope, the local branch of the NAACP. There was prohibition of alcoholic beverages, approved by state ballot in 1916 with Detroit progressives prominent in the fight, the city thus becoming the first city of nearly a million to be voted dry. There was delimiting of factory jobs along racial lines so that black aspiration, promoted in other agencies, would not carry so far as to antagonize white workers and thereby threaten the efficient and harmonious running of the plant. There was residential restriction, in which Detroit real-estate men, builders, and state judicial opinion sought a distinct physical separation of the races, since proximity would increase the likelihood of racial conflict, a calamitous disharmony.

Also for the sake of efficiency Detroit progressives changed the structure of city politics. The relative ease with which this was accomplished is again a function of timing. Because Detroit had little economic importance until after 1900, it had not evolved the tough tradition of boss-feudal-reward to loyalty politics that characterized most burgeoning American cities in the last third of the nineteenth century. The ward and precinct apparatus was there in Detroit, to be sure, and

it occasionally provided the locus for some interesting political conflict,[3] but on balance it lacked the sinew that came, as in other places,
from decades of skilled men playing games for high stakes. So when
progressive forces decided that political efficiency required replacing
Detroit's ward structure with a nine-man common council elected at
large, the transformation was effected rather easily by the new city
charter of 1918. Thus, for Detroit, progressivism in the political sphere
required little energy—certainly nothing like the decade-long battles
against even single ward bosses that characterized urban politics elsewhere—and the success of charter revision reinforced the faith of
Detroit leaders in their ability to confront and solve civic problems.

Because Detroit progressives did not have to expend energy fighting
a corrupt and powerful municipal government, they could instead con-
centrate their attention on various forms of "business progressivism,"
providing as clear an example as anywhere of what was to become a
persistent theme in America's pre-World War progressive movement—the
striving for efficiency through organization in the interest of both profit
and social control. But in destroying the ward and precinct apparatus
Detroit's progressive leaders may have dealt the cause of social harmony
a serious blow. The classic function of the urban political machine was
to provide an organizational framework for co-opting potential dissidents and defusing possibly violent confrontations through the dispensation of gratuities furnished usually by business itself. The political
machines, then, were totally conservative, recognizing that if people
could not be made happy then at least they could be assuaged. Bosses
would remain in power so long as they remembered the needs of the
neighborhoods and distributed a reasonable fraction of what they stole.
By eliminating even a weak ward and precinct machine in Detroit the
city's progressives effectively removed any possible calming function it
might have had. The coincidence of events—the city government being
restructured under a new charter just as the black migration was gathering force and Detroit was beginning to feel its effect—leads one to wonder what the course of local race relations might have been had the
original political machinery remained.

In Detroit, to put this speculation in more concrete form, there was
no institutional apparatus to produce a career like that of Oscar De
Priest's. Born in Alabama shortly after the Civil War to ex-slave parents,

De Priest migrated to Chicago in 1889 and worked as a house painter. With little more than an elementary school education he became involved in real estate and politics and was Chicago's first black alderman. An important part of the Thompson political machine, he was responsible for doling out appointments by the bushel to black payrollers. In 1928 he was elected to the United States House of Representatives, the first black man there since Reconstruction, and would serve three terms.[4]

Leaving aside the standard black-history question of whether Oscar De Priest was a mere party hack or a courageous fighter against racial bias, or both, what is important here is that he had a constituency for which he could provide services, as well as being himself a visible, and audible, "race man" who achieved success within an established institutional framework. In Detroit there was no such political outlet for a black man, or for very many white men who did not subscribe to the progressive ethic; and the new nine-man common council elected at large was generally effective in shutting out such people for decades.

This book, then, is a study of men and institutions and of events which followed from their interaction. The "city" is those who determined public policy and who implemented it and who went along because the policy somehow served their own purposes. "City" embraces those who sat on the Americanization Committee of the Board of Commerce and the recent immigrants who went to the committee night schools because they appreciated the opportunity or because they were fearful of losing their jobs if they did not; it is the Employers' Association and the workers in the factories; it is the Urban League and the blacks who came to it for help. The city's "leaders" are those who exercised "power," "influence," "control," synonymous terms indicating a capability to affect other people, with some predictable effect on the future pattern of events. "Progress" was the ideal moving the city, part of the ethic of the time that efficiency and growth are good and are therefore to be pursued actively.

But was anyone really in control? How ironic it would be if Detroit, which was so well organized, according to the precepts of the day, in its factory life, its social programs, its political forms, had become too highly structured. Can a place be so well machined and hard-driven that events come to take on a momentum of their own and encounter no safeguards to slow their rush because all of the inefficiencies have been removed? Is it possible that men of different race, who in the factories would be pitted against each other for the sake of competition and increased output, might eventually find themselves confronting one another in the street with no institutions left to temper their tendencies toward racial violence?

This theme of forces out of control is hardly a new one. Many American historians, to say nothing of an important segment of American letters, have dwelled on the theme of frenzy, its achievement, and its cost. Scott Fitzgerald's receding green light—perpetually sought after, never attainable—has become a permanent image in twentieth-century American literature. Theodore Dreiser saw the world as a series of slides, some carrying upward, some down, with nothing finally except happenstance dictating whether one rose or fell.

The great historian Henry Adams also, as the world turned into the twentieth century, was concerned more and more with symbols and forces and the sorts of symbols that create fields of force to make history. He was asking the questions: What are the symbols of a period which give rise to a field of force? What are the dead symbols? It was an old insight he was playing with, that symbols are potent historical forces having the power to move men. And he decided that the great symbol of the past, which had the power to build the cathedrals, was the Virgin, and the symbol of the present, the representation of modern technology, was the generator. Steel and electricity could not build the cathedral at Chartres; and piety could not build modern technology. And that was the change he saw in the world.[5]

What this story of Detroit provides, then, is an example of this change and a demonstration of how one city tried to organize and direct its members in answering the call of progress. I have tried as best I can to flesh out the characters, examine their motives, and explore the forces under which they were operating, consistent with the historical record. Sometimes the evidence is impressionistic; mostly it is hard data. If the reader chooses to look at the presentation as a case study of one city's experience in the "progressive era," hopefully there will be some evidence to sustain or even challenge his prior assumptions. Whether or not the story works on any other level of abstraction I cannot be sure, but it does seem to me that Fitzgerald's green light is very much in evidence; though, as he would have us ponder, one wonders whether the light is before men, drawing them, or somewhere in the past, pushing.

II

There came to Detroit in the early years of the present century a great change in the pace of living. It came quietly at first, as it had in England in the 1760s and in Germany some years after that. But soon the quickened tempo, handmaiden of industrialization, was generally apparent; and some reveled in its complexity, others romanticized the past, and still others wondered quietly about the future.

The problems Detroit faced were no less complex for their having been posed elsewhere decades and even centuries earlier. How to organize control of resources and production? How to market efficiently and profitably? How to oversee the new army of workers? There had always been leaders in Detroit to tilt at its problems, gentlemen and ladies, the refined offspring of past commercial successes. But now in the new world, with men and their families spilling daily into the industrial city, the numbers to be led were even greater and the need for control seemingly more compelling than anything the fathers might have imagined. For with the onset of Detroit's modernity there had arisen a whole new set of priorities, turning first on the presumption that harmony in human affairs derives from competition, which produces effort and progress; and focusing ultimately on the belief that because the machine creates wealth, and wealth is good, all effort must be to maximize the efficiency of the machine. So, in keeping with the new credo, progressive leaders fashioned constructs of social control to bend and direct men's lives to the good of the machine, not realizing that in their own acceptance of the ultimate priority they too were being bent and directed.

There was in Detroit a complicating aspect to the already dizzying rush of industrial society. At the onset of the industrial revolutions in England and Germany, the workers who ran the machines were by background and disposition more similar than dissimilar. But in Detroit, transcending the superimposed unity of class, there was the visceral division by race. Blacks and whites were in the city and in the factories. They competed for jobs; they competed for housing. In this competition, with its intense and sometimes visible hatreds, there was the ultimate challenge to those who would devise means of social control: how to subdue the passions, channel the energies, and ultimately increase the power of the machine?

The duty of management was clear. Men no less than pistons had to be fit to close tolerance. What we need, said Henry Ford, is a new managerial competence, "artists in industrial relationship . . . masters in industrial method. . . . We want those who can mould the political, social, industrial, and moral mass into a sound and shapely whole."[6] Because of their orientation, business leaders looked instinctively to the price tags. Labor bore a variable cost. The greater your product, the more labor you needed. The more of it available, the less you had to pay. Simple economics and a commitment to output now pushed hazier considerations, such as payment to social overhead in the form of housing for the work force, aside. A little friction was a good thing, the businessmen thought. It provided worker incentive. But the friction between races over limited available housing would eventually grow to white heat, and along the way the leaders would see that that conflict carried its price tag too, and so did accumulated neglect.

All of that, though, was hidden in the future. In 1915 and thereabouts the automobile men were busy fashioning the performance capability of their city, and from the effort emerged a place which perfectly mirrored the energy of their youth. The physical accomplishment of the ethic was staggering. There is not an index available that does not show quantum leaps almost yearly, whether it be savings deposits, bank deposits, bank clearings, or tax receipts.[7] For example, consider the increase in aggregate valuation of Detroit's taxable property:[8]

Year	Property value
1900	$ 224,371,550
1910	377,335,980
1912	456,816,100
1916	736,552,960
1920	1,699,149,580
1923	2,109,989,410
1926	$3,160,412,150

The city was also growing in sheer physical size: 29 square miles in 1905, 47 in 1915, 85 by 1922, and 119 by 1925.[9]

This was all a reflection of the industrial expansion. By 1925 greater Detroit had 3000 major manufacturing plants, 37 automobile plants, and 250 automobile accessory plants. It boasted the world's largest automobile factory, gasoline motor plant, foundry, tractor plant, automobile wheel factory, automobile spring factory, automobile lamp factory, automobile body hardware factory, automobile windshield plant, adding machine factory, pin factory, coin machine factory, vacuum cleaner factory, seed house, sheet copper and brass rolling mill, stove works, electric iron factory, cigar factory, and insulated wire plant.[10] The value of the city's total manufactured product grew from $764,506,282 in 1921 to $1,438,247,380 in 1923 to $1,599,340,383 in 1925 to $1,736,933,236 in 1927, with the automobile industry accounting for 44.4 percent of the whole in 1921, and for 56.4 percent in 1927.[11] An even more vivid indication of productive capability was the output of the entire Detroit-Wayne County industrial area, which showed a product of $569,519,227 in 1914, growing to $1,803,728,219 in 1919, and increasing to an estimated $2.5 billion in 1926.[12] By these figures the Detroit area's total manufactured output exceeded that of Cleveland, Buffalo, and Toledo combined.[13]

But the most crucial of all the staggering changes, the one which fed and was itself fed by the economic growth, was the population increase. At the turn of the century there had been 285,704 people in Detroit. Ten years later there were 465,766. Ten years after that the population had doubled, to 993,678. By the mid-1920s Detroit was the fastest growing metropolitan area in the country and the fourth largest city in the United States. In 1930 it would have 1,568,662 people.[14]

Immigrants from abroad poured in—91,299 in the century's first decade, 68,450 from 1911 to 1914. The flow subsided to 26,895 from 1915 to 1919 because of restrictions during the war years, but surged again to 85,742 between 1920 and 1924.[15] Detroit was becoming a city of newcomers. From decade to decade the percentage of its Michigan-born population dropped. Strange faces and dark faces were everywhere. In 1920, 90 percent of the city's blacks had not been born in Michigan.[16]

It was a young, working-age city. The people who were coming into Detroit, whether from overseas or from elsewhere in the United States, came to work. In 1920, when the percentage of the total United States population between the ages of 25 and 44 was 29.6 percent, nearly 40 percent of Detroit's population and more than 50 percent of Detroit's black population was of that age.[17]

Detroit was being given a subsidy whose economic value is beyond calculation. People who had been fed, doctored, and educated elsewhere (albeit meagerly) were coming to give Detroit the benefit of that investment. They had cost Detroit nothing. It was a priceless gift, a fact which would often be overlooked or ignored by the recipient.

Many other places worshipping Mammon on a smaller scale stood in awe of this growth. Why? they asked. Why was Detroit the one blessed with the Magic Motor? The customary response was that Detroit was already an important center for the manufacture of carriages, wagons, bicycles, and marine engines, and that it had available a pool of largely nonunionized skilled and semiskilled mechanics. But those circumstances applied to Buffalo, Cleveland, and Toledo as well, cities which also pioneered in the manufacture of automobiles. And Detroit was not unique in other economic and geographic inducements it could offer. Available capital, room to grow, and easy access to established transportation routes were characteristic of many cities at the time. So no one could know for sure why Detroit became the ultimate focal point of the motor industry, but many suspected. What distinguished the city was probably the chance role of personalities. Its automobile men were giants.

There was Henry Ford, who in the 1890s was one of many men building "home-made" cars. Unhappy as a manager of the Detroit Automobile Company (forerunner of the Cadillac Motor Car Company), Ford organized his own concern in 1901 and reorganized it in 1903. He was a perfectionist, always tinkering with the design of his cars and reluctant to deliver any car to a customer until he thought it was just right. Art, he felt, should antecede commerce. But shrewder business heads prevailed, and the company began to make money. In 1909 production was confined almost exclusively to the black Model T—standardizing the consumer, some would say—and the company sold over 18,000 cars in the first year of its new policy.

When a patent difficulty was cleared in 1911 production soared. Sales rose from 78,440 in 1911/12 to 168,304 in 1912/13 to 248,307 in 1913/14; and from that to 730,041 in 1916/17. With the assembly-line technique perfected, the time needed to produce an automobile dropped from ten minutes to five minutes to two minutes, and the money rolled in. A $13.5 million profit in 1912 became more than $27 million in 1913, and more than $57 million in 1916. Even John D. Rockefeller was astonished. The Ford Motor Company, begun in 1903 with a capitalization of $150,000 and cash reserves of only $28,000, would in less than twenty years achieve nearly $3 billion in total sales and net profits in excess of $430 million.[18] Henry Ford became an object of near-worship. Achievement and ideal merged in this one hallowed figure. He had risen in the classic way, from modest origins and rural virtue, and he would live to see the power of his machine inalterably transform the garden of his childhood.

There were others. John and Horace Dodge manufactured engines for Ford and were themselves leading minority shareholders in the Ford Motor Company, having contributed $7000 in materials plus a $3000 note in exchange for 100 shares in 1903. Prosperous, but uneasy at supplying hardware for just one customer under a contract which could be terminated on a year's notice, the brothers began manufacturing their own automobiles in 1914. Within four years the Dodge Brothers Manufacturing Company was the fourth largest automobile producer in the country. When the corporation was sold by their widows to a New York banking house in 1925, it brought $166 million.[19]

And there was James Couzens. Born in Chatham, Ontario—his English father settled there because he did not have enough money to go the fifty extra miles to his original destination, Detroit—Couzens set off for Detroit in 1890, when he was not yet eighteen. (A trip there some months earlier had been abortive.) He got a job as a car checker for the Michigan Central railroad, with wages of $40 a month, working twelve hours a day, seven days a week. The weather was sometimes so cold that the tacks he carried in his mouth for putting labels on the cars froze to his tongue. But Couzens was delighted. He felt he was "running the railroad," and only when he had that feeling was he ever happy.

In the fall of 1895 Couzens went to work for coal dealer Alexander Malcomson as an assistant bookkeeper and clerk for $75 a month. This move was significant because it was through Malcomson, an early investor in Ford automobiles, that Couzens met Ford. The two men impressed each other immediately. Couzens knew next to nothing about automobiles. Once when Malcomson took him for a ride in his car and explained that by turning a knob on the dashboard he was "changing the mixture," Couzens, unaware of the existence let alone function of the carburetor, thought that he was mixing water with the gasoline. But the Ford Motor Company did not need another automotive genius. It needed a shrewd business mentality, and this Couzens provided.

It would be difficult to exaggerate his importance to the company. As business manager it was Couzens' responsibility to handle the great sums of money and to push the sales force. He saw to it that the company's surplus was invested properly. And he initiated a financial plan which probably had no equal then in the business world. Ford monies would be deposited in banks for the specific purpose of being loaned to Ford dealers for buying more Ford cars. The banks charged the dealers regular rates of interest and shared the earnings with the Ford Motor Company. Eventually Couzens would set up a Ford banking subsidiary, and the company would have to share the profits with no one. To Couzens also belongs the credit for initiating the $5-a-day minimum wage in 1914, which drew thousands of people to Detroit.

He was not an easy man to work for. He believed it was impossible to be both a good fellow and good businessman. "I am one of those who hold that it is not worthwhile to attempt to be popular. I should prefer to be a hard taskmaster—but a fair one," he said. "A floor walker in a big department store gets twenty-five or fifty dollars a week because he knows how to be pleasant and shake hands with the trade. But the man in the back room, who buys the goods and runs the business, gets $50,000 to $100,000 a year because *he* knows how *to run* the business."[20] Couzens ran the business, and that was the way Ford wanted it. If anyone came to Henry Ford about a business matter he would say simply, "See Mr. Couzens." Board meetings became perfunctory. "I would not work for a company," Couzens later stated, "where the board did much interfering with actions or policies." He had in mind the Dodge brothers and even Henry Ford. The fact is, if the Ford Motor Company then had a boss, the boss was Couzens.

In 1915, the year the millionth Model T rolled off the assembly line in the Highland Park plant, Couzens left Ford. The news could have been no more shocking to men in Detroit if Henry Ford himself had quit. His leaving came from the inevitable conflict of two strong personalities. By then Couzens had more money than he would ever need. With his original investment and the purchase of Ford stock as others sold, he owned more shares in the company than anyone except Henry Ford. Also he had invested his stock dividends and salary wisely in other ventures. The young man who worked for a coal company in 1903 was now, twelve years later at the age of 43, worth upwards of $40 million. He had built an automobile empire so strong it would withstand even the future mismanagement of Henry Ford himself.[21]

Couzens and Ford demonstrate on a grand scale the possibilities for success in Detroit these years. Businessmen were organizing their operations, making decisions, stepping up output, and making money, some accumulating great wealth and power. This success, because it seemed to derive from talent and method rather than from luck, could only reaffirm progressive men's confidence that they could quickly resolve whatever problems the city's future held.

Evidence to the contrary, however, was going to manifest itself. The mistake in 1915 was in devoting too much attention to plant expansion and high yield return, too little to social overhead, housing. In 1915, before the population increase took on the appearance of a flood, some redirection of priorities might have occurred had a Ford or Couzens called attention to the great need for providing living space for the arriving workers. But no one with their kind of authority knew, and real-estate speculators and developers, attuned only to that day's market, lacked the foresight to commence extraordinary activity on their own.

Some years later, when the housing shortage had become terribly apparent to everyone, both Couzens and Ford addressed themselves to the problem, but in ways that demonstrate more futility than accomplishment. In 1922, Couzens as mayor of Detroit, an office he held on his way to becoming United States senator, suggested that the city of Detroit float a $5 million issue of five-year bonds to build housing for workers. It is obvious, he said, that private initiative and capital are unable to cope with the current situation, so the public sector must step in. The idea was quickly dropped, however, when lawyers convinced him the city could not go into the home-loan business without far-reaching changes in the state constitution.[22]

Henry Ford never was much concerned with worker housing problems. Even after being informed by one of his executive staff in 1916 of increased pressures in the local housing market, he continued to believe that the $5 day, initiated two years before, would enable Ford workers to buy or rent adequate living space without difficulty.[23] When rising costs and congestion in Detroit destroyed this assumption completely, Ford authorized a small experiment. In 1919 Ford Motor Company formed the Dearborn Realty and Construction Company, with Henry Ford's wife and son sitting on the board of directors and his personal secretary in charge. On some land purchased in 1919 in southwest Dearborn, near the beginnings of what was to be the huge Rouge complex, the realty company built about 250 homes from 1919 to 1920. The houses were mostly frame with brick or shingle veneer, three to four bedrooms, priced originally at $8225 to $10,000. At first, Dearborn Realty asked for a down payment of one-half the purchase price, but after the 1921 depression it cut the down payment to one-quarter, then to one-tenth. Prices also were reduced to a range of $6900 to $8500. The company financed the mortgages.

In its first two years Dearborn Realty lost nearly $6000. Eventually it yielded a small profit, but probably no more than 2 percent over a twenty-year period. The parent company and Henry Ford himself were never very enthusiastic about the program, and did nothing to encourage other automobile companies to try the same. Nor would Ford's rate of return from the project be any incentive. While the houses were sturdily built, and attractive to Ford Motor Company employees and others for decades, 250 homes sold and resold in a field in West Dearborn would not have much effect on Detroit's post-World War housing shortage.[24]

But in 1914-15 the attention of Detroit businessmen was on the performance capability of the city and area economy. Lacking not energy nor commitment but vision, they were concerned with the present; and the immediate problem was the threat of foreign immigration to the harmony of the economic machine.

III

The winter of 1913/14 was one of economic depression in the United States. The Princeton professor in the White House called the dislocation "psychological" in origin, but the reality of its effect was grim. Cities throughout the country counted their thousands and tens of thousands of unemployed. In Detroit the automobile factories remained prosperous, but other industries suffered; and that city, like all the others, had an acute poverty problem. Into this dark winter, on the fifth of January 1914, stepped Henry Ford with news that at the time seemed almost beyond belief. The Ford Motor Company had decided to allocate $10 million a year to pay its employees a $5-a-day minimum wage, the highest ever in American history. "This is neither charity nor wages," Ford would tell reporters; it was "profit sharing and efficiency engineering."[25]

To the thousands listening across the country it was salvation. Here was a company with more money than it wanted; a company about to change from two shifts of nine hours to three of eight so it could run all day and all night; a company that needed four thousand or five thousand new men immediately, at higher and higher wages. So the jobless streamed to Highland Park. The announcement had been published Monday afternoon. By two o'clock Tuesday morning men began gathering in front of the Ford employment office. Dawn came, and the streets were packed solid—10,000 men. The company put up a "No Hiring" sign, and this seemed to send many home. But the respite was temporary. Wednesday, despite public notices that no one would be hired, another throng gathered. By this time it included many men from other cities and from other automobile plants. The Ford company announced it would not consider hiring men who formed crowds. Thursday, the job-seekers, trying not to form a crowd, milled loosely around the streets. Ford agents moved among them and surreptitiously handed slips to a number for admission to the employment office. The word was soon out. Hiring had begun. On Friday 15,000 men appeared.

Detroit was becoming frightened at this restless mob that the Ford company had created by its new wage policy. Police had been struggling to maintain order since the first day. City officials were learning that many of the arriving job-seekers were without money and could not afford the return trip home. Newspapers quickly published articles saying that there were no jobs in the Detroit area and asking the unemployed of other places to stay away.

On Saturday signs appeared on the factory announcing in several languages that all hiring had ceased. This and the bitter cold seemed to keep the crowd down—to 4,000—and city and company officials were hopeful that the crisis was over. Their optimism was ill-founded. Monday morning was colder still, but long before dawn men came to gather and wait in the streets around the factory. By seven-thirty there were 10,000 men, and they were impatient and angry. The sight of employees wearing Ford badges arriving for work, pushing through the crowd toward the jobs in the factory, was too much. Accumulated frustration broke into violence, and the crowd surged against the gates, hundreds pushing past the helpless guards onto the plant grounds. More police arrived, but they were unable to restore order. The mob pinned them and the factory guards against the wall, prevented workers from entering, and threatened to break down the doors. A fire hose was dragged out and waved at the mob, but the crowd was unawed. Then someone yelled to turn on the hose, and the water poured full force into the front ranks of the men. The temperature was nine degrees above zero. The disturbance was ended. The crowd broke and ran. But many, out of the range of the hose, stopped to throw stones through the factory windows. Many more ran through the lunch stands in the neighborhood and left them wrecked and empty.[26]

The riot need not have occurred. Had Ford and Couzens simply hired the men they required, they might then have told the world of a plan already in effect. Or they might have made it clear at the outset that no men would be hired for a month until all written applications— there had been 14,000 received the first week while the mob surged at the gates[27]—had been studied. But such restraint was not the style of the men at Ford.

They announced their plan in grandiloquent terms: "The sole and simple aim of the entire scheme is to better the financial and moral standing of each employe and those of his household; to instill men with courage and a desire for health, happiness and prosperity."[28] But the $5, eight-hour day also made perfect sense from a business standpoint. When a company demands docility, as did all the automobile companies, it might get it but at a price. Some years Ford Motor Company's labor turnover rate was nearly 400 percent.[29] And there was the cost of subtler forms of protest. Henry Ford knew that all sorts of discreet sabotage and conscientious withdrawal of efficiency were possible. A better wage might prevent this, and so make the machine even more efficient and even more profitable.

It worked out just that way. "Immediately after the Plan became effective," said the company, "there was a voluntary increase of from 15% to 20% in the production. A better feeling between employe and employer had arisen; employes have shown a greater interest in their work."[30]

The increase in worker productivity pursuant to the $5, eight-hour day had been anticipated by the Ford Motor Company and sought after. In its public pronouncements the company usually contended that the added output had come as a pleasant surprise and that enhanced labor efficiency had not been among the reasons for promulgation of the plan. ("A great many instances of economic benefit to the Company, as a result of the inauguration of the Profit-sharing Plan, showing the appreciation of the men, have developed, entirely as a surprise to the Company."[31]) But according to Ford executive John R. Lee, brought to Detroit from a Buffalo parts firm for his expertise in personnel problems, Ford management had for several years been working toward a delineation of the human factor in production efficiency, and the $5 day was the culmination of this period of corporate thinking. Speaking before a largely academic audience in the spring of 1916, Lee revealed:

> It was along in 1912 that we began to realize something of the relative value of men, mechanism and material in the threefold phase of manufacturing, so to speak, and we confess that up to this time we had believed that mechanism and material were of the larger importance and that somehow or other the human element or our men were taken care of automatically and needed little or no consideration.
>
> During that year there were a number of things that happened that made their impression upon the minds of the executives of the company.
>
> I recall a drop hammer operation that had gone along for a number of years at an even output, when somehow, the standard dropped off. The hammer was in good condition, the man who had operated the machine for years was on the job, but the finished output failed to appear in the old proportions that we were looking for and had the right to expect.
>
> A superficial analysis of things brought no light, but a little talk with the operator revealed a condition of things entirely outside of business, that was responsible for our depleted production. Sickness, indebtedness, and fear and worry over things that related entirely to the home, had crept in and had put a satisfactory human unit entirely

out of harmony with the things that were necessary for production.

This is the type of incident that played an important part in the conclusions that we reached.[32]

The management at Ford sought more, however, than a fractional reduction in disutility. If the bonus pay (added to the worker's customary hourly rate to bring his wage to the $5 minimum[33]) were offered, not outright, but on a conditional basis, it might serve to bend the worker toward a total commitment to efficiency. The wage increase, then, was to be coercive. Said John Lee:

It was clearly foreseen that $5 a day in the hands of some men would work a tremendous handicap along the paths of rectitude and right living and would make of them a menace to society in general and so it was established at start that no man was to receive the money who could not use it advisedly and conservatively; also, that where a man seemed to qualify under the plan and later developed weaknesses, that it was within the province of the company to take away his share of the profits until such time as he could rehabilitate himself.[34]

So, along with the $5 day, the leaders at Highland Park had devised a Ford labor policy under whose aegis all Ford workers—the 12,880 in 1914, 18,892 in 1915, 32,702 in 1916, and on[35] —would fall.

There were two immediate conditions attached to the $5 plan. The first, a result of the riot, was a requirement that no one would be even eligible for employment at Ford until he had lived in Detroit for six months. The second, designed to reward experience and to reduce the enormous turnover of labor, made a half year of company service prerequisite to the new minimum wage. Then, to administer the new wage plan, the Company called on a special agency it had created the year before, the Ford Sociological Department. Under the direction of John Lee, its work was to be the investigation, counsel, and instruction of Ford employees.[36] Said the company to its workers:

A staff of investigators has been chosen whose duties are to explain the profit-sharing plan, and collect information and data from every one of the employes. This information is to be used in deciding who is entitled to benefit in the profit-sharing. It is also used to note from time to time, improvements made in home life, and to know whether the employe is being benefited, and to what extent. The Company simply wants to be assured that the profits are doing a lasting good, and it is for this reason only that investigations are conducted from time to time.[37]

Each sociological department investigator was equipped with a car, a driver, and an interpreter, and was assigned to a district in Detroit mapped to contain the residences of a number of Ford workers. The scope of the investigator's inquiry was wide. There were the standard questions about age (no one under 22 was eligible for the $5 minimum unless he was the support of a family), marital status, number and ages of dependents, religion, nationality, and, if alien, prospects of citizenship. Then, there were questions on economic condition: Did the worker own his own home? If so, how large was the mortgage? If he rented, what did he pay? Did he owe anyone money? If so, how much? How much money had he saved? Where was it kept? Did he have life insurance? How much were the premiums? Then came questions about social outlook and style of living: How was his health? Who was his doctor? What were his recreations? All the while the investigator was making a subjective evaluation of "habits," "home condition," "neighborhood." He would see if there was reading matter around, and note its nature. He would learn whether the family's diet was adequate; whether the family took in boarders, a practice he was to discourage; and whether money was being sent abroad, also to be discouraged. All answers and observations were recorded on blue and white forms.[38]

On the basis of material gathered each Ford employee was classified under one of four headings: those fully qualified for the $5-a-day minimum; those disqualified on the basis of age or length of service; those disqualified by bad personal habits; and those disqualified by unsatisfactory home conditions combined with improper habits. Moderate use of liquor was frowned upon but not forbidden. "Excessive use," however, came under the ban. So did gambling. So too did "any malicious practice derogatory to good physical manhood or moral character." A household which was dirty or comfortless; an unwholesome diet; the destruction of family privacy by boarders; an excessive amount of money sent to foreign relatives—all were cause for condemnation.[39]

Any worker for whom the $5 minimum was, in Lee's words, "a menace rather than a benefit" was placed on probation and watched closely. If he changed his deviant habits or home conditions within thirty days, he received all bonus money which had been withheld from his pay envelope. If reformation took sixty days, he got 75 percent; if ninety days, 60 percent; if four months, 40 percent; and if five months, only 25 percent. If after six months the worker had not, again Lee's words, "found the folly of his ways," he was "eliminated as an employe of the Ford Motor Company." The unearned profit shares were used for charity.[40]

Through its investigators the company encouraged workers to open savings accounts, improve their living conditions, and better feed and clothe their families. It reviewed the progress its employees were making and it was pleased. Almost all workers who had been living in substandard housing when first visited were subsequently found to be much more comfortably situated. Worker home ownership had increased by 99 percent the first year and a half; bank deposits by 205 percent.[41] So, confident that it had effectively delineated a proper life style for its employees, the company now penned in the fine detail.

> Employes should use plenty of soap and water in the home, and upon their children, bathing frequently. Nothing makes for right living and health so much as cleanliness. Notice that the most advanced people are the cleanest . . . .
>
> Improved garbage cans, of which there are several good types on sale, should be used. The can should be covered at all times, especially during the summer time, to prevent the carrying of disease germs by flies, dogs, cats and rats. . . .
>
> From 12 years of age to 18 especially is a time when they [children] should be guarded well, and not allowed to contract habits and vices injurious to their welfare and health. . . .
>
> Do not spit on the floor in the home. . . .
>
> Do not allow any flies in the house, as they are carriers of germs. . . .
>
> A double purpose is served under the profit-sharing plan. First, to provide money for future needs; second, to foster self-control. The second is the more important of the two, because, having that, the first is quite assured. . . .

Avoid, as much as possible, making purchases upon the installment plan. . . .

A good understanding should be had between husband and wife as to expenditures and savings. . . .

Cases have been brought to the Company's attention indicating that some young men, in order to qualify as profit-sharers, have hastily married without giving serious thought to such an important step in their lives. Seldom does such a marriage prove a happy one. If they would give some thought to the uncertainty of business affairs and the certainty of the obligations and responsibilities assumed in the marriage vows, there would be less work for the divorce courts.[42]

Ford education also took more traditional forms. To expedite Americanization of its immigrant workers, many of whom knew no English and lived in parts of the city where the language was seldom heard, the company established its English School in May 1914. It hired Dr. Peter Roberts of the Young Men's Christian Association, trained in immigrant education, to organize the staff and set up the curriculum. Instructors, volunteers without pay, were taken from Ford supervisory and office personnel and trained in the Roberts method of group recitation and "acting out" the meaning of words. Workers attended classes before or after their shift for an average of six to eight months, and upon completion of the course received a diploma at graduation exercises. A graduate of the school was acknowledged by Federal authorities to be qualified for first citizenship papers without further examination. By the end of 1916 some 2700 students were being instructed by 163 volunteer teachers.[43]

John Lee was sensitive to allegation that a worker's unwillingness to attend the school meant loss of his job. He said in June 1914: "No man is discharged or changed in status or relationship with the company because he does not speak English or is not naturalized, but the advantage to be derived from both are explained to him and the opportunity given at the company's expense to learn the English language and to do the things necessary to become a citizen of Uncle Sam."[44] Seemingly Lee described a program for voluntary self-betterment; but attendance at the school was mandatory, and workers who did not make a proper effort to learn the English language were presently discharged.[45] The determining factor in effecting coercion was probably the business cycle. In flush times, when the labor pool available to Ford was shallow, the company was probably more willing to overlook a worker's refusal to take advantage of its extracurricular offerings than in times when such workers were more easily replaced. When the company greatly reduced the English School's activities in 1917, business leaders in Detroit—members of the board of commerce—understood the reason to be that Ford was no longer having difficulty hiring English-speaking workmen.[46]

Why did the company have the school? The reason most frequently given was the absolute necessity for all Ford employees to be able to take orders in English, because safety and shop efficiency depended on it.[47] But the school also served a socializing function. The sociological department investigators discovered that non-English-speaking workmen and their families tended to live in ethnic ghettos, and that by patronizing shops within these clusters, they paid exorbitant prices for food, clothing, and furniture. "We have actually found in Detroit petty empires existing," said John Lee.

> For instance, we know it to be true that when a group of Roumanians, we will say, arrive in New York, in some way or other they are shipped to Detroit and the knowledge of their coming imparted to someone in our city, who meets them at the station and who confiscates the party, so to speak, persuades them to live in quarters selected for them, to buy their merchandise in markets other than their own choosing and to live unto themselves and apart from the wholesome environment of the city, so that the instigators of all this may benefit through rentals and large profits on food, wearing apparel, etc.[48]

So the immigrant was the victim of unscrupulous practice, and he succumbed, thought the men at Ford, not because he might have welcomed familiarity in language and environment, but because he was kept ignorant of anything better. The problem could be resolved, they thought, by educating the victims to their bondage.[49] Thus the Ford English School was begun.

The overriding image of the school was the melting pot. In a graduation exercise held in February 1916 at the Light Guard Armory in Detroit, a pageant was presented to some two thousand people, including many Detroit business leaders. Across the stage to the rear sat the hull and deck of an ocean steamship. In the center of the stage, taking up about half of the entire area, was an immense cauldron bearing the words "Ford English School Melting Pot." A gangway led from the deck of the steamship down into the cauldron. Suddenly a figure appeared at the top of the landing. Dressed in foreign costume and carrying his possessions in a bundle suspended from a cane, he looked about with bewilderment, hesitated, and then slowly descended into the melting pot. He held aloft a sign which told the country from which he had come. Then another figure appeared, and then another—"Syria," "Greece," "Italy," "Austria," "Poland," "Roumania," "Norway," "Palestine," "Russia"— all the different countries represented in the graduating class, filing in their turn down the ladder. Then came the transformation. From the cauldron the men emerged, now neatly dressed in American clothes, their faces "eager with the stimulus of the new opportunities and responsibilities opening out before them." Each carried a small American flag in his hand. The crucible of the melting pot had triumphed, the symbolic purging process was complete, and rising over all was a banner proclaiming "E Pluribus Unum."[50]

The activities of the men at Ford were not the only efforts at Americanization in Detroit at the time, nor perhaps were they even the most significant. Other leaders in the city also saw a threat in the foreigners, and they too felt that something had to be done. In the spring of 1915 the Detroit Board of Commerce commissioned Raymond E. Cole of the Committee for Immigrants in America to write a survey of the immigrants in Detroit. The report was finished in May 1915, and within its pages, in flat, unadorned, statistical statements that the men who would read it had been trained to appreciate, there were the facts all had long suspected. Using 1910 census statistics Cole reported:

Seventy-four percent (344,820) of the population of Detroit were either foreign-born or children of foreign-born parentage (one or both parents foreign-born).

Therefore, only 26 percent (115,106) of Detroit's population could call themselves native Americans of native parentage.

More than 43 percent of the total population of the city were

non-English-speaking by birth (born in a non-English-speaking
country or the child of two non-English-speaking parents).

Fifty percent of Detroit males of voting age were born on foreign
soil. Of this number only 44 percent were naturalized. The remaining
56 percent (42,432 persons) had to be naturalized. "Whenever there
is in a municipality a large male population of voting age who have
not a voice in the government," said Cole, "there is not pure democracy, but rather fertile soil for the seeds of anarchy and violent
socialism."[51]

The responsibility of the leaders was clear: teach the newcomers to be
citizens, for in citizenship the seeds of anarchy might be crushed. "The
aim," wrote Cole, "is to assimilate the immigrant into the body politic
of the city and so into American life. . . . [The work] must be primarily
protective and educational in nature, must be undertaken with a view
of conserving all the desirable qualities and energies of the immigrant
while eliminating the undesirable tendencies and with the purpose of
maintaining American standards."[52]

The men reading Cole's report were members of the standing Committee on Education of the Detroit Board of Commerce, the committee
soon to be called the Americanization Committee. They were

Henry W. Hoyt, chairman of the Americanization Committee, and
    vice-president and secretary of the Great Lakes Engineering
    Company.
Frank S. Bigler, vice-president and general manager of the Michigan
    Bolt & Nut Works.
Frank Cody, assistant superintendent of schools.
John R. Lee, of the Ford Sociological Department.
Ernest F. Lloyd, president of the Lloyd Construction Company.
Oscar B. Marx, mayor of Detroit.
Horace H. Rackham, listed as "attorney and capitalist." He had no claim
    to the latter until the day in 1903 when, as a young lawyer in
    the employ of Alexander Malcomson's coal company, he invested
    $5000 ($3500 down, $1500 in installments) in the new Ford Motor
    Company. Five percent of the paper secured his position of power.
Adolph G. Studer, general secretary of the Young Men's Christian

Association. The YMCA had helped organize the English classes at
Ford and had itself for some time been holding classes in English and
citizenship in various parts of the city. Studer would be on the Americanization Committee for only a short time. He told what he knew,
and he departed.
Arthur J. Tuttle, judge, United States District Court.[53]

These were the men who were members of the Americanization Committee at the time of its inception. They set the tone and policy. There are
two more men, soon added to its membership, who deserve mention.
One is Fred Butzel, a Detroit attorney, Jewish, always interested in
social causes, and a man who will appear in the story of the leadership
of the Detroit Urban League. The second man is Chester M. Culver,
general manager of the Employers' Association of Detroit. Culver too
will appear in the affairs of the Detroit Urban League, but he is one of
those many men whose importance is less as an individual than as representative of an organization. The Employers' Association of Detroit was
unquestionably the most powerful group in the city. Every worker,
whatever his nationality or race, was in some way dependent upon it.
Often he was dependent in ways he would never know.

The EAD was formed in 1902, the child of Detroit manufacturers'
anti-union urgency. By 1904 it had enlisted sixty-seven firms, and each
year saw more and more companies joining. (Ford signed the articles of
agreement in 1903 and became active in 1910.) The need to defend
factories and city against the thrusts of organized labor prompted the
association to use its power without scruple: it organized blacklists, put
political pressure on the state government to stifle proposed child labor
and factory inspection legislation, pressured the city government, used
the Detroit police force as a virtual arm of its anti-union policies, and
created the Employers' Association Labor Bureau. It was the Labor
Bureau which all agreed was the main source of EAD strength. By 1906
the bureau listed in its index about 40,000 workers, half of the entire
Detroit labor force. With this army of men the association was able to
break strike after strike merely by throwing large work forces into the
shops that unions were trying to organize and close to nonunion labor.

By 1910 most unions were effectively dead in Detroit. With native
and foreign immigrants pouring into the city, jobs plentiful and turn-

over high, unionmaking would have been difficult enough with no opposition. Against the Employers' Association of Detroit, labor organizers had no chance. The association was convinced that the rapid expansion of the automobile industry in Detroit and the attractiveness of the place to new industry of all sorts was due to the absence of effective trade unions. There was probably a good deal of truth to the claim. Thus the mission of the Employers' Association was ongoing—to assure a continuing supply of labor for the burgeoning automobile factories and to see the open shop perpetuated.

In the spring of 1911 the association computed the Detroit labor force to be 175,000 men. Of these, 160,000 were manageable men ("independent workingmen with clean records") on the bureau's index.[54] If 91 percent of the work force is certified, control would seem to be complete. But part of control is uplift, or recasting, and new arrivals had to learn what was expected. So Chester Culver of the Employers' Association sat on the Board of Commerce Americanization Committee.

Basic to the committee's program of Americanization were the night schools. In more than twenty-five public schools in immigrant neighborhoods throughout the city, classes were held in the Roberts Dramatic Method of Teaching English. Since the Roberts Method was used at the Ford English School the content of the lessons is familiar: simple words and sentences taught by repetition and by "acting out," the words and sentences usually conveying some message about personal hygiene, the American social system, and, in more advanced classes, the procedure for taking out citizenship papers. Enrollment in the classes was secured through the cooperation of employers of immigrant labor. Nearly 4000 students from 386 Detroit manufacturing firms enrolled in the elementary evening schools for the 1915/16 term.[55]

The principal concern of the Americanization Committee was to get as many foreigners as possible into the schools. It eagerly endorsed Frank Cody's suggestion to erect a red, white, and blue beacon on each night school to "enable the prospective pupil to quickly locate the schools and . . . be a constant reminder to passers-by of the work being done in connection with the Americanization movement in Detroit."[56] Other methods were more direct. When an immigrant child took a book out of a branch of the Detroit Public Library or went onto any

Detroit city playground, he was likely to be given a pamphlet on the front of which was printed in large block letters:

CAN YOUR MOTHER AND FATHER SPEAK ENGLISH WELL?

Take this card home; it will tell them where to go to learn English.

Inside the pamphlet was a sentence, printed in various languages, addressed to the parents telling them where to register for night school.[57]

Beyond that there was coercion. "If you let your men know both collectively and individually that you prefer men to work for you who understand and speak English," said the board of commerce to its members, "and that in dull times preference will be given men according to their attendance at night schools, the result will be for the good of the men, your company and your city. They will stick to the night schools, learn English and eventually become American citizens."[58] Again, the business cycle dictated the extent of coercion. In flush times, hiring was generally pursued indiscriminately. But given a production lag, or a localized labor surplus, firms like the Packard Motor Car Company, whose chief executive officer was a vice-president of the board of commerce, would announce to job-seekers that no one would be hired unless he passed a company-administered test proving he could speak, read, and write English, and would similarly announce to its non-English-speaking employees that their jobs depended on regular attendance at night school.[59]

Employers' Association policy followed a like course. Unemployed night school pupils did not automatically get a job from the EAD Labor Bureau, but if they held up their night school registration card they were at least guaranteed to be taken from the line outside the building and given a place inside the employment office.[60] The lesson was not lost for long on the nonmatriculated unemployed.

So the men of the Americanization Committee went about their manipulations, and met the occasional demurrers from below with contempt. When a Polish daily newspaper claimed that the Americanization program was really an attempt to destroy national spirit and ethnic identity, committee secretary I. Walton Schmidt dismissed the allegation by impugning the source. In rhetoric familiar to the day he said: "The paper is decidedly pro-German and pro-Catholic."[61] Thus in the troubled winter of 1915/16 at least one problem was pushed aside.

NOTES

1. See John Higham, *Strangers in the Land: Patterns of American Nativism, 1860-1925* (New York: Atheneum, 1963), esp. pp. 234-63; also Edward G. Hartmann, *The Movement to Americanize the Immigrant* (New York: Columbia University Press, 1948); and Howard C. Hill, "The Americanization Movement," *American Journal of Sociology* 24 (May 1919): 609-42.

2. See Samuel Haber, *Efficiency and Uplift: Scientific Management in the Progressive Era, 1890-1920* (Chicago and London: University of Chicago Press, 1964). Haber deals with the Frederick W. Taylor system of scientific management, its adherents and implications for a wider society. The Detroit area had its own apostle of factory efficiency who was eager to delineate the social applications. See Henry Ford, *My Life and Work* (Garden City, N.Y.: Garden City Publishing Co., 1922); Ford, *My Philosophy of Industry* (New York: Coward-McCann, 1929); *Ford Ideals, Being a Selection from "Mr. Ford's Page" in The Dearborn Independent* (Dearborn, Mich.: Dearborn Publishing Company, 1922).

3. Melvin G. Holli, *Reform in Detroit: Hazen S. Pingree and Urban Politics* (New York: Oxford University Press, 1969), surveys the late nineteenth-century political history of Detroit and Michigan with Pingree as a focus.

4. Richard Bardolph, *The Negro Vanguard* (New York: Vintage Books, 1961), pp. 196-97; Allan H. Spear, *Black Chicago: The Making of a Negro Ghetto, 1890-1920* (Chicago and London: University of Chicago Press, 1969), pp. 78-79.

5. See Henry Adams, *The Education of Henry Adams* (New York: Modern Library, 1931), esp. pp. 379-90; for the effect of economic and population changes on Adams and others of his social class, see Barbara M. Solomon, *Ancestors and Immigrants: A Changing New England Tradition* (New York: John Wiley and Sons, 1965).

6. Ford, *My Life and Work*, p. 104.

7. *Manual, County of Wayne, Michigan, 1926* (Detroit: Board of County Auditors, 1926), p. 40; Adcraft Club of Detroit, *A Study of the City of Detroit* (Detroit: Adcraft Club of Detroit, 1929), pp. 59-65.

8. *Annual Report for the City of Detroit for the Year 1930* (n.p., n.d.), pp. 41-42; also Lent D. Upson, *The Growth of a City Government* (Detroit: Detroit Bureau of Governmental Research, 1931), p. 22.

9. *Detroit City Directory, 1927-28*, p. 11.

10. *Detroit City Directory, 1925-26*, pp. 34-37; also *Manual, County of Wayne, Michigan, 1926*, p. 40.

11. Adcraft Club, *A Study of the City of Detroit*, p. 65.

12. *Manual, County of Wayne, Michigan, 1926*, p. 40.

13. Ibid.

14. U.S. Department of Commerce, Bureau of the Census, *Thirteenth Census of the United States Taken in the Year 1910* (Washington, D.C.: Government Printing Office, 1913), vol. 1, *Population*, p. 208, vol. 2, *Population*, p. 953; U.S. Department of Commerce, Bureau of the Census, *Fourteenth Census of the United States Taken in the Year 1920*, vol. 3, *Population* (Washington, D.C.: Government Printing Office, 1922), p. 488; U.S. Department of Commerce, Bureau of the Census, *Fifteenth Census of the United States: 1930*, vol. 3, pt. 1, *Population* (Washington, D.C.: Government Printing Office, 1932), p. 1183; *Detroit City Directory, 1925-26*, pp. 46, 47.

15. *Fifteenth Census* (1930), vol. 2, *Population*, p. 540.

16. Ibid., p. 200; *Fourteenth Census* (1920), vol. 2, *Population*, p. 662.

17. *Fourteenth Census* (1920), vol. 2, *Population*, pp. 155, 365.

18. Sidney Glazer, *Detroit: A Study in Urban Development* (New York: Bookman Associates, 1965), pp. 81-83; Harry Barnard, *Independent Man: The Life of Senator James Couzens* (New York: Charles Scribner's Sons, 1958), esp. pp. 35, 68, 69; Allan Nevins, *Ford: The Times, The Man, The Company* (New York: Charles Scribner's Sons, 1954), esp. pp. 237-38, 471-76, 487-91, 644-50. The Ford Motor Company was nominally capitalized in 1903 at $150,000. Only $100,000 in stock was actually issued; the remaining $50,000 was held as treasury stock. Nevins, *Ford: The Times, The Man, The Company*, p. 237n.

19. Clarence M. Burton, *City of Detroit, Michigan, 1701-1922*, vol. 4 (Detroit and Chicago: S.J. Clarke Publishing Co., 1922), pp. 308-13; Clarence M. Burton, *History of Wayne County and the City of Detroit, Michigan*, vol. 2 (Chicago and Detroit: S.J. Clarke Publishing Co., 1930), pp. 1374, 1377; John B. Rae, *American Automobile Manufacturers: The First Forty Years* (Philadelphia and New York: Chilton Company, 1959), pp. 162-65; Lawrence H. Seltzer, *A Financial History of the American Automobile Industry* (Boston and New York: Houghton Mifflin Company, 1928), pp. 240-42. Nevins, *Ford: The Times, The Man, The Company*, p. 238, lists shareholders

of the Ford Motor Company as of the date of incorporation (June 16, 1903).

In 1919 Henry Ford bought back all outstanding shares in the Ford Motor Company. The Dodge brothers received $25 million for their 2000 accumulated shares. Allan Nevins and Frank Ernest Hill, *Ford: Expansion and Challenge, 1915-1933* (New York: Charles Scribner's Sons, 1957), p. 110. For the legal warfare between Ford and the Dodges, see ibid., pp. 86-105.

20. Quoted in Barnard, *Independent Man,* p. 51; for Couzens on the success ethic, see his speech to 300 Boy Scouts, *Detroit Journal,* January 26, 1915.

21. Barnard, *Independent Man,* pp. 7-94; Nevins and Hill, *Ford: Expansion and Challenge,* pp. 10-11, 22-24. Couzens' net worth as of 1915 may well be understated at $40 million. His biographer (Barnard, *Independent Man,* p. 8) estimates it to have been $40-$60 million, taking into consideration Couzens' Ford Motor Company stock, cash dividends, salary, and outside investments. When Couzens, along with the other shareholders, sold his stock back to Henry Ford in 1919, he received $29,308,857.90, probably much less than its actual worth at the time. For the details behind the repurchase, see Nevins and Hill, *Ford: Expansion and Challenge,* pp. 105-13.

22. *Detroit News,* September 19, 1922.

23. Nevins and Hill, *Ford: Expansion and Challenge,* pp. 347-48.

24. Ibid., pp. 347-49; Ernest G. Liebold to Robert Gair Company, Brooklyn, New York, December 21, 1920, Accession 62-2, Box 4, FA; *Detroit News,* August 15, 1974, p. 1C.

25. *Detroit News,* January 5-7, 1914; Nevins, *Ford: The Times, Man, The Company,* pp. 533-34; Barnard, *Independent Man,* pp. 91-93.

26. *Detroit Times,* January 7-14, 1914; *Detroit News,* January 12, 1914; *Detroit Free Press,* January 12-14, 1914; also Nevins, *Ford: The Times, The Man, The Company,* pp. 543-44.

27. Nevins, *Ford: The Times, The Man, The Company,* p. 544.

28. Ford Motor Company, *Helpful Hints and Advice to Employes to Help Them Grasp the Opportunities Which Are Presented to Them by the Ford Profit-Sharing Plan* (Detroit: Ford Motor Company, 1915), p. 3; see too the Ford Motor Company publication *Ford Factory Facts* (Detroit: Ford Motor Company, 1915), pp. 43-51; also D. Kenneth Laub, *An Investigation of Ford Profit-Sharing at the Close of the First Year,* reprint from the *Detroit Evening News,* November 24, 1914 (Detroit: Ford Motor Company, n.d.).

29. Nevins, *Ford: The Times, The Man, The Company,* p. 549.

30. *Ford Factory Facts* (1915), pp. 47-49.

31. Ibid., p. 47.

32. John R. Lee, "The So-Called Profit Sharing System in the Ford Plant," *The Annals of the American Academy of Political and Social Science* 65 (May 1916): 299. On John Lee's background see Nevins, *Ford: The Times, The Man, The Company*, p. 458.

33. *Ford Factory Facts* (1915), p. 47.

34. Lee, "The So-Called Profit Sharing System in the Ford Plant," p. 302.

35. Nevins, *Ford: The Times, The Man, The Company*, p. 554. The work force figures are yearly averages.

36. Ibid., pp. 546-57; Nevins and Hill, *Ford: Expansion and Challenge*, p. 13; Barnard *Independent Man*, p. 94.

37. Ford Motor Company, *Helpful Hints and Advice to Employes*, p. 9.

38. Ibid., pp. 7-8, 9-11; Nevins, *Ford: The Times, The Man, The Company*, p. 554; Lee, "The So-Called Profit Sharing System in the Ford Plant," pp. 302-03. Lee noted (ibid., p. 309): "One of the greatest crimes a man of the Ford organization can commit is not to keep us posted as to change of address."

39. Nevins, *Ford: The Times, The Man, The Company*, pp. 555-556; Lee, "The So-Called Profit Sharing System in the Ford Plant," p. 307.

40. Lee, "The So-Called Profit Sharing System in the Ford Plant," p. 307.

41. Ibid., pp. 308-09; *Ford Factory Facts* (1915), pp. 49, 51.

42. Ford Motor Company, *Helpful Hints and Advice to Employes*, pp. 8-28.

43. Nevins, *Ford: The Times, The Man, The Company*, pp. 557, 558; Gregory Mason, " 'Americans First': How the People of Detroit Are Making Americans of the Foreigners in Their City," *The Outlook* 114 (September 27, 1916): 200; *Ford Factory Facts* (1915), pp. 51-53; "Assimilation Through Education," *Ford Times* 8 (June 1915): 407, 410-11; also see Peter Roberts, "The YMCA among Immigrants," *Survey*, 29 (February 15, 1913): 697-700.

44. John R. Lee to Boyd Fisher of the Detroit Board of Commerce, June 24, 1914, Accession 62, Box 3, FA.

45. Nevins, *Ford: The Times, The Man, The Company*, p. 557; Nevins and Hill, *Ford: Expansion and Challenge*, p. 340.

46. Americanization Committee, Detroit Board of Commerce, Min-

utes, October 9 [1917], Detroit Board of Commerce and Americanization Committee Papers, MHC.

47. *Ford Factory Facts* (1915), p. 51; "Assimilation through Education," p. 407; "A Motto Wrought into Education," *Ford Times* 9 (April 1916): 409; Lee, "The So-Called Profit Sharing System in the Ford Plant," p. 305; Nevins, *Ford: The Times, The Man, The Company,* p. 558.

48. Lee, "The So-Called Profit Sharing System in the Ford Plant," p. 305.

49. See "Assimilation through Education," p. 407. Said John Lee:

> Of course, it is to the interest of such men [the "instigators"] that these foreigners shall know nothing of the English language, of American ways and customs, or of local values, as these are things which would liberate them from the bondage (and it is nothing more or less) under which they have unconsciously been placed.
>
> Now, in facing this problem we decided that the only way to work out the things that we wanted to do was to put these men in position to understand directly from us all what we wanted them to know. ["The So-Called Profit Sharing System in the Ford Plant," pp. 305-06.]

50. "A Motto Wrought into Education," pp. 407, 409, and photograph, p. 408.

51. Raymond E. Cole, "The Immigrant in Detroit" (Report prepared for the Detroit Board of Commerce, May 1915), pp. 1, 4, 17. Copy in Americanization Committee Papers, MHC.

52. Ibid., p. 27.

53. Membership lists and communications in Americanization Committee Papers, MHC; *Detroit City Directory, 1914;* Barnard, *Independent Man,* pp. 36, 40; Nevins, *Ford: The Times, The Man, The Company,* pp. 237-38.

54. Nevins, *Ford: The Times, The Man, The Company,* pp. 376-80, 512-18, 523n; Jacob Nathan, "Detroit Employers Waging Fight for Detroit Workingmen," *Detroit Saturday Night,* May 15, 1915; also Myron W. Watkins, "The Labor Situation in Detroit," *Journal of Political Economy* 28 (December 1920): 840-52. A collection of Employers' Association literature, clippings, etc., can be found in the EAD scrapbooks (111 vols.), BHC.

55. List of Free Public Evening Schools, Detroit, Michigan, September 1, 1916, distributed by the Detroit Board of Commerce, Americanization

Committee Papers, MHC; City of Detroit, Board of Education, *Courses in the Detroit Evening High Schools* (Detroit: Board of Education, 1919), pp. 52-53; "List of Manufacturers and Number of Employees from Each in Elementary Evening Schools, 1915-1916," October 15, 1915, Americanization Committee Papers, MHC.

56. Americanization Committee, Minutes, June 15, 1916, Americanization Committee Papers, MHC.

57. National Americanization Committee, *Americanizing a City: The Campaign for the Detroit Night Schools Conducted in Co-operation with the Detroit Board of Commerce and Board of Education, August-September, 1915* (New York City: National Americanization Committee and the Committee for Immigrants in America, December 15, 1915), p. 14; Americanization Committee, Minutes, August 10, 1916, Americanization Committee Papers, MHC.

58. Memorandum of Byres H. Gitchell, Secretary, Detroit Board of Commerce, "Attention General Manager: Regarding Night Schools," November 18, 1915, Americanization Committee Papers, MHC. Americanization Committee concern with building night school attendance did not abate with Gitchell's communiqué (see, for example, Americanization Committee, Minutes, December 16, 1915, January 14, 1916, ibid.), but a tactical approach had been set down.

59. "Report by Mr. [Harvey] Saul, Packard Motor Car Company, Regarding Night Schools," in the Americanization Committee memorandum, "Information for the Committee on Education," January 17, 1916, ibid.; see also Mason, "'Americans First,'" p. 196.

60. Americanization Committee, Minutes, January 6, 1916, Americanization Committee Papers, MHC.

61. Memorandum of I. Walton Schmidt, Secretary, Committee on Education, "Information for the Committee on Education," January 10, 1916, ibid.

chapter
TWO

Rumblings: Houses and Newcomers

I

"I have never considered the Board of Commerce merely as a commercial body," said its president, Charles B. Warren, in the year 1915. "We have a very definite work along purely social lines. One of our slogans is, 'Every industrial employee a home-owner,' and we hope to realize that before long. The housing conditions in Detroit are excellent. We have 150,000 manufacturing employees here, but there is not a tenement-house in Detroit."[1] If Detroit's leaders were boastful and self-satisfied, so too could they be myopic. The housing situation in Detroit in the middle years of the century's second decade was not "excellent" at all. It was desperate. In the railway yards of the city there were perhaps 200 carloads of household goods just sitting there. The owners were not destitute; they had jobs in the automobile and munitions plants. They simple had no place to live. Families crowded into one room in the downtown tenements and disposed of their sewage through rain leaders. Men walked the streets, with no place to sleep between shifts on the job. Flophouses rented rooms by the hour; even fetid mattresses were at a premium. The local federation of labor sent a resolution to President Woodrow Wilson asking that Fort Wayne be opened to homeless families. The rejection surprised no one.

Of course, symbolic gestures toward solving the housing problem had been made in the years preceding 1915. The Detroit Housing Association, an agency of the board of commerce, was a permanent fixture. It sponsored an occasional speaker. It established an inspection bureau in 1913 and staffed it with six investigators. And it supported a 1914 Michigan law applying to cities of over 10,000 population which fixed minimum standards for light, ventilation, and sanitation in dwellings to be erected. But little else was done. Buildings continued to deteriorate, yet no firm commitment to meet future housing needs was made. Perhaps no one could have worked out and adopted a comprehensive housing policy in those years. Perhaps the problem of housing all people satisfactorily was just too crushing, especially in a rapidly growing city like Detroit. But Detroit business leaders, caught up in the euphoria of the economic boom, made no substantive effort to confront the problem mainly because cries for the future never much interested them. It was the present which occupied their energies, and it was the present which caught them.[2]

There had been several city plans for Detroit in the past, all of them dealing with the monumental. But parks, boulevards, and causeways were not to be the focus of concern in the dozen years from 1915 to 1926. Rather, there would be a much more fundamental type of construction going on, a frenzy of building activity, as Detroit tried to build its long-neglected physical plant.

As always, the city's leading men were concerned for their image and sensitive to their choice of words. "No doubt," said the report of the city building department in 1916, "as Detroit's building record reaches the ears of outsiders, only a 'building boom' will be the first thought. Let it be fully understood that this remarkable record is not a 'boom,' as the term implies, but a good, sturdy example of Detroit's marvelous growth into the circle of large cities of America."[3] But whatever the choice of words, resources were being poured into building—offices, stores, and especially housing. Sometimes it seemed like an impossible undertaking, for the more housing that was built, the more people seemed to be attracted to Detroit, and the more housing was needed. The war years of 1917 and 1918 intensified the problem, for most building material and money had to be diverted to the war effort, and the population flood did not decrease much. By the end of 1919 the situation appeared to be even worse than it had been four years earlier.

The shortage in dwelling places, despite the frenzy of construction and renovation, was increasing as fast as the population, or so it seemed. The figures are blunt enough, and they ignore the deficit existing in the base year of 1915 (Table 1).

TABLE 1

POPULATION AND HOUSING FIGURES
FOR DETROIT AND VICINITY, 1915-1919

Year	Estimated population[a]	Population increase	Dwelling places needed for increase[b]	No. of new dwelling places built	Shortage in dwelling places
1915	723,926				
1916	820,778	96,852	19,370	18,123	1,247
1917	914,896	94,118	18,823	8,514	11,556
1918	986,690	71,794	14,359	1,587	24,328
1919	1,086,700	100,010	20,002	13,928	30,402

Source: *Annual Report for the City of Detroit for the Year 1919* (n.p., n.d.), p. 95. Several arithmetic errors in the source are corrected here.
[a]Population figures for Highland Park and Hamtramck included.
[b]Calculated on the basis of one per five inhabitants.

How, then, to make a dent in the problem? The answer was more money and more effort. It was an impressive and even awesome display of Detroit energy, as the "building boom" continued into the 1920s. Pride in the accomplishment was pervasive. "The past year has been a record one in increased building activity," boasted one source concerning the year 1923.

Accommodations for approximately 100,000 persons, in 14,163 places of residence, such as apartment houses, flats and dwellings, were provided. Aside from the pronounced increase in dwellings constructed, there were an additional 14,614 business places built, including factories, warehouses, stores, garages, and other mercantile and industrial establishments. Statistics show that the number of persons employed attained a new maximum during the year.

This encomium to Detroit's economic progress was written into the annual report of the Detroit police department.[4]

The achievement was indeed stunning. The postwar depression years of 1920-21 saw a decrease from 1919 levels of performance, but then activity resumed. Housing was constructed for 16,689 families in 1922; for 23,153 families in 1923; for 26,377 in 1924; for 26,679 in 1925; and for 27,287 in 1926.[5] Similarly with the amount of money spent for new housing:[6]

Year	Housing expenditure	Year	Housing expenditure
1919	$39,378,850	1923	$76,725,813
1920	24,203,150	1924	91,062,431
1921	21,317,061	1925	98,821,514
1922	49,640,479	1926	99,386,023

For the sum of all building construction in Detroit see Table 2. Not until after 1926 would there begin the tailing-off of activity which characterized the construction industry throughout the entire United States and presaged, for the few who were listening, the beginnings of the Great Depression.

Detroit, however, was listening only to the whirring of its own progress, and it scarcely could be blamed. With enormous resources, both financial and human, being spent on construction, the general economic boom was inevitably intensified. The value of the annual product of Detroit area industry soared into the billions of dollars. Money was invested, profits made and invested and reinvested again and again. All classes seemed to benefit, if disproportionately. Jobs had to be done, giving men work and wages to spend, men who would need and could afford still more services, still more goods. And so there would be still more growth. Whatever the magic was in the building boom and its "backward and forward linkages," there would

TABLE 2

BUILDING CONSTRUCTION IN DETROIT, 1920-1926

Year	No. of new buildings	Value of building construction
1920	14,023	$ 77,737,365
1921	12,146	58,087,081
1922	19,397	94,615,093
1923	28,768	129,719,731
1924	32,970	160,064,794
1925	34,021	180,132,528
1926	32,555	183,721,438

Source: Adcraft Club, *A Study of the City of Detroit,* p. 60.

be still more growth, and with it, its concomitants: more power, more people, still more growth, still more power, still more people.

The housebuilding took a predictable direction: mostly outward. Detroit's central areas were already thick with tenements, distinguishing it not at all from other cities at the time, and a builder wishing to erect an apartment house near downtown would usually first have to clear the land of a deteriorated, vermin-ridden structure. To be sure, this was often done, and frequently involved what was to become a classic problem in urban redevelopment—the displacement of families who probably would be unable to afford rents in the new building when it was completed. But most of the time the builders opted for new land on the city's periphery. There, demolition was unnecessary, condemnation proceedings not required; and the increasingly ubiquitous automobile enabled large numbers of people now to commute extended distances from home to work in a city conspicuously lacking in rapid public transportation.[7]

The bulk of the resources poured into housing from 1919 to 1926 was spent, not for apartments, but for the construction of single-family

homes and duplexes. This is one index of the widening prosperity in
Detroit during these years. Many of the houses, in the haste of construction, may have been shoddy, without adequate foundations, and built
in barracks-like colonies by professional builders who were just beginning to refine techniques of mass construction.[8] But at least they were
houses, new and clean and within the grasp of many Detroit workers.
No house remained vacant for long, as men who worked in the factories
hastened to place their down payments and move their families into
what was, at last, their own home.[9]

It is difficult to determine the precise extent of increase in home
ownership among Detroit working men in the period 1910-30. The
decennial census did not use "working men" as a separate designation
in its information on "families" and "homes," so the figures which are
available for the entire period, lacking breakdown by occupation or
class, are merely suggestive (see Table 3). The drop in percentage of
families owning homes in 1920 is predictable because the population
was increasing at a much faster rate than houses were becoming available. But there was, as Table 3 shows, a great absolute as well as percentage increase in the number of home-owning families in the decade
1920-30, and it might be assumed that a sizeable part of this increase
was the result of purchasing by laboring men and women.[10]

TABLE 3

HOME OWNERSHIP IN DETROIT, 1910-1930

Year	No. of owned homes	No. of families	Percentage of families owning homes
1910	40,471	100,356	40.3
1920	82,679	218,973	37.7
1930	153,027	370,293	41.3

Sources: *Fourteenth Census* (1920), vol. 2, *Population*, pp. 1271, 1286, 1287,
1293; *Fifteenth Census* (1930), vol. 6, *Population, Families*, pp. 665-66.

Other sources seem to substantiate this. In the summer and fall of 1920 the Detroit Board of Commerce initiated a study of housing conditions among working-class families. Questionnaires were sent to the heads of all firms in the city employing more than twenty persons, and replies were received from approximately 275,000 of the 350,000 persons estimated to have been employed in Detroit at the time. The survey included Highland Park and Hamtramck, two autonomous communities completely surrounded by the city of Detroit. The survey showed that 33.6 percent of the families responding owned the houses they lived in, and 4.2 percent owned their flats. The total of 37.8 percent is nearly identical to the 37.7 percent derived from the Bureau of Census figures for 1920.[11]

All of this meant a general movement of population to the outer edges of the city. Land which not too many years before had been unused, unplatted acreage was now dotted with houses. Even if the land was vacant, it had no doubt been earmarked for development. After 1925 the city of Detroit stopped listing in its annual report the number of unplatted acres in the city; they were too few to mention. The semicircular periphery of the city was filling in and extending outward,[12] with one commentator noting that Detroiters evidently preferred to commute twenty miles a day six days a week into the city to work than to live within it and drive the same distance out on Sunday to play.[13]

The story, however, is not idyllic. There is a great temptation to look at the statistics of enormous activity in housing construction and to conclude with satisfaction that the problem was being solved. Yet at a given point in time thousands of people in Detroit had no decent place to live. For example, in August 1919, one house on St. Antoine Street, just off Adams, was occupied by fifteen regular tenants and a varying number of transients. The place had six rooms, no toilet or bath, and rented for $75 a month.[14] The ultimate achievment of Detroit's economic progress mattered less to these people than it did to many others. They all were black and were living in a Detroit black ghetto already filled to bursting. For them there was no place else to go, and there would likely be no place else soon, regardless of the activity on the periphery.

But from another perspective the frenzy of construction and its accomplishments at a point in time did matter, and the irony is that it mattered greatly to both races. While the housebuilding was the response of real-estate men to a perceived market need, its thrust—mostly one-family and two-family dwellings on the outskirts for whites only—suggests another consideration. On any given day the housing shortage in the city was a potential source of racial conflict. If the strictures of limited dwelling space in the ghetto became too tight, and as a result blacks sought housing in white neighborhoods, there could be violence. A sufficient number of homes thrown up fast enough would ease population pressure and diminish the likelihood of confrontation. And as much as that mattered to whites, it was also important to blacks needing a place to live and not anxious to endanger themselves finding it.

There is no doubt that the business, civic, and real-estate leaders of Detroit were aware of the ever-increasing number of blacks in the city and were concerned about the consequences of racial proximity. There are a number of ways to document this. One is that, like the Americanization Committee some years before, they wanted a current count. So in 1919 the Detroit Community Union, the city's monolithic social service agency, initiated a census. The stated reason for the undertaking was the sixfold increase in the city's black population since 1910. "One of the problems the census will assist to some extent in solving," reported a Detroit newspaper, "is that of housing conditions. It will reveal whether the negro population is scattered over the city or whether it has been contracted into a densely populated settlement, with the inevitable unsanitary conditions resulting from such a situation."[15]

The rate of increase in the number of blacks living in Detroit was indeed dizzying. A population of 5741 in 1910, and not much more than that in 1915, grew to 40,838 by 1920, a decennial increase of 611.3 percent. By 1925 the number of blacks in the city had risen to 81,831, and by 1930 was 120,066. Only Gary, Indiana, which went from 383 blacks in 1910 to 5299 in 1920, had a greater decennial increase among U.S. cities in that decade; and no U.S. city with more than 5500 blacks had a greater percentage increase than Detroit (194.0 percent) from 1920 to 1930.[16]

Another way the city's leadership verbalized the consequences of proximity was the threat of disease. Writing about a scarlet fever outbreak in Detroit in March 1917, a local newspaper reported: "With the epidemic of scarlet fever now spreading unchecked over the city and the congested housing conditions known to exist among Negroes it is likely that action will be taken at once by health authorities and charity organizations to guard against a condition that might prove dangerously infectious in every part of the city." Predictably, housing patterns were seen to be closely related, and the article ended with an interesting speculation in the light of policy to come: "Real estate dealers are known to be talking of opening a subdivision for colored residents and this plan may be adopted as a final solution of the problem."[17]

The clearest indication, however, that racial proximity and the housing shortage were matters of great concern and that the city's leaders did not have to be prescient to fear violence was that blacks were periodically breaking from the ghetto and meeting white resistance.[18] One such incident occurred in June 1920. The bottom apartment of a duplex in an exclusive residential area on West Philadelphia Avenue suddenly fell vacant. The landlord of the building, a musician named Bayer, had lived in the apartment while renting the upstairs to a physician. The doctor had signed her lease when rents were much lower, Bayer had tried to void the document and issue a new one, the doctor refused to sign, and Bayer sued. The validity of the original lease was confirmed by the court.

So the landlord sought extralegal means of revenge. He vacated his downstairs apartment, and on the evening of June 15 a black family moved in. News of the event immediately spread through the neighborhood, and the rage began to build. By the next day residents were gathering in groups in the street. A committee of property owners was formed to call on the new neighbor, but before the committee could reach the door the black man who had rented the apartment, sensing the danger, came into the street and asked what he should do. He was given twenty-four hours to move out. Within five minutes the man, his wife, and seven children came out of the house and headed in the rain toward Woodward Avenue. The children carried their shoes and stockings. The furniture, which had been moved from a ghetto address on Macomb, was left in the apartment, abandoned.

Before the black man departed with his family, he had explained to the "indignation committee" that he had agreed to pay $6 a week for one room in the house, and that he had contracted to rent the other rooms to other black families at a similar rate. Efforts to reach the landlord Bayer were fruitless. He had left no forwarding address, neighbors said.[19]

Nor was this the earliest incident. Three summers before, an apartment had become vacant in a four-family brick dwelling on Harper Avenue. The neighborhood once had been upper-middle-class housing, but by 1917 was quite perceptibly run-down. It was not an all-white neighborhood. Several houses away from the vacant apartment lived a black family who had been there for years. Other blacks resided in the area. The house at 202 Harper had been occupied by four white families. The landlord was a policeman named Curtis. He had become dissatisfied with the way his white tenants were caring for the property and with the capricious way in which they were paying the rent. So with one apartment now vacant he decided to try black tenants. He contacted a black man named Trigg, who lived at the corner of Riopelle and Lyman, not far from the Harper Avenue house. Trigg, an employee at Dodge, agreed to take over the entire house as it became vacant, and paid $45 rent for the one apartment already available plus $7 for the kitchen furniture.

Trigg had no intention of living in the apartment himself. He had evidently seen an opportunity to make some money by acting as a middleman between Curtis and prospective black tenants, which he himself would supply. The tenants would pay rent to Trigg, and Trigg would in turn pay Curtis a previously stipulated amount. The more people Trigg could squeeze into the apartment the more profit he stood to make. So he began moving families out of a house on Lyman Street, with another group coming from a place at the corner of Trombly and Riopelle. All were going to be tenants in the one vacant apartment.

Black people began arriving and moving in furniture and other belongings early in the day and were still moving in that evening when a crowd of about 200 white people gathered in front of the house and began to jeer and call names. Two men acting as spokesmen for the crowd went to the rear of the house and informed Trigg that the white people of the community would not allow any of the blacks to stay even overnight. The spokesmen further told Trigg that they were going to get trucks and move the furniture out. Trigg and one of his lodgers went to find the landlord; but upon their return they discovered that the furniture had already been loaded onto four trucks, taken back to Lyman and Riopelle, and dumped there. Trigg appealed to a policeman who was present, but the officer told him he ought to leave and not make any trouble. Trigg then asked if the women could stay overnight? The policeman shook his head and said that none of them could stay and that they all would have to sleep in the alleys if they could not do any better. Someone in the crowd shouted, "Before we'll stand for these niggers staying here, we'll turn this house upside down during the night." Four more policemen arrived, watched the ejection, and did nothing. The whites were successful. All the blacks left. Some twenty-five of them moved back to two rooms on Lyman, and they waited, willing to return if the chance arose.[20]

In the middle of the century's second decade blacks in Detroit shared their ghetto with Jews. The thirty-block area bounded by Leland on the north, Macomb on the south, Hastings on the east, and Brush on the west was 70 percent black, the rest Jewish.[21] With the closeness of inadequate housing, life, in classic ghetto fashion, spilled into the streets. If privacy was to exist at all it had to be a cerebral construct; it was impossible as physical reality.

Thousands of separate incidents—of baiting, petty theft, and sullen stares, real and imagined—must have occurred daily as the races shared their ghetto. In themselves the incidents were of minor importance, recorded only on the sensibilities of the individuals involved. Accumulated, they nourished the fear and the hatred each group felt for the other. Not surprisingly there was an occasional major breakdown in the uneasy coexistence, one of which occurred on August 1, 1915.

At six o'clock in the evening a white woman stepped off a streetcar at Hastings and Division streets. Two blacks approached her. One of them drew a knife from his pocket and cut the strings of the woman's handbag. The incident did not go unnoticed. Several small boys, sons of Jewish merchants in the neighborhood, shouted an alarm. The blacks became startled. The man with the knife dropped the purse and ran after the streetcar, which was just getting underway; the other fled down a side street. By this time a crowd of Jews had gathered. They saw that the black who was chasing the streetcar had grabbed the casing of an open window and had pulled himself inside. A Jewish man, a resident of Hastings Street, raced after the car and caught it in the next block. He grasped the rope to the trolley pole and pulled the pole off the overhead wire. The car stopped. The crowd of Jews surrounded it.

Bricks, sticks, and stones were hurled at the car. The passengers fled in terror; all but the robber. He drew his knife and stood in the empty car. A Jewish man leaped inside with thoughts of capturing the black man, but he was stabbed in the back and staggered out. The robber followed him from the car and with wide, arcing sweeps of his knife kept the crowd in a semicircle as he stood with his back to the trolley door.

At this point another black, Charles Hamilton, came hurtling through the crowd with a drawn revolver and took a stand with the other. "You better back up until I get this man out," he shouted. The crowd gave way, but not because of Hamilton's warning. Just at that moment a reinforcement of twenty-five blacks descended on the Jews from behind, armed with knives, revolvers, and bricks. The Jews scattered and fled down Hastings Street, blacks in pursuit. Several shots were fired. One man was hit with a bullet, another stabbed. Cheers and applause rang from above, as black women leaning from the upper-story windows along Hastings Street showed their approval.

When the mob—the pursuers and the pursued—reached Division Street, Hamilton entered his rooming house with the robber. Moments later the police arrived. A detective went into the rooming house and was met by Hamilton, who pressed his revolver against the policeman's stomach and said, "Get out or I'll shoot right through you." There was a struggle, and the detective managed to disarm his assailant. In the confusion the robber escaped.

The police arrested four blacks, including Charles Hamilton, and loaded them into a patrol wagon. By this time nearly 2000 persons had surged into the street. Most were Jews. The blacks hurriedly sought refuge in nearby rooming houses. Cries of "Lynch 'em" came from the mob as it pressed forward in an attempt to drag the now thoroughly frightened captives from the patrol wagon. The police struggled to protect their prisoners and finally forced the mob to disperse. They returned to the precinct house, where the blacks were charged with felonious assault.

An hour later another call for the police was sent from Division and Hastings streets. Fearing the disturbance had broken out once more, the police inspector in charge quickly dispatched three automobiles filled with patrolmen and detectives to the scene. The call proved to be of minor importance. Uneasy calm prevailed again.[22]

II

Blacks had been among the pioneers of Detroit. As slaves, they constituted part of the population almost from the earliest days of settlement,
numbering nearly 200 by the 1780s. One of them, in 1792, was the first
man to be legally executed in the region.[23]

Slavery in Michigan Territory ceased to be viable in 1807 when,
after a long legal debate, the area was closed to further slave ownership,
with only those bondsmen officially registered to British settlers at the
onset of American rule (July 11, 1796) retaining slave status. Over the
next three decades these blacks died, escaped, or were manumitted. The
legal end came in 1837, when the institution was expressly forbidden by
the constitution of the new state of Michigan. By the 1840s Michigan was
a bastion of abolitionism, having founded antislavery societies which
disseminated speakers and written matter with a zeal characteristic of
their Massachusetts brethren. Detroit was a northern terminus for slaves
escaping the South, and when Congress passed the Fugitive Slave Law
in 1850 the city became a funnel for blacks seeking the legal safety of
Canada.[24]

Yet racial attitudes changed little. In April 1861 the *Detroit Free
Press* expressed the alarm and amazement of white citizenry at the sight
of a "negro military company, armed with muskets and bayonets and
fully uniformed," parading at midnight. "The first time in our knowledge
that an armed organization of such a character was ever seen in the
streets of Detroit," came the cry.[25] Two years later the pressures of
civil war became more than a few white men could bear, and in March
1863, scarcely two months after the president had issued his Emancipation Proclamation, violence erupted.

A mulatto named William Faulkner had been accused of committing
an assault on a white girl. Whites were incensed. When Faulkner was
being returned to jail at the end of the first day of his trial, a mob—
mostly Irish, some Germans—gathered in the streets and stoned him.
The trial concluded the next day, and Faulkner was sentenced to life
imprisonment. Again the trip from the courthouse to the jail was inter-
cepted by enraged whites. The provost guard helping the sheriff protect
the prisoner was attacked and in self-defense fired on and killed one of
the mob. The prisoner was safely locked in jail. In their fury the white

men marched on the third-ward black neighborhood, set fire to houses and shops, and beat any black people who appeared. Property damage was extensive; some thirty-five houses were destroyed, more than 200 people left homeless. Two blacks were killed, at least sixteen others seriously injured. Seven years later William Faulkner was found to be innocent and given a pardon.[26]

The years from the end of the Civil War to the beginning of the Great Migration in 1915 were years of relative stability and of easing tensions for Detroit blacks. Their number grew very slowly—2235 in 1870, 2821 in 1880, 3431 in 1890, 4111 in 1900, and 5741 in 1910. The white population of Detroit was growing at a much faster rate in these years,[27] and it was easy for some blacks to believe that their small, well-established number was gradually being accepted into the community and respected for their contribution.[28] There were many instances of blacks living peacefully side by side with immigrant whites,[29] and so, for a few at least, the old wariness black men felt toward white men began to relax just a little.

Yet Detroit before 1915 was hardly an integrated community. Long before the onset of the Great Migration, most blacks were clustered in a clearly defined residential area on the city's near east side. From 1860 to 1900 never fewer than 82.5 percent of Detroit's blacks lived there.[30] In 1910, the first year for which decennial census population data by wards is available, the pattern still held. Sixty-eight percent of 5741 blacks lived in the east side's third and fifth wards, with 4870 blacks (84.8 percent) living in the first, third, fifth, and seventh wards combined.[31]

Just as black clustering in Detroit anteceded the Great Migration, so too did dilapidated, filthy housing and exorbitant rents. In the area of several blocks bounded by Beaubien and Hastings on the east and west and Napoleon and Brewster on the north and south lived the black "alley dwellers." The year was 1911. In the rear of a Beaubien Street lot stood an old shack, measuring some fifteen by thirty feet. It had two levels.The lower part was used as a shed and stable and the upper part was intended for storage of hay. The lower part remained a shed, but the hay loft had been converted into a dwelling, partitioned off with rough lumber to make two rooms and two recesses. In this rookery were housed five persons—a man, a woman, a young girl, and two

adult lodgers. The windows looked out onto an alley where refuse collected through the winter. At the entrance to the building was a large
box of manure which had been thrown out of an adjoining stable.

A similar shack stood in an alley between Alfred and Brewster
streets. Built of rough boards and resembling a chicken coop, it was
divided into four rooms housing two black families. Each paid $5
a month rent. The total value of the shack could not have been more
than $25. Another alley shed between Hastings and Rivard streets,
occupied by two families and a varying number of lodgers, paid its
owner a rental of $18 a month. The families had long since given
up trying to keep out the filth.[32]

There were some black Detroiters, however, who stood apart.
Identified by a local newspaper in 1902 as fifty-one families and
individuals ("Detroit's Most Exclusive Social Clique, The Cultured
Colored '40'"), they were generally professionals, businessmen, or
public servants. Often college-educated and thoroughly middle-class in
life style and outlook, they lived in a world unknown to the preponderance of Detroit blacks, an integrated world where whites were met
on a daily basis and business conducted between seeming equals. They
were proud of their accomplishments and of the respect they were
given by responsible white people, but they were always fearful that
the fragile distinction in the white man's mind between them and other
blacks might blur and the insidious stereotype come to cover them
both.[33]

Their pattern of church membership offers a clue to their self-image.
A few belonged to white congregations. Most of the rest chose St. Matthew's Episcopal, finding dignity in its quiet mass, safety from the poor
in its rented pews, and comfort in the fellowship demonstrated by
brethren in white Episcopal congregations. Whatever his church affiliation, however, no member of the black elite could abide the frenzied
fundamentalism favored by the lower social order.[34]

The elite walked a tight line on public issues. As black men they
were concerned about discrimination, and battled it,[35] but they always
recognized that their position above the throng was marginal and that
to remain recognizable they had to keep their dignity. So none of
Detroit's leading black citizens would participate in the 1871 com-
memoration of the Fifteenth Amendment, and in 1875 a meeting of

the elite approved a resolution recommending no further celebration of "all days that are only celebrated by them [blacks], as the tendency is to perpetuate caste feeling."[36]

Because image was important to them, so too were words that produced images. "Negro" was a particularly opprobrious term since it suggested the white stereotype. For this reason the *Plaindealer*—a newspaper founded in 1883 by five young members of the black elite, including brothers Robert and Benjamin Pelham—initiated a campaign to substitute "Afro-American" for "Negro" in Detroit. "The word 'Negro' as commonly used in America and as scientifically applied," said the journal, "means everything low and degraded." It was hoped that "Afro-American" would carry the implication that blacks were simply another hyphenated American ethnic group.[37]

The elite's housing reflected their social standing and economic accomplishment. They chose sturdy, usually brick, single-family structures in neat neighborhoods among middle-class whites, generally near the outer edges of the city's settlement. The Benjamin Pelhams, for example, moved from Alfred Street, near downtown, to Frederick Street in 1907 because the old neighborhood was beginning to deteriorate. The new neighborhood was white, middle-class, with no first-generation Americans. Across the street was the D. M. Ferry experimental seed farm. Sitting on the front porch the family could look across four blocks to Hendrie Street. They would live in this house until 1921, when Benjamin Pelham sold it to the Couzens Foundation, which was going to build an expanded Children's Hospital on the site. They then moved to Burns Avenue and again were one of the few black families within a six- or eight-block radius.[38]

Another black professional man in Detroit moved out even closer to the edge of the city, to where a neighborhood did not yet even exist. He was Arthur William Palmer, whose family lived in the first house on the block on Mount Vernon, just east of Woodward. The people who moved in later would be white, creating within a few years a racially and ethnically mixed neighborhood, a neat reversal of the classic pattern of inundation. The irony of this was not lost on Palmer.

He was a barber, but this trade was a dying one for blacks in the United States in the 1890s. White Americans were turning more and more toward Europe for their standards of civility and emulating

Europe in its choice of imaginative literature, currency, and modes of personal service. Respectable people on the Continent used whites for domestics and barbers, and so too it would be in the United States. By necessity, therefore, Arthur Palmer, who had always been interested in politics, got a job in the county treasurer's office and worked there for years. He spent much of his life amid the contacts and conflicts of the central city, and he recognized early that he did not cherish this sort of existence for his children. In 1902 his family acquired the home on Mount Vernon. For a long time he would not allow his children to go into downtown Detroit.

Arthur Palmer was a second-generation Detroiter at a time when many of the city's subsequent first families were just arriving. His father had been a slave whose own sire was freely acknowledged to be the white owner. The young slave William Henry Palmer (a name he later assumed; his slave name is lost) grew up in his owner-father's house on the Virginia plantation. He played with his younger half-brothers and sisters, with whom he was identical in skin color. But harmony ended when William was fourteen years old. It was time for his brothers and sisters to be sent off to school, but no such plans were in the works for young William. He was to be sent into the fields. So he ran away. He got to Detroit via the Underground Railroad with the pursuers his father had dispatched literally two blocks behind. The safety of Canada was in front of him, but in between was the Detroit River. There was a ship tied up to a dock. He jumped aboard, scrambled down into the coal bin, covered his body with coal dust, and reemerged. His pursuers did not recognize him: he was too black. They turned away and began to search elsewhere, and William Palmer escaped to Canada. In Toronto he assumed his name and met Augustina Jefferson, a girl who could trace her ancestry, more circuitously, back to another Virginia plantation owner. She had been born and raised in Jamaica, the daughter of a black American minister sent there as a missionary. Her father's term ended, and their return home to the United States blocked by the Civil War, they emigrated instead to Toronto. In that city William Henry Palmer and Augustina Jefferson were married. Some time after the close of the war, the couple returned to Detroit. William Palmer's name and his occupation—cook—can be found in the *Detroit City Directory* for 1869.

Arthur Palmer, who often thought of his parents' history, was jealous for his family's privacy and determined to protect his children—two sons and a daughter—from indignities in any way he could. The family's house on the city's periphery meant his children could go to the best public schools—to the brand-new Breitmeyer School and prestigious Northern High School—and have open fields on which to play. There was time enough later to learn about the great problems of housing and discrimination, of human deprivation and human depravity.[39]

The good life did not come easily for Arthur Palmer, as it did not come easily for any of Detroit's established Old Guard blacks. It had to be protected. Unquestionably, they were frightened by the arrival of migrants from the South, black people who did not know how to live in a city and who might, by their presence and demeanor, cause whites to take recourse in the stereotype.[40] So when Eugene Kinckle Jones, black representative of the New York-based National League on Urban Conditions Among Negroes, stepped off the train in Detroit one day in 1916 to establish an Urban League branch office, the Old Guard blacks took his visit to be symbolic of what was happening in Detroit. To them Kinckle Jones' arrival was less a mission of interracial goodwill than a visitation from an agent of doom. So, with the frenzy born of fear and of the need to protect themselves and what they had accomplished from the demon, the Old Guard blacks ran Kinckle Jones out of town.[41]

III

Nevertheless, the deluge—not even exorcising Kinckle Jones could stop it. There were a thousand new black faces a month; sometimes twice that many in a single week. A city-wide population of fewer than 7000 blacks in 1915 grew to 40,000 in 1920, 80,000 in 1925, and 120,000 in 1930. Blacks from the rural South who a few years before had scarcely heard of the Wonder City of the Magic Motor now found themselves living there.[42]

It seemed as if whole counties of the rural South were being depopulated. "There has been lots of darkies left here and nearly all the good ones is gone," grumbled a white Alabama farmer in 1917,[43] and the flight northward continued. A United States Department of Agriculture survey of April 23, 1923 showed that in the year preceding 15,000 black farmers had left Arkansas for points north, and that in seven months, 22,750 blacks had left South Carolina, giving that state a white majority for the first time in generations.[44] Fifty separate highway construction projects had to be abandoned in North Carolina in the spring of 1923 because in one month 5000 unskilled black laborers had disappeared.[45] Hardest hit by the exodus was Georgia. A hundred thousand blacks left in 1921 and 1922, and 80,000 more through mid-summer 1923, with no sign of abatement. By September 1923 there were more than 46,000 farm dwellings vacant in the state, 55,524 plows idle, and a farm labor shortage in excess of 70,000 men. Farm land that had brought from $40 to $75 an acre in 1919 now met no demand at all; it lay unused and grew only weeds. The damage to the state's economy was staggering—an estimated $25 million in agricultural revenue alone in 1923.[46] But there was a far greater cost—the cost of the departure of the young. Forty-five percent of the black males between the ages of fifteen and thirty-four in Georgia in 1920 would be gone by 1930.[47] The presence of these men had been taken for granted. Whites had assumed they would remain forever to do the state's work. Now they were leaving to contribute to northern industrial development.

The contribution was often solicited. Before 1915 northern industry had been absorbing nearly one million immigrants a year. When the war came and cut off this flow of cheap labor, industry began to look southward for an alternative supply. Labor agents from nearly every major northern city—representing industries, railroads, and groups like the Employers' Association of Detroit—traveled the South in search of black labor. They sang the praises of factory life and the $5 day. They offered to pay for transportation for blacks willing to migrate to the North and frequently chartered whole trains to handle the numbers.[48] Often blacks were skeptical of the enraptured stories of the North told by the sometimes venal white men. "I've get [sic] no confidence in some of these so-called agents," wrote a black from New Orleans.[49] But succumbing to the promise of the riches beyond is something Americans have done since the beginning of their history, and so it was too with southern blacks. Their skepticism submerged by hope, they left in droves for the promised land.

The South did not view the exodus with equanimity. To be sure, some, like Judge Gilbert Stephenson of Winston-Salem, North Carolina, saw reason for rejoicing: "Many of these young bucks already have criminal records and, going North, add to their bad reputation. They are the ones who cause riots."[50] But most southerners were disturbed. Towns and cities frantically set up interracial councils in an attempt to dissuade blacks from migrating and to convince them that they were indeed cherished members of the community. Indicative of such efforts was the sign stretched across the main street of Canton, Mississippi, proclaiming: "Come White and Colored People and Let's Get Together."[51] "Magnolia State Invites Wandering Negroes Home," read a Mississippi newspaper headline.[52] But throughout the South most blacks saw through the sham, and the migration continued. Whites became more desperate. Commissions of white men were dispatched from southern states northward on the errand of luring migrant blacks back to the South. They offered railroad fare to those who had found northern opportunity an illusive mirage. Few blacks chose to return. "If I've got to be killed, I would rather be killed by my friends," was the way one man put it.[53] So white southerners, often not reluctantly, turned to a more direct means of persuasion: coercion and violence. Blacks no longer dared openly to solicit information about migrating.[54] Labor agents were frequently arrested, fined, imprisoned, and beaten.[55] The city of Macon, Georgia, passed an ordinance requiring labor recruiters to pay a license fee of $25,000 and barring their admission entirely except on recommendation of ten local ministers, ten manufacturers, and twenty-five businessmen.[56] Even the frequently racist administration of Woodrow Wilson attempted to limit the migration of the South's labor supply. The wartime United States Railway Administration, under the direction of Georgia-born William Gibbs McAdoo, secretary of the treasury, issued an order preventing anyone in the North from prepaying the transportation of a southern black who wanted to migrate. Only when pressure was brought by the NAACP and by Senator Warren G. Harding and Representative Henry I. Emerson of Ohio did the Railway Administration finally rescind its order.[57]

Why the Great Migration? No one can say for sure. A song suggested one reason why so many blacks left the South:

De boll weevil say to de farmer:
  "You better leave me alone;

I done eat all yo' cotton, now I'm goin'
   to start on yo' corn,
I'll have a home, I'll have a home."[58]

And in an older song there was another reason why some did not leave:

Ole Aunt Dinah, she's just like me
She work so hard she want to be free
But old Aunt Dinah's gittin' kinda ole
She's afraid to go to Canada on account
   of the cold.[59]

There were the deplorable social conditions in the South—the Jim Crow regulations, the all but nonexistent chance for education, the constant threat of mob violence, the near peonage of the agricultural system, and the horror of a legal structure whose purpose seemed only to punish, never to protect. By 1910 every southern state had effectively disfranchised the black man. Between 1900 and 1914 an average of seventy-two blacks a year were lynched.[60] And there were the jobs and the promise of the North.

Somewhere between the squalor of the present and the vision of the future came the decision to move. But why did it happen then? There is no evidence that social conditions, as bad as they were for the black man in the South, were any worse from 1915 to 1926 than they had been earlier. Jim Crow segregation was already decades old, and the rate of lynching fell short of the levels reached in the last years of the nineteenth century.[61] Nor was severe agricultural depression, which prevailed in the South before American entry into the World War, new to the region. Even if it could be shown that in certain counties the depths of depression exceeded that of previous trough periods—and cotton prices and production figures over three decades suggest the possibility unlikely[62]—a student of the migration would still be hard put to prove that the suffering was sufficiently more acute to account for the great, sudden shift of population.

So perhaps the vision rather than the squalor was the critical consideration: that the industrial cities, already growing at a frantic rate and now also preparing for war, desperately needed a new labor supply, offered black men the chance for steady employment, and were willing to pay good wages. The migrants themselves seemed to express their yearnings in these terms. "Being a poor man with a family to care for, I am not coming to live on flowry Beds of ease for I am a man who works and wish to make the best I can out of life," said one.[63] "We are not particular about the electric lights and all i want is fairly good wages and steady work," said another.[64]

Urban opportunity was present not only in the North but also in the South, and some southern cities experienced a considerable increase in black population. Birmingham went from 52,305 blacks in 1910 to 70,230 in 1920 to 99,077 in 1930; Memphis from 52,441 to 61,181 to 96,550; and Atlanta from 51,902 to 62,796 to 90,075. But Richmond lost 1053 blacks from 1920 to 1930, and Norfolk gained just 550.

So southern towns were one alternative for the black migrant. But, as a whole, they did not have the appeal of places further north. Indeed, were one to look at farm-to-city movement from 1910 to 1930 for the South only, nothing unusual would appear to be happening. Blacks had been leaving rural areas for southern cities for generations; the numbers now simply kept pace. Throughout the period the percentage of blacks in the total populations of Birmingham, Memphis, and Atlanta remained roughly constant.[65] Also, many blacks who were now migrating to southern cities may well have stayed only a short time. Once familiar with the way of the factory they would leave again, this time for the North and the "real" opportunity. Others behind them would in turn follow the same pattern—the temporary stop for education and then resumption of the journey, though as the migration sped into the 1920s these intermediate stops were probably made with less and less frequency.[66] And, in contrast to the increase in the southern cities, the increase in the black populations of northern cities due to the migration was staggering (see Table 4).

Something had happened to the southern black man, something which struck dumb many white southerners who were watching. Black men who for generations had stoically endured, who to whites had been easily recognizable as creatures of languor and lethargy, suddenly had become unrecognizable in their restlessness. Whites once had been able smugly and confidently to berate the black for his apathy and laziness.

TABLE 4

INCREASE IN BLACK POPULATIONS OF NORTHERN CITIES, 1910-1930

City	1930	1920	1910
New York, N.Y.	327,706	152,467	91,709
Chicago	233,903	109,458	44,103
Philadelphia	219,599	134,229	84,459
Detroit	120,066	40,838	5,741
Cleveland	71,899	34,451	8,448
Pittsburgh	54,983	37,725	25,623
Gary, Indiana	17,922	5,299	383
Buffalo	13,563	4,511	1,773
Toledo	13,260	5,691	1,877
Akron	11,080	5,580	657

Source: U.S. Department of Commerce, Bureau of the Census, *Negroes in the United States, 1920-32*, p. 55.

Now whites were frightened and awed. "Where is that happy-go-lucky, banjo-playing attitude toward life?" asked the *Richmond News*.[67] What was happening to the system, they were really asking, the system which so effectively stifled the ambition of the black and made him—happily, comfortably—nigger to us? What was happening to the system that told whites from the minute they became aware that the niggers were better off because of it and them, and told them too that the niggers were their burden and whites had to do their duty, even if it meant eliminating dissidents and apostates from either race? The system which had even been able, with its constant threat of punishment, to justify itself to many black men and to convince them too of its merit now indeed seemed to be cracking,[68] and the great trek northward continued.

One thing that had happened to the black man was that he had been to France. Not all black men, of course, but enough to write letters home; enough for the burgeoning black press to do stories about; enough, that is, for many times their number to share—somehow, even if only with opaque understanding—the experience of being treated like a human being. The southern system, in its totalitarian presence, worked efficiently so long as no promise of improvement was held out to the black man. Then, he would be grateful for an occasional dispensation. But if just once the vision of a better, or at least a different, sort of life were allowed to creep in, so too would creep in dissatisfaction and the determination to escape. Such was the result of the war experience.[69]

It had happened before to a few American blacks. "From the day I set foot in France," wrote the poet and novelist James Weldon Johnson,

> I became aware of the working of a miracle within me. I became aware of a quick readjustment to life and to environment. I recaptured for the first time since childhood the sense of being just a human being. I need not try to analyze this change for my colored readers; they will understand in a flash what took place. For my white readers . . . I am afraid that any analysis will be inadequate, perhaps futile. . . . I was suddenly free; free from the conflict within the Man-Negro dualism and the innumerable maneuvers in thought and behavior that it compels; free from the problem of the many obvious or subtle adjustments to a multitude of bans and taboos; free from special scorn, special tolerance, special condescension, special commiseration; free to be merely a man.[70]

What Johnson described happened to others. Seeds were planted, and dissatisfaction grew.

The United States government had feared that blacks might glimpse a new freedom over there and thus become restless back home, and for that reason the Army of Woodrow Wilson ordered the French liaison to issue a directive to the French Army. Called "Secret Information Concerning Black American Troops," it sketched the ongoing premises of American race relations and called on the French military to exercise its influence in keeping the native cantonment population from "spoiling" black American soldiers. "The increasing number of Negroes in the United States . . . would create for the white race in the

Republic a menace of degeneracy were it not that an impassable gulf has been made between them," said the directive in part.

>   As this danger does not exist for the French race, the French public has become accustomed to treating the Negro with familiarity and indulgence.
>   This indulgence and this familiarity are matters of grievous concern to the Americans. They consider them an affront to their national policy. They are afraid that contact with the French will inspire in black Americans aspirations which to them [the whites] appear intolerable.[71]

When the French Ministry heard of the distribution of the document among the Prefects and Sous-Prefects of France it ordered that copies of the directive be collected and burned. But destroying the documents was as futile a gesture as having had them distributed, for the damage would be done regardless. The vision of "freedom" would be clearly infused, the migration powered, and the course of American history fundamentally changed.[72]

NOTES

1. Quoted in "'F.O.B. Detroit': The Romance of the Wonder City of the Magic Motor," *The Outlook* 111 (December 22, 1915): 984-85.

2. *Social Service Directory of Detroit, 1917* (n.p., n.d.), p. 36; Detroit Housing Association, *Right Methods in a Housing Bureau* (January 1915); Charles B. Ball, "Homes of Today and Citizens of Tomorrow" (Address at the Detroit Museum of Art, April 15, 1915, Detroit Housing Association reprint); *Detroit Journal,* February 16, 1917; *Detroit News,* March 13, 1917.

3. *Sixth Annual Report of the Department of Buildings of the City of Detroit, Year Ending December 31st, 1916,* p. 6, in *Annual Reports . . . of the City of Detroit for the Year 1915-1916* (n.p., n.d.).

4. City of Detroit, Department of Police, *Fifty-Eighth Annual Report* (1923), p. 1.

5. *Annual Report of the City Plan Commission* (Detroit, 1928), p. 15; Adcraft Club, *A Study of the City of Detroit,* p. 60. The City

Plan Commission put the number of families provided for in 1923 at 23,151, the Adcraft Club at 23,153.

6. *Annual Report of the City Plan Commission* (1928), p. 15.

7. Barnard, *Independent Man*, pp. 24-25, 103-05, 115, 126-33; Graeme O'Geran, "A History of the Detroit Street Railways" (Ph.D. diss., University of Michigan, 1928); *Sixth Annual Report of the Department of Buildings of the City of Detroit . . . 1916*, p. 8; Jerome G. Thomas, "The City of Detroit: A Study in Urban Geography" (Ph.D. diss., University of Michigan, 1928), figs. 10, 11, 66, pp. 58-59; Detroit Urban League Board, Minutes, December 18, 1919, Detroit Urban League Papers, Box 1, MHC.

8. *Annual Report of the City Plan Commission* (1928), p. 15; Glazer, *Detroit: A Study in Urban Development*, pp. 94-95; Cyril Arthur Player, "Detroit: Essence of America," *New Republic* 51 (August 3, 1927): 274; *Detroit News*, August 15, 1974.

9. Player, "Detroit: Essence of America," p. 274.

10. In the 1910 and 1920 censuses, breakdowns were offered on homes owned "free" and "encumbered," and if one could assume that comparatively few workingmen owned their homes outright, the statistics on encumbered homes might have been helpful. But the designations were dropped in 1930, so no overall comparison is possible. In the 1930 census, information was given on "value" of homes. Had this data been available in 1910 and 1920, and an upper limit to the cost of a laborer's house arbitrarily set for each of the two decades under consideration, a good estimate of the increasing incidence of worker home-ownership might have been made.

11. National Industrial Conference Board, "The Cost of Living among Wage-Earners, Detroit, Michigan, September, 1921," *Special Report Number 19, October, 1921* (New York: National Industrial Conference Board, 1921), pp. 6-7.

12. *Fourteenth Census* (1920), vol. 3, *Population*, pp. 496-97; Detroit Board of Education, "The 1925 Detroit City Census," *Research Bulletin No. 9, October, 1925* (Detroit: The Detroit Educational Bulletin, 1925); building, housing, and assessment data in the *Annual Reports for the City of Detroit* for the years 1916-26, 1930; National Industrial Conference Board, "The Cost of Living among Wage-Earners, Detroit, Michigan, September, 1921," pp. 7-8; Eric Kocher, "Economic and Physical Growth of Detroit, 1701-1935," Division of Economics and Statistics, Federal Housing Administration, November, 1935, pp. 64-66, maps in app., typescript carbon in

MHC; Thomas, "The City of Detroit: A Study. in Urban Geography," figs. 10, 11, pp. 57-59.

13. Player, "Detroit: Essence of America," p. 274.

14. Unsigned [John C. Dancy] memorandum on housing, August 1919, Detroit Urban League Papers, Box 1, MHC; see too John C. Dancy, *Sand against the Wind: The Memoirs of John C. Dancy* (Detroit: Wayne State University Press, 1966), pp. 56-57.

15. *Detroit Free Press*, May 14, 1919, p. 1; see also *Detroit News Tribune*, July 22, 1917.

16. U.S. Department of Commerce, Bureau of the Census, *Negroes in the United States, 1920-32* (Washington, D.C.: Government Printing Office, 1935), p. 55; Detroit Bureau of Governmental Research, *The Negro in Detroit*, sect. 2, *Population* (Detroit Bureau of Governmental Research, 1926), p. 15.

17. *Detroit News*, March 17, 1917, p. 5.

18. Another manifestation of racial tension not directly related to housing but apparent to anyone was the increasing, and disproportionate, regularity with which police and blacks were shooting at each other. In the thirty days ending November 13, 1920, five policemen were wounded in Detroit; four of the assailants were black. Over the same period two policemen were shot and killed, both by blacks. Over a longer period the figures are similarly contorted. From January through November 1923, three policemen were killed by blacks, two by whites; five officers were wounded by black men, none by whites. Blacks comprised roughly 6.5 percent of Detroit's total population in 1923. James W. Inches, commissioner of police, to John R. [*sic*] Dancy, November 13, 1920, Detroit Urban League Papers, Box 1, MHC; memorandum of William P. Rutledge, superintendent of police, to F. H. Croul, commissioner of police, December 20, 1923, Mayor's Office Papers, 1924, Box 1, folder "Police Department (2)–1924," BHC. The violence was reciprocal. In 1925 fourteen blacks were killed by policemen in Detroit, compared to three in New York City. Detroit's black population that year was approximately 82,000; New York City's about 183,000. Detroit Bureau of Governmental Research, *The Negro in Detroit*, sect. 9, *Crime*, p. 38; also Walter White, "Negro Segregation Comes North," *The Nation* 121 (October 21, 1925): 458-460.

The face of the law in Detroit was white. As of September 21, 1926, out of a total force of 2848 men, the Detroit Police Department employed 14 black officers, or 0.5 percent. In this Detroit compared unfavorably with such cities as Chicago (114 black officers, or 2.1 percent

of the force), Columbus (18 black officers, or 6.7 percent), and Pittsburgh (36 black officers, or 4.7 percent). Of ten major northern cities
with an appreciable black population at that time (Boston, Chicago,
Cleveland, Columbus, Detroit, Kansas City, Los Angeles, New York,
Pittsburgh, St. Louis), none had fewer blacks on its police force per
1000 blacks in the city than did Detroit. Detroit Bureau of Governmental
Research, *The Negro in Detroit*, sec. 9, *Crime*, p. 38, apps. I, II B. Whether
the racial composition of the Detroit Police Department contributed to
an inordinate amount of shooting between police and blacks is problem-
atic. What is clear is that hostility was open, and that no observer could
have failed to be aware of it.

19. *Detroit Free Press*, June 18, 1920.

20. Memorandum of Forrester B. Washington to the Detroit Urban
League Board, August 25, 1917, Detroit Urban League Papers, Box 1,
MHC.

21. Detroit Bureau of Governmental Research, *The Negro in Detroit*, sect. 2, *Population*, p. 10; Ulysses W. Boykin, *A Hand Book on
the Detroit Negro* (Detroit: The Minority Study Associates, 1943),
p. 54.

22. *Detroit Free Press*, August 2, 1915, pp. 1-2.

23. Detroit Bureau of Governmental Research, *The Negro in Detroit*, sect. 2, *Population*, pp. 1-2; Burton, *City of Detroit, Michigan,
1701-1922*, vol. 1, pp. 475-84; Dancy, *Sand against the Wind*, pp. 37, 38;
George B. Catlin, *The Story of Detroit* (Detroit: The Detroit News,
1923), pp. 738-39; *The John Askin Papers*, vol. 1, *1747-1795*, ed.
Milo M. Quaife (Detroit: Detroit Library Commission, 1928), p. 410n.

24. Detroit Bureau of Governmental Research, *The Negro in Detroit*, sect. 2, *Population*, pp. 1-2; Dancy, *Sand against the Wind*,
pp. 39-40; David M. Katzman, *Before the Ghetto: Black Detroit in
the Nineteenth Century* (Urbana, Ill.: University of Illinois Press,
1973), pp. 5-7, 40-41.

25. *Detroit Free Press*, April 13, 1861, p. 1.

26. Boykin, *A Hand Book on the Detroit Negro*, pp. 13-14; Burton, *History of Wayne County and the City of Detroit, Michigan*,
vol. 2, pp. 1129-30; *The Late Detroit Riot, March 3, 1863: A Thrilling Nar-
rative from the Lips of the Sufferers* (Hattiesburg, Miss.: The Book
Farm, 1945); Katzman, *Before the Ghetto*, pp. 44-47.

27. Detroit Bureau of Governmental Research, *The Negro in Detroit*, sect. 2, *Population*, p. 3; *Thirteenth Census* (1910), vol. 1, *Population*, p. 208.

28. Detroit Bureau of Governmental Research, *The Negro in Detroit,* sect. 2, *Population,* pp. 2, 16; Katzman, *Before the Ghetto,* pp. 135-68.

29. Katzman, *Before the Ghetto,* esp. pp. 67-70, 78; interview of Mr. John Panzner by William A. Sullivan, University of Michigan—Wayne State University Institute of Labor and Industrial Relations, April 20, 1959, p. 5, MHC.

30. The most thorough study of blacks in Detroit in the nineteenth century, including residence patterns, is Katzman, *Before the Ghetto.* See esp. pp. 25-28, 59-61, 67-80, and the caveat on the quality of demographic data available for Detroit nonwhites before 1910, p. 61n.

31. *Thirteenth Census* (1910), vol. 2, *Population,* p. 953.

32. "The Alley Dwellers of Detroit," *Detroit News Tribune,* June 4, 1911.

33. *Detroit News Tribune,* April 27, 1902, p. 7; Katzman, *Before the Ghetto,* pp. 135-68, 177-206; Detroit Bureau of Governmental Research, *The Negro in Detroit,* sect. 2, *Population,* pp. 2-3, 16-17, 19-21; Dancy, *Sand against the Wind,* pp. 51-52; Francis H. Warren, *Michigan Manual of Freedmen's Progress* (Detroit: Freedmen's Progress Commission, 1915). Also see "Drawing the 'Color Line' in Detroit," *Detroit Tribune,* January 15, 1890. The black elite in Chicago are treated in Spear, *Black Chicago,* pp. 51-89, though more impressive, to my mind, is St. Clair Drake and Horace R. Cayton, *Black Metropolis: A Study of Negro Life in a Northern City,* 2 vols. (New York: Harper Torchbooks, 1962), 2: 658-715. The classic tract is E. Franklin Frazier, *Black Bourgeoisie: The Rise of a New Middle Class in the United States* (Glencoe, Ill.: The Free Press, 1957); also see August Meier, *Negro Thought in America, 1880-1915* (Ann Arbor, Mich.: University of Michigan Press, 1963).

34. Katzman, *Before the Ghetto,* pp. 136-47; Detroit Bureau of Governmental Research, *The Negro in Detroit,* sect. 10, *Religion,* pp. 9-10.

35. Katzman, *Before the Ghetto,* esp. pp. 175-206.

36. Ibid., pp. 163-64; *Detroit Tribune,* March 16 and 25, 1871, March 31, 1875, p. 4.

37. Katzman, *Before the Ghetto,* p. 164; *Plaindealer,* April 11, 1890, p. 4. For another view on the relationship between the name and the thing, see W.E.B. DuBois editorial, "The Name 'Negro,' " *Crisis* 35 (March 1928): 96-97.

38. *Detroit News Tribune,* April 27, 1902; Katzman, *Before the*

Ghetto, pp. 77-78; interview with Mr. Alfred H. Pelham, Detroit, Michigan, November 7, 1967.

39. Interview with Mrs. Anne A. Lewis, Detroit, Michigan, April 13, 1967; Mrs. Anne A. Lewis to David A. Levine, June 1, 1967; *Detroit City Directory, 1869-70.*

40. Detroit Bureau of Governmental Research, *The Negro in Detroit,* sect. 2, *Population,* pp. 16-17, 19-21; Dancy, *Sand against the Wind,* pp. 51-52; Forrester B. Washington, notes to speech delivered at Round Table of Negro Migration into Northern Cities, National Conference of Charities and Corrections, June 13, 1917, Detroit Urban League Papers, Box 1, MHC. Also see Forrester B. Washington, "A Program of Work for the Assimilation of Negro Immigrants in Northern Cities," *Proceedings of the National Conference of Social Work,* Pittsburgh, Pa., June 6-13, 1917, pp. 497-500.

41. Eugene Kinckle Jones to John C. Dancy, October 11, 1944, letter on file in the Detroit Urban League offices, Detroit, Michigan; interview with Mr. John C. Dancy, Detroit, Michigan, April 13, 1967; Dancy, *Sand against the Wind,* pp. 86-89.

42. Detroit Bureau of Governmental Research, *The Negro in Detroit,* sect. 2, *Population,* pp. 5-6, 14-15; *Fifteenth Census* (1930), vol. 3, pt. 1, *Population,* p. 1183; U.S. Department of Commerce, Bureau of the Census, *Negroes in the United States, 1920-32,* pp. 34-36.

Georgia sent the most black migrants to Detroit, followed by Alabama, Tennessee, and South Carolina. In the 1930 census, nearly 50 percent of Detroit's native U.S. blacks listed one of these four states as place of birth.

43. Quoted in Helen B. Pendleton, "Cotton Pickers in Northern Cities," *Survey* 37 (February 17, 1917): 570.

44. "Negro Migration," *Monthly Labor Review* 16 (June 1923): 1186.

45. Martha Bensley Bruere, "Black Folk Are Coming On," *Survey* 50 (July 15, 1923): 434.

46. "Negro Migration from Georgia," *Monthly Labor Review* 18 (January 1924): 32-35; untitled editorial, *The Nation* 117 (September 12, 1923): 254.

47. Karl E. Taeuber and Alma F. Taeuber, "The Negro Population in the United States," in *The American Negro Reference Book,* ed. John P. Davis (Englewood Cliffs, N.J.: Prentice-Hall, 1966), pp. 112-13.

48. Glen E. Carlson, "The Negro in the Industries of Detroit" (Ph.D. diss., University of Michigan, 1929), pp. 49-50, 52-53, 189; Boykin, *A Hand Book on the Detroit Negro,* p. 15; Dancy, *Sand against the Wind,* p. 56; Taeuber and Taeuber, "The Negro Population in the United States,"

p. 111; Rollin Lynde Hartt, "When the Negro Comes North," *The World's Work* 48 (May 1924): 84; George E. Haynes, "Negroes Move North," *Survey* 40 (May 4, 1918): 116.

49. Emmett J. Scott, "Letters of Negro Migrants of 1916-1918," *The Journal of Negro History* 4 (1919): 331. On venality, see pp. 330-31; also see Emmett J. Scott, *Negro Migration during the War* (New York: Oxford University Press, 1920); and Louise V. Kennedy, *The Negro Peasant Turns Cityward* (New York: Columbia University Press, 1930).

50. Quoted in "Negro Migration as the South Sees It," *Survey* 38 (August 11, 1917): 428.

51. "Social Progress," *Crisis* 20 (October 1920): 291; see also "Negro Migration from Georgia," pp. 32-35.

52. Walter F. White, "The Success of Negro Migration," *Crisis* 19 (January 1920): 112.

53. Ibid.; see also "New Negro Migration," *Survey* 45 (February 26, 1921): 752; and Hartt, "When the Negro Comes North," p. 86.

54. Scott, "Letters of Negro Migrants of 1916-1918," pp. 306, 311-12; Emmett J. Scott, "Additional Letters of Negro Migrants of 1916-1918," *The Journal of Negro History* 4 (1919): 417, 426.

55. Carlson, "The Negro in the Industries of Detroit," pp. 52-53n.

56. Charles E. Silberman, *Crisis in Black and White* (New York: Vintage Books, 1964), p. 26.

57. Charles Flint Kellogg, *NAACP: A History of the National Association for the Advancement of Colored People,* vol. 1 (Baltimore: Johns Hopkins University Press, 1967), p. 221n.

58. In Carl Sandburg, *The American Songbag* (New York: Harcourt, Brace and Company, 1927), pp. 8-10.

59. In Ralph Ellison, "The Art of Fiction: An Overview," *Shadow and Act* (New York: Signet Books, 1966), p. 173.

60. C. Vann Woodward, *Origins of the New South, 1877-1913* (Baton Rouge: Louisiana State University Press, 1951), p. 321; *1952 Negro Year Book,* ed. Jessie Parkhurst Guzman (New York: Wm. H. Wise & Co., 1952), p. 278; also Meier, *Negro Thought in America, 1880-1915;* and C. Vann Woodward, *The Strange Career of Jim Crow* (New York: Oxford University Press, 1957).

61. *1952 Negro Year Book,* p. 278; W.E.B. DuBois editorial, "Lynching," *Crisis* 32 (May 1926): 10.

62. U.S. Department of Commerce, Bureau of the Census, *Historical Statistics of the United States, Colonial Times to 1957* (Washington, D.C.: Government Printing Office, 1960), p. 301.

63. Scott, "Letters of Negro Migrants of 1916-1918," p. 297.

64. Ibid., p. 292. Some students of the migration see its cause solely in the economics of job opportunity. See Donald Ramsay Young, *American Minority Peoples: A Study in Racial and Cultural Conflicts in the United States* (New York and London: Harper and Brothers, 1932); and Thomas J. Woofter, Jr., *Races and Ethnic Groups in American Life* (New York: McGraw-Hill Book Co., 1933).

65. U.S. Department of Commerce, Bureau of the Census, *Negroes in the United States, 1920-32*, p. 55.

66. Hartt, "When the Negro Comes North," pp. 84-85; "Negro Migration in 1923," *Monthly Labor Review* 18 (April 1924): 763; Bruere, "Black Folk Are Coming On," pp. 432-33.

67. Quoted in "The Bourbon South," *Crisis* 30 (June 1925): 88.

68. The nature of the system of the single truth traced from its beginnings is told in W.J. Cash's brilliant *The Mind of the South* (New York: Alfred A. Knopf, 1941); also Lillian Smith, *Killers of the Dream* (New York: Anchor Books, 1963).

Some indirect evidence on this point is the wave of violence that swept the South (in addition to the violence in the North) in the summer of 1919, coincident with the return of black soldiers. Some southern whites, upset over a perceived stirring of the black man from the passivity which the system had always demanded, reacted with vengeance. The Ku Klux Klan revived. More than seventy blacks were lynched. Ten black soldiers, several still in their uniforms, were hung by white mobs. Fourteen blacks in the South were publicly burned. See John Hope Franklin, *From Slavery to Freedom: A History of Negro Americans* (New York: Vintage Books, 1969), pp. 478-86.

At least four of the many racial incidents in the South in 1919 can be classified as riots. They were in Charleston, South Carolina; Longview, Texas; Knoxville, Tennessee; and Phillips County, Arkansas. For an account of these and other racial incidents within a larger theoretical framework, see Arthur I. Waskow, *From Race Riot to Sit-In, 1919 and the 1960s: A Study in the Connections between Conflict and Violence* (Garden City, N.Y.: Doubleday & Company, 1966).

69. Robert L. Vann, for one, was convinced that the war experience directly accounted for the migration. The child of ex-slave tenant farmers, Vann grew up so submerged in the back country of North Carolina that he was ten years old before he saw his first train. Ultimately, however, he reached the North and built the *Pittsburgh Courier* into a major black newspaper. "The chief cause of the migration at present," said Vann in 1924,

is the disillusionment that has spread far and wide through our black race since the war. Ignorant Southern Negroes in the camps encountered the word "democracy" for the first time, and wondered what it meant. Later on, in France, they saw white people willing to eat beside them in restaurants and sit beside them in trains, and wondered what that could mean. Then it struck them. "This must be democracy," they said. "It's that mysterious thing we're fighting for. It's what we're going to have in America when we get home." Their discovery that the black man was Jim-Crowed in the South after the War, precisely as he had been Jim-Crowed in the South before the war, bred a great discontent, a great restlessness, a great determination somehow to escape. [Quoted in Hartt, "When the Negro Comes North." p. 85.]

For further information on Vann, see Bardolph, *The Negro Vanguard,* pp. 192-96.

70. Johnson is describing his experiences circa 1906. James Weldon Johnson, *Along This Way* (New York: Viking Press, 1933), p. 209. The ellipses in the quotation are in the original.

71. "Documents of the War," collected by W. E. Burghardt DuBois, *Crisis* 18 (May 1919): 16-18.

72. Because he, like many white Americans, was fearful that blacks had developed habits and preferences in France which would be detrimental to interracial stability when they returned to the United States, President Woodrow Wilson sent Robert Russa Moton, Booker T. Washington's successor at Tuskegee Institute, to France in December 1918 to "inspect" the black troops. There was, and is, considerable speculation over what exactly Moton told his black audiences. The record of his remarks as offered in his autobiography (Robert Russa Moton, *Finding a Way Out* [Garden City, N.Y., and Toronto: Doubleday, Page & Co., 1920], pp. 261-65) is brief and maddeningly interrupted by ellipses. But it seems likely that his words followed the Booker T. Washington philosophy: do not assume you will find the same freedom at home you have found here, work hard, settle down on a small piece of land, do not push too hard, and so on. Moton himself quotes the appreciative letter for a mission well done sent him by President Woodrow Wilson from Paris on January 1, 1919:

Dear Principal Moton: I wish to express my appreciation for the service you have rendered during the past few weeks in connection with our coloured soldiers here in France. I have heard, not only of the wholesome advice you have given them regarding their conduct during the time they will remain in France but also of your advice as to how they should conduct themselves when they return to our own shores. I very much hope, as you have advised, that no one of them may do anything to spoil the splendid record that they, with the rest of our American forces, have made. [Ibid., p. 265.]

But clearly the war experience had had its effect. Editorials and articles on the delightful freedoms of France dotted America's black press. The *Washington Bee,* August 23, 1919, p. 4, editorially explained "Why We Love France" ("Any oppressed people will honor and respect their benefactors"). The *Chicago Defender,* city edition, September 27, 1919, p. 10, told its readers "Why French Girls Adore Our Men." And the ideology of the war aroused black hopes and demands in America. "America has got to do a whole lot better in its treatment of our race in the future," wrote a black corporal from France to his mother in Baltimore, "if it intends to come up to the standard of this country in pure democracy. These people over here do not draw the color line anywhere you go. A man is a man with these people regardless of race, color or creed." [*Afro-American* (Baltimore), November 1, 1918, p.4]

Similarly black writers—particularly W. E. B. DuBois, at the time editor of *Crisis,* the journal of the NAACP—were forever talking about the need to extend democracy at home. One example from DuBois in *Crisis:*

> This is the country to which we Soldiers of Democracy return. This is the fatherland for which we fought! But it is *our* fatherland. It was right for us to fight. The faults of *our* country are *our* faults. Under similar circumstances, we would fight again. But by the God of Heaven, we are cowards and jackasses if now that the war is over, we do not marshal every ounce of our brain and brawn to fight a sterner, longer, more unbending battle against the forces of hell in our own land. [W.E.B. DuBois editorial, "Returning Soldiers," *Crisis* 18 (May, 1919): 14.]

See also the famous poem written in 1919 by Harlem Renaissance poet and novelist Claude McKay ("If we must die . . . ") for the mental transfer that having saved the world for democracy, blacks must turn their aggressiveness to the home front. Claude McKay, *A Long Way From Home* (New York: L. Furman, 1937), p. 227. That poem, according to historian John Hope Franklin, "expressed the feelings of a great many Negroes" in postwar America. Franklin, *From Slavery to Freedom,* p. 484.

chapter
THREE

Direction and
Diversion

I

In Detroit in 1916 progressive men and women, conscious of their
responsibility to provide leadership and direction for the city, assem-
bled with renewed vigor. Aware of the increase in Detroit's black
population, an increase some among them were actively soliciting, they
decided to create an organization to facilitate the adjustment of the
newcomers. This was the Urban League. Its program would stress moral
uplift, economic efficiency, and social control, precisely the rationale
behind the city's Americanization work. But because the latest newcomers were black, and the business and social service leadership of the
city white, a tactical change was effected. Intermediaries were assigned
to carry the message from the white men to the black, intermediaries
themselves black, chosen for their local prominence and evident re-
spectability, invested now with the status of "leader," but ultimately
responsible to the white men who appointed them. It would be a
narrow line for these black respectables to walk, trying to help others
of their race adjust to the new conditions of the North while still seeking to maintain their own dignity within a framework in which they
were essentially powerless.

By a number of means Detroit would become as highly structured in its social and political forms as in its economic organization. To educate the black man to the expectations of northern factory life there was the Urban League, itself intimately tied to the Employers' Association and part of a city-wide network of social supervision. Because the housing market was extremely tight and the potential for racial violence apparent to all, real-estate developers, supported by the courts, built subdivisions on the city's periphery with specific racial restrictions written into the deeds. In politics, because the ward and precinct machinery was clumsy, potentially corrupt, and therefore inefficient, Detroit progressives restructured city government; and the new nine-man common council came to be dominated by realtors, reflecting the boomer spirit and tensions of overcrowding. In this way inefficiencies in Detroit were systematically removed, and no institutions were left to deflect passions into harmless rhetoric. Events thus took on a brutal logic of their own, and men of good hope would soon wonder what went wrong.

II

Eugene Kinckle Jones was a persistent man. He had been traveling around the country for the National League on Urban Conditions Among Negroes since 1913, interviewing social work agencies and prominent citizens with a mind toward establishing Urban League offices in their cities. He was a man on a mission, and as the migration began its sweep northward, he realized the increasing importance of what he was doing. He was purposeful and dedicated, and such men are not easily put off, at least not by other blacks. Who then could he go to in Detroit for a hearing? The black elite had driven him out, and what, after all, was their influence in the community? There was only one option, and he was amenable to it. He would go to the white leaders. Who but they had the power and the money to initiate an organization of social uplift? Who but they had the experience and the ability in such matters, and so would know how to run an efficient and business-like operation?

And the whites, although Kinckle Jones could not really understand this, would leap at the chance. Outwardly they would be calm and restrained and genially pleasant, and they would listen to the story of his people's need for education, leadership, and guidance. But inwardly, beneath their reserve of dignity, they were eager, for they were learning again of their responsibility to lead and to educate.

The man whom Kinckle Jones saw, and who began to mobilize activity, was Henry Glover Stevens. The "great and good Henry Stevens," as Kinckle Jones would call him,[1] was the sort of man cities point to with pride and call "civic leader." He never had to spend his energies making money, for his father had accumulated a vast fortune in western mining. But the son did not allow himself to be pampered. He was physically frail as a boy and was determined to build strength into his body. In preparatory school and as an undergraduate at Yale he was a cross-country runner. Speed was a gift; stamina could be developed. In college he majored in forestry, although he probably knew he would never practice it as a profession. Back in Detroit he became one of the best local amateur tennis players. The rest of his energies and the rest of his life he devoted to charities, philanthropies, and the arts.[2] The boy who proved he could overcome his own adversities was now prepared to be generous to those who could not. He sat on the governing board of a number of Detroit charities, and was a founder and trustee of the Detroit Museum of Art.[3] At least one black leader in Detroit knew that the best way to get Henry Stevens' attention directed to what you wanted was to start him talking about painting.[4]

Mrs. Roscoe B. Jackson was another civic leader present at the onset of the Urban League. The story of her family could have come from Horatio Alger or Edith Wharton. Her grandfather was Richard Hudson, an immigrant who left England for Canada in 1853 and that country for the United States in 1860. Her grandmother, Elizabeth Lowthian Hudson, bore Richard Hudson eight children, seven of whom survived to adulthood, among them Joseph Lowthian, the second eldest, and Mary Eleanor. After the Civil War, Richard Hudson, with financial backing from the flamboyant Christopher Mabley, a pioneer in men's ready-to-wear clothes, opened a small retail dry-goods store in Ionia, Michigan. Soon Hudson bought out Mabley's interest and was able to induce son Joseph, nineteen years old, to take over the store's management. In 1873 Richard Hudson died, and the business, which had been built to a comfortable $40,000-a-year volume, folded in that year's depression. But Joseph had caught the spirit of merchandizing. He managed a clothing store in Detroit for a while for his father's former partner, accumulated some capital, and in 1881 went into business for himself. Under his direction the retail dry-goods store operating from the ground floor of the Detroit Opera House grew into a mercantile giant, the J. L. Hudson Company.

He died suddenly in 1912, never married. Assuming management of the business were his four nephews—Richard, Oscar, James, and Joseph Webber—all sons of his sister Mary Eleanor and her husband, Joseph T. Webber. Louise Anna Webber, Mrs. Roscoe B. Jackson, was the daughter of Mary Hudson and Joseph T. Webber. Her husband, Roscoe Jackson, was a young engineer who at the University of Michigan had been close friends with Roy D. Chapin and Howard Coffin, two early automobile pioneers. Jackson, like so many others, spent some early years working at the Olds Motor Works and then went east to Buffalo, where he was factory manager of a small motor company. He returned to Detroit in 1909 to join his old associates, Chapin and Coffin, who were forming— with Hudson capital—the Hudson Motor Car Company. He was made general manager at the start, married Louise Webber, and would in 1923 become president of the company. The Hudson—Webber family grew in power. Given its circle of acquaintances it could hardly avoid doing so. Louise Webber Jackson's first cousin (her mother's sister's daughter, Eleanor Lowthian Clay) married Edsel B. Ford, son of Henry Ford. Their children were William Clay Ford, who married Martha Parke Firestone, and Henry Ford II, who subsequently became chief executive officer of his paternal grandfather's company.[5]

There were others, each offering affiliations or expertise necessary for the efficient operation of the new Urban League branch. Among them, either present at the outset or joining within the first several years, were the following:

Mrs. August Helbig, wife of a Detroit real-estate and investment broker.[6]
Mrs. George Stedman Hosmer, the former Frances Bagley, a past president (1909-11) of the Detroit Mount Vernon Society and the daughter of a former governor of Michigan. Her husband, George Stedman Hosmer, was a lawyer and judge of the Wayne County Circuit Court.[7]
Mrs. Julian H. Krolik, wife of a dry-goods wholesaler (A. Krolik and Company, Detroit). Her husband was prominent in the city's federated Jewish charities.[8]

Clara T. Livermore, chief probation officer, girls' division, Wayne
County juvenile court.[9]

Rachel Haviland, social worker in residence at The House on High
Street, a clubhouse for working girls. The House offered instruction in domestic science and the social graces.[10]

Fred M. Butzel, lawyer, involved with local charities and progressive
improvement; member of the Americanization Committee of the
Detroit Board of Commerce. His advice in Urban League meetings
on legal matters, budgets, and the most sensible, economic ways of
expanding League services was an important factor in placing the
organization on a respectable, business-like footing.[11]

The Reverend Eugene Rodman Shippen was, for the brief time he was
on the Urban League Board, the most radical member of that body.
Pastor of the First Unitarian Church in Detroit, he was himself the son
of a Unitarian minister. He had been educated at Harvard, the Harvard
Divinity School, and Oxford, and had preached in Boston for thirteen
years before coming to Detroit in 1910. He enjoyed nettling his congregations. "It is the duty of the church," he once said, "to take an active
part in all movements for social uplift. The pews must not be allowed
to prevent the pulpit's utterances in favor of anything that will tend to
raise mankind to a higher plane, even though it may cut into the
profits of a contributor to church work." Another time he remarked
similarly: "The church can do society no greater service than teaching
the people the injustice and inhumanity of permitting selfish and
greedy men to build unsanitary tenements into which are crowded
scores of human beings, and which must inevitably become breeding
places for disease and crime."

Sometimes he carried his militance into the arena, spending election
days at the polls trying to prevent illegal voting or seeking to gain a seat
on the city charter commission. But it was from the pulpit that he felt
he could do the most for the cause of progressivism. When he spoke of
Jesus he spoke of him as a great social, rather than spiritual, reformer.
And as Jesus was a social reformer, so too should his followers be, trying to make a kingdom of heaven as best they can in this world rather
than waiting for social wrongs to be righted in some vaguely defined
hereafter. "The world is growing better," the Reverend Shippen would
say, "not worse." There is no more slavery among civilized people. The

condition of women and children has been improved. And since much of this must be credited to the Christian church, Christianity is not the complete failure some insist it is. "But who can truthfully deny," he would add, "that it would not have been more of a success had our Teacher not been submerged into a mysterious being who is neither God nor man?"[12]

A few decades earlier these men and women probably would have pursued their charitable impulses as individuals or in small groups operating out of a member's parlor. They would have dispensed their gratuities and advice in amounts of their own choosing, been self-supporting, unsupervised, and responsible only to themselves. But social service in Detroit was not like that any more. "No longer," reminisced a local journal in 1922,

> does a large lady with a lorgnette descend from a brougham—or a limousine, before the humble cot of the toiler who toils not and ask the good woman if her husband drinks. Learning that the bread-winner stepped into the flowing bowl whenever he had the price of a pint in his jeans, the large lady wept a few tears into her lace handkerchief and then told Ruggles, the second footman, to slip the housewife a basket of pineapples and alligator pears. That kind of charity is out.[13]

What was in its place was organization—highly structured, machined to close tolerances, and efficient—all the prevailing characteristics of Detroit's economic progress. The social service leadership of Detroit had created supervisory bodies to oversee the vast majority of the city's small charities. The reason is rooted in the progressive intellect: to render things orderly is to render them manageable; organization facilitates control. Out of the complex intertwining of social welfare agencies there emerged a pyramid of leadership which effectively loosened control from the hundreds of individual charities and centralized policy-making and major decisions about collection and disbursement of funds in the hands of a few. The large lady of the past was still a factor in the new game, but now the energy of her tears was harnessed and her noble impulses directed. She was being supervised. By whom and for what is crucial to understanding sources of leadership in the Urban League.

The administrative agency immediately superior to the Detroit Urban

League was the Associated Charities. It was to the people of the Associated Charities—Henry G. Stevens chief among them—that Kinckle Jones had gone to mobilize activity. A legend in block letters on Urban League stationery defined the relationship between the two organizations: "The Associated Charities of Detroit at 31 Warren Avenue West, Through Its Administrative Bureau, Receives and Disburses All Funds." The board of trustees of the Associated Charities was a conclave of civic leaders, including:

Alexis C. Angell, a noted attorney, president.

Henry G. Stevens, vice-president.

Claire M. Sanders, social worker, secretary.

Frank M. Klingensmith, vice-president and treasurer of the Ford Motor Company, treasurer.

Richard H. Webber, president of the J. L. Hudson Company, chairman of the finance committee.

Frank S. Bigler, vice-president and general manager of the Michigan Bolt and Nut Works; member of the Americanization Committee of the Detroit Board of Commerce.

Fred M. Butzel.

Luman W. Goodenough, attorney.

George T. Hendrie, read-estate man.

Mrs. Roscoe B. Jackson.

Horace H. Rackham, of the Americanization Committee and the Ford Motor Company.

William P. Stevens, real-estate man, treasurer of the Stevens Land Company; brother of Henry G. Stevens.

Joseph B. Schlotman, retired treasurer and general manager of the Ray Chemical Company, director of the First and Old Detroit National Bank, and full time financier and socialite.

John J. Whirl, for more than thirteen years (1902-16) secretary of the Employers' Association of Detroit.

Claire Sanders, in addition to Henry G. Stevens, Fred Butzel, and Mrs. Roscoe B. Jackson, sat on the board of directors of the Detroit Urban League.[14]

For the eight formative years of the Urban League's existence the umbilical connection with the Associated Charities remained. It was

1924 when the Urban League received permission to incorporate, thereby eliminating its need for an outside organization to receive and disburse all of its funds.[15] Respectable legal status, however, did not make the Urban League autonomous. Other connections had been forged and would remain.

The Detroit Community Fund was the agency most familiar to Detroiters who contributed to charity. Begun in 1918 (as the Detroit Patriotic Fund) it served as fiscal clearinghouse for some seventy welfare institutions requiring public contributions for their total or partial support. Once a year the Fund would hold a drive whose goal was the sum of the needs of the affiliated organizations plus an additional amount for the Fund's own operating expenses. Rarely were the campaigns anything but completely successful. The drive for the 1922 calendar year was held in October and November 1921. A total of $2,161,174.89 was raised ($2,135,202.04 in pledges, the rest in interest, dividends, and profits on the sale of U.S. government certificates). From this was deducted $104,112.61 for administrative, campaign, and collection expenses. The remainder was available for distribution, some going to national organizations like the American Red Cross, the bulk ($1,791,494.43) earmarked for allotment to local members of the federation. These included the YMCA and YWCA; the Detroit Urban League (with money allocated to the Associated Charities, which in turn reallocated it to the Urban League); the Detroit Urban League Community Center, a settlement house supervised by the league and funded out of its budget; the Dunbar Memorial Hospital, an institution staffed and patronzied by blacks; the Phyllis Wheatley Home for aged black men and women; the Visiting Nurse Association; the Visiting Housekeeper Association; the Children's Aid Society; the League of Catholic Women; the Salvation Army; the Society of St. Vincent de Paul; the Methodist Children's Home; the United Jewish Charities; the Americanization Committee of Detroit (the Detroit Board of Commerce relinquishing primary financial responsibility to the Fund in 1922); the Florence Crittenton Home for destitute, homeless, and wayward women; the Detroit Tuberculosis Society; the humane society; the Boy Scouts; and the Girl Scouts and Campfire Girls. The list is by no means exhaustive. Nearly every Detroit charity except those that were completely inconspicuous or else financially self-sufficient came under the purview of the Community Fund.[16]

The leadership of the Fund is familiar: Henry Glover Stevens, Richard H. Webber, Joseph B. Schlotman, Julian Krolik, Roy D. Chapin, Edsel Ford, James Couzens, corporation presidents, bank executives, real-estate men, lawyers.[17] But the driving force behind the Community Fund was none of these. This agent was William John Norton, Maine-born Phi Beta Kappa from Bowdoin College, social worker, practical, hard-headed, efficient. His genius was his ability to run the multimillion-dollar Community Fund organization and keep operating costs at 4 percent of the yearly subscription. Such talent the city's business leaders admired. Norton was secretary of the Community Fund, director of the Associated Charities, and a member of the Detroit Urban League Board.[18]

The pyramid continues upward. In 1918 a council of social agencies called the Detroit Community Union was begun. In its membership were all the private and governmental agencies involved with welfare work in the city. The stated purpose of the council was to coordinate social work and to develop a balanced program. Here was an amalgamation of the public and private sectors under one leadership. Not only were all of the private charities under the Community Fund represented, but also the school board, the juvenile court, and the departments of health and public welfare. Within ten years the union would take in the probation department and psychiatric clinic of the criminal court, the Detroit House of Correction, the police department, the recreation department, and the public library.[19]

Secretary and administrator of the Community Union was William John Norton. His responsibility here was to supervise distribution of the money raised in the Community Fund drive to the union's member organizations not supported by public funds. Under Norton's direction allotments were made monthly rather than yearly, for frequent disbursement of smaller amounts enabled the union to keep a close watch on federation members and allowed it to cut back financial support almost immediately on evidence of waste or inefficiency.[20]

Norton's associate on the Community Union staff was Fred R. Johnson. Born on a farm in Minnesota in 1886 of Swedish parents, Fred Johnson for years lived the uncluttered, busy life of a farm boy. He went to the rural school and then to high school at Waseca. His first urban experience came in Minneapolis at the University of Minnesota, where he majored in history and social science. He became heady with the rush of the city, and carried along by the ethic of the time, he took a part-time job as a social worker during his senior year at college. "Nineteen-five to 1910 were stirring days," Johnson recalled. "Those were the days of trust busting, of progressiveness, and every young fellow had some notion of going into 'public service.' Yes, I wanted to get into this field ever since I was old enough to think for myself." He did social work in Kansas City, Bridgeport (Conn.), and Boston before coming to Detroit in 1919 to work for the Community Union. Fred Johnson also sat (replacing Norton) on the board of directors of the Detroit Urban League.[21]

The rest of the leadership of the Community Union is predictable: the president of the Merchants National Bank, the superintendent of the Detroit Public Schools, the vice-president of a realty company, Henry G. Stevens, Joseph Schlotman, Claire Sanders, Fred Butzel, Mrs. Roscoe B. Jackson.[22]

Henry G. Stevens' position in the Community Union deserves special attention. Along with holding a seat on the board of directors, he was chairman of the union's Central Budget Committee, the body to which the budgets of the Community Fund member organizations were annually submitted for approval. The Union Budget Committee would accept or pare the statements of estimated expenses for each Fund member and then would turn the approved total over to William J. Norton's office for allocation.[23] Here was the seat of ultimate power in Detroit charity, for the hand that approved the budget ruled the organization. The money filtered down, the leaders channeled its flow, and sometimes the absolute totality of supervision could become crystallized in one small exchange, as when Henry Stevens, chairman of the Detroit Community Union Central Budget Committee, wrote to Henry G. Stevens, chairman of the board of the Detroit Urban League, requesting that the proposed budget for the coming fiscal year be promptly submitted to the union for consideration.[24]

Another important white man on the Urban League Board in those years was Chester M. Culver, general manager of the Employers' Association of Detroit. Culver grew up in Kansas, graduated from Kansas State Normal School in 1890, taught high school in Topeka for a short time, and in 1894 matriculated at the University of Chicago. Though without a degree from Chicago (he would receive it in 1925), Culver enrolled at Harvard Law School, graduated in 1899, and moved to Detroit to practice law. He stayed until 1912, when he moved to Arizona to manage a sugar company. He returned to Detroit in 1916 and accepted the executive position to which he would devote his life.[25]

The Employers' Association helped finance the Detroit Urban League. More precisely, it was paying for a service. The league almost from the beginning of its existence operated an employment bureau through which blacks, generally recently arrived migrants, were funneled to jobs in the factories. The Employers' Association financed the operation of the bureau at the cost of several thousand dollars a year. In return, the association was assured a constantly replenished supply of labor for its members—labor which was largely ignorant of unions and which could serve as strikebreakers in time of dreaded turmoil. There was no conflict of interest in this Employers' Association-Urban League entente. Rather, there was an identity of interest. Blacks got jobs, and so the Urban League was happy. Blacks given jobs would be grateful, tractable workers. If some were not they were easily replaced by those who would be. So the purpose of the Employers' Association—"the mutual protection of its members from unjust action from any source"—was also served.[26] Amelioration and mutual gain—they were far too important to be left to the vagaries of migration. So an agent of the Detroit Urban League was dispatched to Cincinnati, to be stationed there permanently for the sole purpose of persuading black migrants arriving at that transfer point to entrain for Detroit rather than for other northern cities.[27]

The black members of the Detroit Urban League Board were sliced from the upper ranks of the black community. The following were among those chosen within the first several years:

Lillian E. Bakeman, a physician's bookkeeper.
Roscoe S. Douglas, bank clerk.
Eva Loomis, notary public.
George E. Smedley of the Smedley Realty Company, and editor and
    publisher of the *Detroit Herald.*
Mrs. Charles S. Smith, member of one of Detroit's Old Guard black
    families, whose husband was bishop of the African Methodist
    Episcopal Church.

George H. Green, postal carrier and later undertaker.

William P. Kemp, printer, and editor and publisher of the *Detroit Leader.*

Dr. Albert H. Johnson, physician.

Mrs. Albert H. Johnson.

Dr. Charles F. Green, physician.

Birney W. Smith, postal carrier and later a probation officer for the Wayne County juvenile court.[28]

C. Henri Lewis, born in Munich, North Dakota, and educated at Virginia Union University, Richmond, Virginia. He entered Detroit College of Law in 1909, graduated in 1912, and was admitted to the Michigan bar shortly thereafter. Lewis was senior partner in the firm of Lewis, Rowlette, and Dunning, which was located on St. Antoine Street in the heart of the black ghetto. He was also active in the Masonic lodge.[29]

Cecil L. Rowlette, born in Petersburg, Virginia, and also educated at Virginia Union University. He graduated from Howard University Law School in 1912, came to Detroit two and a half years later, and was admitted to the Michigan bar in October 1915. He was law partner of C. Henri Lewis.[30]

Laura Pelham, wife of Benjamin B. Pelham, the son of one of the old Detroit black elite families. Benjamin Pelham, after graduating from the Detroit public schools, worked on several Detroit newspapers and with his brother and three others founded the *Plaindealer* in 1883. In 1890 he took a job with the Internal Revenue Service, and then was employed for several years as secretary to a contractor. In 1895 he entered local government service, where he would spend the rest of his life. He worked for eight years in the county treasurer's office, then in the office of the recorder of deeds. 1909 he became county accountant, with the responsibility of auditing all books and records of Wayne County, signing bonds, and acting as clerk to various finance committees. His ability became legend. The duties of citizenship and the Pelham birthright of civic leadership were prevailing themes in Benjamin Pelham's household. They affected his wife and would imbue his children.[31]

William C. Osby, trustee and general manager of the Dunbar Hospital, officer (president from 1911 to 1916) of the Detroit branch of the NAACP, trustee and secretary of the Second Baptist Church of Detroit. William Osby was a building engineer, virtually self-educated,

having completed only a correspondence course (1900) in electrical
and steam engineering. He went to work for the Detroit Realty
Company in 1902, was given responsibility for one building, and by
1916 was the company's chief engineer and supervisor of operations
in a number of large apartment complexes. "I had about fifteen or
eighteen people under my supervision, and the majority of them was
white," he said. Like his colleagues on the Urban League board, Osby
was proud of his place in the community. "The Negro people knew
all the outstanding men of their race," he would recall years later.
"Of course I kinda stood out, like the lawyers, like the doctors, like
the other professional people. . . . The Negro community was small,
and we knew one another and knew well, you know, and everything
we had I was in on it."[32]

These people, members of the black middle class, had worked hard to
be respected as individuals in a white city. They were concerned with what
others—especially successful whites—thought of them, and their self-esteem
rested on the conviction that they stood alone, exempt from popular con-
ceptions about their race. But as the migration continued to pour black
people into Detroit, they became troubled. Virtue, which presumably once
was self-evident, now perhaps was becoming more difficult to see. How
then to reassure one's self and again convince others of personal distinction? One way was to sit as a partner on an interracial board for the improvement and control of the migrants, to discuss and make judgments.
So those middle-class blacks who were invited to join, did. The meetings
generally were congenial and friendly, as Henry Stevens and Fred Butzel
and Chester Culver sat and listened before they spoke. But underneath
the congeniality there was a tension, because the white men were, after
all, white.

Sometimes racism was there to be seen through the veil of harmony.
When Benjamin Comfort, the principal of Cass Technical High School
in Detroit, wrote to William Norton accepting a place on the Urban
League board he mentioned what he thought were his qualifications.

Social service among the negroes fits into my experience somewhat as I was in business in Louisiana for seven years from 1891 to
1898, and employed from 50 to 150 negroes during that time, and,

also, my mother's ancestry were Kentuckians and had numerous
slaves in their homes, so that I have some background in the negro
problem which is becoming more serious each year in our whole
country.[33]

Even if the black board members did not read this particular letter they
would have recognized the attitude. But generally they chose to sit
quietly, for to say anything would have been to appear spiteful. The
Benjamin Comforts, they were convinced, would learn when they came
in contact with blacks and saw how intelligent blacks could really be.
"The more the opposite race comes in contact with the intelligent and
refined members of my race," said one of them on a later occasion, "the
better it will be for all concerned."[34]

Inevitably, though, someone had to explode. It happened once in the
tense depression winter of 1920/21. The city of Detroit's Department of
Public Works had always refused to hire blacks except as garbage men.
Appeals by the Urban League's black staff to the department's head
produced no promise of any permanent change in employment practices, but did result in the department's hiring 500 blacks for two days
to shovel snow. A paragraph describing the discrimination and appeal
was included in the report read to the monthly board meeting. When
Henry Stevens heard the word "discrimination" used to characterize
the city's hiring practices, he became furious. It is not the Urban League's
function, he said, to investigate matters of discrimination as discrimination. That sort of thing is the responsibility of the NAACP. The wording
of the report has to be changed, he insisted, to read only that jobs are
being sought for colored men. At this, board member Lulu Rainwater,
a black schoolteacher, became livid. She asked that Stevens explain the
function of the league to her, since she evidently did not understand
what it stood for, if not to challenge discriminatory hiring practices.
Slowly and with his rage suppressed, Henry Stevens replied that the
league was a coordinating agency, and that its program was made with a
view toward establishing better housing, employment, recreation, and
health.[35]

Within two years Lulu Rainwater would be retired from the board.[36]
The blacks who remained would be more circumspect. What else could
they do? The Chester Culvers provided the jobs. But beyond that, the

black respectables would sit quietly because most of them embraced
the guiding ethic of all respectables: no scenes. In dignity and bearing they
had sought distance, and distance was precisely the quality that the
whites required of those who would seek entry into the chambers of
leadership.

"I have come to Detroit at the request of the Associated Charities
Board to discover the needs of the colored people of Detroit, and interpret them to the public. . . . The committee will be financially responsible for my work and will act as consultant for my policies."[37] In this
way Forrester B. Washington explained his duties as the first executive
director of the Detroit Urban League. Like other newcomers to Detroit
he was young—twenty-nine years old. He had been born in the archetypal
Yankee town of Salem, Massachusetts, and had been educated at Tufts
College, a white institution near Boston. He also attended graduate
school at Harvard before coming to Detroit in 1916, and while in Detroit
at the Urban League would be working toward a master's degree in
social work at Columbia University. Forrester B. Washington was highly
educated by any standards of the time. He was urbane; he was articulate.[38]

And he was pestered by his employers. A prevailing assumption of
white (and black) respectables in Detroit was that organizational profi-
ciency was equated with being white. So while Washington was conceded
some latitude in mingling with the migrants, he could not be allowed
autonomy in business dealings. Every Urban League office transaction,
no matter how minute, was subject to the scrutiny of the Employers'
Association. He would read in his mail:

> Please understand that the Association will not be responsible for
> any expense incurred by the Urban League unless it is done upon the
> written authority of this office. . . .
>
> As authorized verbally some time ago, you may incur the nominal
> expense of having a couple of slides made for use in the moving
> picture theatre.[39]

> After thoroughly considering the matter of telephone service for
> the Employment Department, we have concluded that for the
> present, an extension from your phone upstairs will answer the
> purpose. You will therefore kindly request the Associated Charities

to arrange for the extension, with the understanding that the cost
will be assumed by our Association, and will be included in our
monthly payment to the Associated Charities.[40]

Confirming our telephone conversation of to-day-, you may
arrange to incur such nominal expense as is necessary to purchase
curtains for the front windows of the bureau. . . .

You may also arrange to have the necessary connections made
for the gas heater. If the connection is made on a separate meter
from that which supplies the upstairs rooms, you will also be required
to make application for service at the Gas Company.[41]

"Efficiency" was one watchword. "Thrift," "sobriety," "cleanliness,"
"industry," and "calm" were others. These were the universal values of
middle-class America, and Detroit's leadership held them out to the
latest arrivals. The city's progressives were operating on the assumption
that a smoothly running apparatus like the Urban League to inculcate
the ideal was necessary for the newcomers' speedy adjustment, and that
that adjustment, once achieved, would mean harmony in city race relations. But perhaps the progressives were twice deceived. Perhaps the black
man, in the country for so long, had already developed values and aspirations not so very different from their own.[42] And perhaps too there were
circumstances in prospect for the black man in Detroit that would sully
the ideal and make questionable facile pronouncements about virtue and
its inevitable reward.

But that was in the future, and the economic and social service leadership of Detroit, innocent of the possibilities, geared for action. Their
agent, the man whose job it was to preach the norm, the man whose
statements would foreshadow Urban League public policy from then
on, was Forrester B. Washington of Salem and Harvard.

III

"You are the people who are going to make Detroit a great city for
the Negro. You are the yeast who are going to leaven the loaf. We are
directing our onslaught not against you, but against those who have not
the ambition you have." The words were Forrester B. Washington's. He

was addressing the blacks of the Detroit Dress Well Club. The Dress
Well Club had been formed by the Detroit Urban League in conjunction
with the Loyal Christian Brotherhood of the Second Baptist Church
and the Young Negroes Progressive Association, a group of thirty-four
young men who were attending various schools and colleges in the
Detroit area. It was the Urban League's organ for spreading the new
message.

"This is not a meeting arranged for Northern Negroes to criticize
Southern Negroes," Washington said. Every one of us, he said, came
either directly or indirectly from the South. Our stress, rather, is on
advice, and "this meeting was called by people who have a better right
to advise the newcomer than any one else." "On the whole the Negro
is making good in this city," he went on, "but there is room for vast
improvement." The Urban League, he said, receives complaints daily
from the police commissioner and other city officials concerning the
behavior of some Negroes in public. These Negroes act the way they do
because "the freedom of the North and especially of Detroit have been
heralded so thoroughly," and they don't know any better. So they have
to be advised.

Washington cited some of the things he had seen that he thought
needed correcting: black workmen crowding inside street cars in dirty
overalls; black men sitting around during the summer months bare-
foot; blacks talking loudly in public places. White people, Washington
said, complain about such things and they are justified in doing so.
Color prejudice does not enter into the situation.

The solution Washington offered was the Dress Well Club organization. "This organization will be one which welcomes to its membership
all people in Detroit who have the welfare of their people at heart," he
said. The way the organization shall be operated "is by printing cards,
upon which is a statement of the importance of dressing well. Members
should ask any person who is making himself a nuisance by vulgar clothing or loud mouth, to digest this card and hand it to others. . . . We be-
seech you to impress these doctrines on every Negro you come in contact
with who you think needs them."

There would always be the " 'you can't club,' " Washington went on.
There would always be "people who call every movement to help the

Negro segregation." But "segregation is increasing in this city" in
theatres, restaurants, hospitals. "Why is this segregation increasing [?]
Partly on account of southern whites. But chiefly on account of the
loud, noisy, almost nude women in 'Mother Hubbards' standing around
on the public thoroughfares. The public doesn't see people like you.
You stay at home or are not conspicuous. [One hundred] of the bad
class do more to shape public opinion than 10,000 like you. There
are dirty white people of course, but white people are the judges and
colored people are being judged."[43]

At the conclusion of the meeting the Dress Well Club brochure
was handed out for dissemination among the newcomers. Here
is what they would read:

New Comers' Attention. Read Carefully.
    Detroit Dress Well Club.
    Why Formed.

    This organization is composed of earnest race men resolved to
create a better impression of the Negro by attention to dress, personal
appearance and public behavior.

By Whom Formed.
    It is formed under the auspices of the Loyal Christian Brother-
hood of the Second Baptist Church, Young Negroes Progressive Association and the Detroit Urban League. It is not confined however, to
any denomination or even to Church-goers.

Members.
    The Detroit Dress Well Club welcomes to its membership all
Negroes in Detroit who have the welfare of their people at heart and
extends its welcome to natives as well as newcomers.

The Way We Work.
    By accepting this card you become at least an honorary mem-
ber of this Society authorized to spread its doctrines wherever you
see a Negro making himself conspicuous by bad behavior or improper
dress.

No Ducs— No Fees—
Just to help the Negro to make good.

Become a regular member by communicating with the Urban League, 297 St. Antoine Street, Cherry 1325 or with the officers of the Loyal Christian Brotherhood of the Second Baptist Church.

ADVICE FROM THE DRESS WELL CLUB
The importance of dressing well.

Complaints are being received by the Police Commissioner and the officials of the street railway companies regarding the unclean clothing, etc. of Negro workmen on the car lines. This sort of carelessness in regards to dress will lead to discrimination and segregation unless steps are taken to improve conditions.

Employers have more respect for a man and are more apt to give him a good job if he dresses neatly. This does not mean that a man must be a "dude." Flashy clothes are as undesirable and as harmful as unclean clothes.

Dress-Well Don'ts.

Don't crowd inside of a street car filled with people in your dirty, greasy overalls. Stay on the platform as do the majority of white men in such apparel or wear a coat over your clothes when you are going back and forth to the foundry.

Don't wear overalls on Sunday.

Don't sit barefooted in front of your house or loll around in public at Belle Isle etc. with your shoes off.

Don't allow your women folks to go around the streets in bungalow aprons and boudoir caps if you want white people to respect them.

Don't do your children's hair up in knots, alleys and canals if you don't want other children to make fun of them.

VERY IMPORTANT DON'TS

Don't loaf. Get a job at once.

Don't carry on loud conversations in street cars and public places.

Don't keep your children out of school.

Don't send for your family until you get a job.

Don't think that you can hold your job unless you are industrious, efficient, prompt and sober. ["Sober" was printed in extra heavy type.]

Don't forget that cleanliness and fresh air are necessary for good health.

Don't fool with patent medicines in case of sickness, but send immediately for a good physician.

Don't fail to become an active member in some Church as soon as you reach the city.

Don't start buying on the installment plan.

Don't fail to start a savings account with some good bank or with a building loan association.

Don't spend all of your money for pleasures. Save some of it for extra clothing and fuel for the winter.

Do not fail to call upon the Urban League if you are a stranger in the city—if you want a job, if you want a place to live, if you are having trouble with your employer, if you want information or advice of any kind. No charge, no fees, we want to help you.

To do these things means to help yourself and 20,000 more of your own people in this city to make good in your jobs, to get better jobs and to keep down prejudice, race friction and discrimination.

Detroit League on Urban Conditions Among Negroes.
        297 St. Antoine Street   Cherry 1325

READ CAREFULLY[44]

Despite the ulterior motives of the blacks and whites who issued it, the brochure undeniably contained some good advice. Installment buying could be an insidious trap. Provision for the Detroit winter had to be made. But when members of the Young Negroes Progressive Association, under Washington's direction, went into the factories to distribute cards, the message they spread was less than honest.

Why He Failed.
        He watched the clock.

> He was always behind time.
> He asked too many questions.
> His stock excuse was "I forgot."
> He wasn't ready for the next step.
> He did not put his heart in his work.
> He learned nothing from his blunders.
> He was contented to be a second rater.
> He didn't learn that the best part of his
> salary was not in his pay envelope—SUCCESS. . . .[45]

The implication was clear enough. Success attends virtue properly culti-vated. Unspoken, however, was the reality of the time: the position of the black man within the system had already been determined, and suc-cess, if achieved at all, could be had only within the narrowest of limits.

Detroit's economic leaders saw the migrant as an input, a rough-hewn laborer of considerable potential who needed now to be cast to the specifications of the machine. Urban League education, with its procla-mation of the ideal, was necessary to facilitate this transition, to make the black man at once more useful economically and less threatening socially. There was no consideration on the part of white business lead-ers of any larger possibilities for the black migrant, despite their persis-tent calls for his self-improvement. The economic machine did not re-quire distinction from its laborers; it required merely effort.

In a strange way the language that white progressives in Detroit used to define their burdens and responsibilities as leaders could also be used to define the place, assigned almost by default, of the black man in the system. "What we need," wrote Henry Ford of himself and his com-patriots, "is to see that one strain is equipped to do for the other what it cannot do for itself, and set it upon the road of living a life which ful-fills its destiny; and the strain equipped to do this must do it, or suffer the consequences of neglected duty."[46] Because responsibility for orga-nization and uplift had already been accepted by the dominant "strain," the black man would get the jobs that were left after most whites had been supplied. There were "nigger jobs," just as there were "hunkie jobs" for Poles and "wop jobs" for Italians. These "nigger jobs" were jobs so hot, noisy, dusty, dirty, hazardous, or physically exhausting that few white men would do them, and none out of choice. But these jobs, according to those who ran the factories, were the responsibility of the laborer, especially of the black laborer. They were his special province.[47]

The great majority of blacks in the automobile industry—65 percent, as opposed to 25 percent of the whites, reported one investigator—were classified as unskilled laborers, and these blacks filled the iron-smelting, iron-pouring, furnace-tending, sweeping, sand-wheeling, frame-spraying, shakeout, and metal-cleaving jobs so categorized. But distinctions based on skill are deceiving, for even in the semiskilled occupations blacks were confined to the most hazardous or otherwise undesirable parts of the particular operation—filling such jobs, for example, as shear operator, heater, sprayer, chipper, rough-snag-grinder, and sand blaster.[48]

Discrimination pertained specifically to job classification, not to wages. Neither Forrester B. Washington, in his 1920 study of blacks in Detroit conducted for the Associated Charities, nor the Detroit Bureau of Governmental Research in 1926 found any overt discriminations in wage scales on those occasions when blacks and whites performed the same job. Both studies found, however, that blacks tended to work longer hours for less money than whites because of the nature of the work available to them, though specific discriminations in wages and hours did not apply.[49]

The automobile companies did not pursue identical employment policies with regard to blacks. Fisher Body for many years was almost totally restrictive in its hiring. In 1926 the company's two plants in Detroit, which employed thousands of workers, reported only forty blacks on the payroll; and fewer than forty would work for Fisher nearly two decades later.[50] Ford Motor Company, however, employed 10,000 blacks by 1926, and would try to maintain a racial balance in its labor force proportionate to that of the Detroit metropolitan area.[51] And Ford did not irrevocably limit all blacks to foundry and similar jobs. Black men were employed in most departments, and on occasion, even in supervisory capacities. But this was simply token dispersal. There was no new departure at Ford, for at Ford as elsewhere the overwhelming number of blacks were employed and would continue to be employed only in those jobs and processes where the general nature of the work was the least desirable.[52]

The restriction of blacks to particular jobs, generally the case at Ford and almost universally true elsewhere, was conscious policy on the part of industry leaders. The black man's ambition had to be trimmed because his labor served its most useful function just where it was. So an arbitrary limit was established beyond which the black man could not go. In drop forge shops he could be a helper but never a hammerman. In stamping departments he could be a trucker but not a press operator. Few would claim he was incapable of running the restricted machines. It was simply that "Negroes can't work on presses." Plant policy dictated it.[53] "We brought the Negro to this plant," said the superintendent of one automobile factory, "to do the dirty, hard, unskilled work. If we let him rise, all of them will want better jobs." Was this fair, he was asked? "No," came the reply, and the response was typical of men who at once ran and yet were totally defined by the machine: "But we can't try any experiments here. We are competing with other automobile firms and we've got to keep our men satisfied to keep up the competitive pace. Personally I'd like to help them, but what can I do?"[54]

Keeping up the competitive pace, however, sometimes meant exacerbating rather than lessening race rivalry among the workers. For a number of years the foundry of this same automobile company pitted black crews against white. Under the praise and pressure of the foreman the black crews began—as the phrase then current had it—to "work like niggers" and soon were turning out considerably more tonnage in castings than were the white workers, who had speeded up very little for fear of rate cuts. Ultimately black labor completely displaced white labor in the company's foundry. The company continued to kid and prod the black labor, the lines were steadily speeded up, and production continued to soar—from 225 to 650 tons of castings per day. There was, however, no increase in wages. The superintendent of the plant stated that although some improvement in mechanical technique may have accounted for part of the astonishing boost in productivity, "most of the increased tonnage was because these niggers will work their fool heads off if we handle them right."[55]

"We ought to keep niggers out," said a Pole.[56] "Negroes smell like goats, and I hate them anyhow," said an Italian laborer.[57] And enmity did not come only from white workers who felt threatened. There was hatred too in the eyes of other black men. "These damn southern niggers have spoiled the jobs for all of us," complained a skilled black molder in one automobile shop. "Some of us used to have good jobs here but so many unskilled niggers from the South have come in that none of us have a chance now. They think we are all the same. I used to do all sorts of skilled molding but now I'm kept on the machines."[58] Even personal liberties, so long taken for granted, were gone. "These southern Negroes just don't know how to act," said a black working in an employment office. "I have always eaten my lunch in that little restaurant at the corner with other people [white] from the office. But they [the Southern blacks] went in and messed up the place, and now no colored men can eat there. It's a damn shame. No, I don't blame the manager much; he told me to come back later."[59]

The sullen stares, the problem of finding a less crowded place to live, the filth and heat of the job, the enormous power the foreman held over all workers[60]—there had to be a release from all this somewhere, and for tens of thousands it came in religion. No one can know precisely the extent of religious participation among blacks in Detroit in those years. In 1914, just before the beginnings of the Great Migration, there were only nine black religious bodies in the city, and of these, two were missions and three others very small. By 1919 more than 21,000 black people were registered as church members. The number doubled, to nearly 45,000, by 1926. Churches that did not even exist in 1916 and 1917 had thousands of people in their congregations a few years later. Despite perpetual enlarging and rebuilding programs there were hardly seats for half the city's total enrolled membership. The value of all black church property was estimated in 1926 to be nearly $2,300,000, three times that of 1919; and still, on a given Sunday, thousands of blacks waited in line to get into a church.[61]

Churches sprang up in basements, attics, houses, and stores. They vanished, they reappeared. "We are the higher educators of glory," ran the legend across the door of one,[62] and many black people wanted to believe it. These were the churches that both black and white civic leaders would denounce as trafficking in religious hysteria. But there was no denying that the fervent, highly emotional, evangelic religion they offered had great appeal to many Detroit blacks recently arrived from the South.[63] The Fire Baptized Holiness Church gathered enough members to form three congregations by 1926; the White Horse and Riders' Church had two.[64]

The basement churches also attracted what Forrester B. Washington

called "a number of emotional and unbalanced white people."[65] Many
of these were mountain southerners, carried to Detroit by the migration
in search of jobs, who needed a church in the city that would supply the
sort of religious service they had known at home. Some found what they
wanted in the black churches, and they joined. Nor were southerners the
only white people attracted. One Sunday members of the black Church
of God and Saints of Christ sect visited a white Lutheran service. At its
conclusion they were offered the traditional public opportunity to
join the Lutheran church. The blacks refused, explained that the Lutherans were not worshipping God rightly, and proceeded to give a short
demonstration of their own manner of service. Then they invited the
Lutherans to visit the Church of God the following Sunday. A number
of the whites did and so enjoyed the fervor of the service that they not
only joined the church themselves but subsequently brought enough of
their French and German friends to warrant holding special services in
these languages.[66]

Progressive men in Detroit shook their heads at blacks who participated in such emotional release in the name of religion. They are "extremely ignorant" individuals "who form the membership of these
hysterical churches," was the claim, with proof "the noisy and irreligious
manner in which they carry on their services." "There seems to be a
general impression among them," the observation continued,

> that shouting, dancing hither and thither, groaning, howling, crying,
> protracted prayers, frantic embracing, the waving of handkerchiefs,
> grovelling on the floor, the throwing up of arms, and similar "hyster-
> ical" outbursts are the sole means of expressing devotion to God.
>
> Not only are the members of these churches ignorant, but the
> ministers are rarely more intelligent than their flocks. They are usu-
> ally persons who have had little or no educational training. Their
> greatest ambition seems first to be [to] so arouse the emotion of
> the so-called "saints" as to produce a general uproar in the Church;
> second, to exploit for their own personal profit the barbaric super-
> stitions of the class of Negroes who make up their congregation.
> Frequently sexual indulgence is a third motivation.
>
> It is probably true that the individuals who take part in these
> exercises get much emotional satisfaction from them, but those who

have become addicted to this type of service often become so unbalanced mentally that they lose all sense of reason and, as a result,
are not able to control their passions. Often those who shout, cry
and groan the most and pray the longest prayers are the most im-
moral and hypocritical people in the community, who are constantly
getting into trouble for stealing and for committing other crimes
which are supposed to be contrary to their religion.

A visit to one of these churches would convince those who have
some knowledge of psychiatry that quite a number of the adherents
are abnormal and that these services only contribute toward the
further dis-organization of their minds.[67]

Middle-class black leaders agreed. "It is impossible to find in the
Christian religion any justification for such barbaric practices as go on
in these so-called churches," wrote Forrester B.Washington, who by
then was gone from the Urban League to the employ of the Associated
Charities.

The situation has its very pathetic side and there is no doubt that in
the wailing and shouting of these people they bring to their souls
which are so circumscribed some satisfactory expression. But it is all
very harmful, nevertheless, because it unquestionably produces an
abnormal type of individual. Time and time again . . . investigators
have seen examples of mental disorganization resulting from the
protracted hysteria encouraged in these "churches." These highly
emotional services seem to produce an unbalanced state which robs
the individual of inhibitions which would make him a reasoning being
and capable of self-control in sudden uprushes of passion.[68]

"It takes sunlight to cure miasma," echoed William T. Vernon, African
Methodist Episcopal bishop of Michigan, Illinois, Indiana, Ontario, and
Bermuda. "Mental development will cure these people of their weakness
for barbaric forms of worship."[69]

Among members of Detroit's black clergy, then, there were standards
of liturgy as conservative as any found among white people. "You'll
find that there is always a crowd at a circus," said the black minister of
a modestly attended church.

The museum of art is not always crowded.

The service that appeals only to the emotions, not to the mind, more often debases than it uplifts. I do not believe much in pulpit oratory. The truth, simply stated, is forceful enough to sustain any faith that is worth while.

I do not deem it my mission to afford entertainment at Sabbath service. Those who flock to church for entertainment alone are likely to flock out again without having absorbed one iota of religious truth. It may be a good way to attract crowds. But crowds, lacking a serious purpose, don't interest me. The acquiring of true religion is a gradual development, just as is the acquiring of an education. It does not come as a flash from the blue. I like to think that the members of our church, though not so large in numbers, are steadily advancing toward a high religious level. This level I can describe best by saying it would leave a man on Monday in the same state of mind as he was on Sunday, at the hour of worship.[70]

Because the Ford Motor Company was hiring black newcomers in large numbers, religion and jobs soon became intertwined in several black churches. The men at Ford, as always, sought to ensure a supply of sober, efficient, dependable workers. The sociological department bore the main responsibility for this; and when the company began to hire blacks in large numbers, the department expanded its operations to include supervision of black men. But problems seemed to arise which had never occurred when only white men were being investigated. What was to be done, for example, about black workers who were living with common-law wives? In the early 1920s the company's solution was to force such men to marry the women with whom they were living on penalty of being discharged otherwise. The tactic was soon abandoned, however, for the sociological department discovered that frequently black employees had wives in the South for whom they had never sent. The company could hardly allow itself to be an agent in the enforcement of bigamy.[71]

More and more Henry Ford came to rely on another means of screening workers. He developed close relations with Detroit's respectable black clergy. The clerics served him as job agents. It was an arrangement profitable to both. Ford Motor Company got tractable workers, and the ministers got prosperous congregations, which insured prosperity for the churches. Two clergymen were particularly active in this regard: the Reverend Robert L. Bradby of the Second Baptist Church and Father Everard W. Daniel of St. Matthew's Episcopal. Within the black community a recommendation from either of these two men was considered tantamount to securing a Ford job. The Reverend Bradby was a personal friend of some of the top Ford officials and Father Daniel was a favorite of Henry Ford himself. Mr. and Mrs. Ford visited St. Matthew's annually, and Ford made several substantial contributions to the church. The St. Matthew's parish house was Ford's gift. Moreover, the Negro-relations executive of the Ford Motor Company, Donald Marshall, was a member of St. Matthew's. He held several minor positions in the church over a period of years and for a while administered the Sunday School. It seems entirely likely, therefore, that of the large number of young blacks who joined the Second Baptist Church and St. Matthew's Church in those years, many did so with an eye to securing a job at Ford.[72]

Gambling on numbers was another way in which many Detroit blacks tried to escape despair. The practice of playing numbers did not take firm root in the United States until the 1930s, when the repeal of prohibition forced underworld organizations to find a profitable substitute for selling now no-longer illicit alcohol and when, in the height of depression, there seemed for most Americans to be no hope at all and many needed to believe there was some chance—however remote—that things could get a little better very quickly. But culture patterns derived from number playing were already emerging in the 1920s on the streets of Detroit's black ghetto. The customary form of greeting among the cognizant was no longer "Good evening" or some trite remark about the weather. Rather it had become "What was it?" with the answer "327," "389," "426," or whatever the number happened to be on that particular day.[73]

Words took on meanings which derived from their special usage among numbers players. "Squawk"—in the argot of the gambler, an individual who fails to hit his number and returns to the confidence man for a refund—began in everyday language to mean one who was in the habit of making a commotion over small matters. Entirely new words were created from the jargon. "Gig," which was a type of play in policy involving three numbers, became synonymous on the street with the number *3*.[74]

Gradually too there came into existence in the Detroit black community an entire folklore based on numbers and number playing. There were at least three identifiable themes. In one, the traditional enemies of number playing, usually policemen or ministers, were made unwitting agents for its promotion. In these stories the player would bet the number on a policeman's badge or the number on a minister's doorway and invariably would hit and win a large sum of money. Then he would notify the moral guardian either by mail or by a note in the collection plate and thank him for his compliance. A second theme had the individual obtaining a number from some usually tragic or gruesome event, such as an automobile accident or murder. He plays the number and of course wins, thereby capitalizing on misfortune. The third theme involved dream numbers. An individual has a dream which he interprets by consulting a dream book. After locating the proper number, he conveys the information to his friends, all of whom play the number heavily. The number hits, and great wealth comes to the players along with ruin to the bankers.[75]

Black ministers strongly disapproved of number gambling and periodically held militant crusades against the practice. "Number gambling is a vice and we should act to do away with it," said one minister. "It is an insidious practice which feeds upon the poverty and ignorance of the masses," said another. "We must unite to do away with this cancer that pauperizes our people," echoed a third.[76] Their attitude would change completely in the 1930s. Suddenly the white man's institutions seemed much less worthy of emulation and envy. And suddenly too, gamblers, who had risen to the middle class by one of the few routes available to blacks, were becoming benefactors of desperately poor black churches. So there developed a new orthodoxy to fit these circumstances. Clerics who once inveighed against the paractice now claimed that numbers playing was a kind of charity.[77]

More than a few in the ghetto scoffed at such diversion and instead sought release in programs for racial uplift. "Whether it is proper or not it is the custom of man to view races or individuals from the angle of possession," said a special "business" edition of a black Detroit newspaper in 1920. "You are important in proportion as you possess. Our problem is largely one of ownership. We do not own; so consequently we are in most cases owned." The ideal then was restated epigrammatically: "The man who buys and sells is the man reckoned with. Business is color blind and money talks. Our people must quit begging and invest."[78]

Others, sensing that uplift necessitated recasting, followed the logic of racial self-improvement all the way to separatism. These were disciples of Marcus Garvey, Jamaican immigrant to New York City, who was espousing black nationalism. His message was simple and direct. There can be no hope for the black man in America because the country is cancerous with white prejudice. The only recourse is a return to Africa.[79] To promulgate his ideas and promote his program Garvey created the Universal Negro Improvement Association. Perhaps a half million blacks in thirty cities joined the New York-based UNIA.[80] In Detroit 5000 black people were members, and many more undoubtedly felt allegiance.[81]

There was a great deal in Garvey's black nationalism which must have comforted many white men. "I believe in a pure black race," he proclaimed, "just as how all self-respecting whites believe in a pure white race, as far as that can be." The dangers inherent in social equality seemed to him to be manifest. "Some Negroes believe in social equality," he warned whites. "They want to intermarry with the white women of this country, and it is going to cause trouble later on. Some Negroes want the same jobs you have. They want to be Presidents of the nation." "All true Negroes are against social equality," he said elsewhere, "believing that all races should develop on their own social lines." So intent was Garvey on the goal of strict racial separation that he would abandon all black economic rights in America. He warned white leaders that if they persisted in allowing blacks to become elected officials, artisans, or skilled laborers while any white workers were unemployed, the result could only be "bloody . . . wholesale mob violence."[82] For Garvey it was above all "this danger that drives me mad. It must be prevented."[83]

In Detroit, the few thousand Garveyites there echoed the separatist message. "It is time that the Negro wakes up," wrote a woman, one of the city's faithful. "Give one Negro a job in a white man's office, even if it is to shine his shoes, [and] he feels that the race problem is solved; not seeing the mass of his people who are suffering. The so-called big

Negroes will sell you out for a cigar that is bigger than his mouth to see the smoke as it goes up."[84] The Garveyites in Detroit held meetings, ran excursions, staged parades.[85] Members were largely working people from the ghetto—laborers, factory workers, laundresses, dressmakers. When they contributed to UNIA "rehabilitation and expansion" programs, the donations were rarely more than a dollar, often much less.[86]

The executive secretary of the Detroit division UNIA was Joseph A. Craigen, a confidant of Marcus Garvey himself. Born in British Guiana, Craigen came to the United States about 1918 as a Spanish interpreter for the navy department at Muscle Shoals, Alabama. Sometime after the armistice he migrated to Detroit and worked for a while in the automobile factories. Later (ca. 1932) he entered law school and became an attorney; in 1937 he was appointed by Governor Frank Murphy to the Michigan Workmen's Compensation Commission, a position he held until his death in 1962.

As the Garvey leader in Detroit Craigen called on black men to direct themselves toward a specific kind of self-improvement. It is a materialistic age, he said in 1927, an age in which, if a race is to advance, it must assert itself in the worldly spheres of finance and business. Too much black energy in the past, he claimed, has been devoted to spiritual things, and the danger is that blacks continue to do this.

> As a race we have prayed louder and longer than all other races combined, and have received less of the world's goods than any race.
>
> To expect more churches to solve our problem is to ignore every lesson of history. . . .
>
> Standing erect we may demand, defy, dare and do; in the church, on our knees, we can only confess to the world that we are a race of . . . cowering and whimpering slaves who give thanks for stones when we beg for bread.[87]

To the United States government—and, one suspects, to the white leaders of Detroit[88] —a black man like Marcus Garvey, organizing self-respect for black Americans on a large scale, was dangerous and best eliminated. When the UNIA formed the Black Star Line in 1919 to establish trade between blacks in America and those in the West Indies and Africa, the government watched closely. Soon it became apparent that management

of the steamship line was inept and fraudulent, and so in 1922 the
United States brought suit against Garvey on the charge of using the
mails to defraud. He was convicted in 1923 and sentenced to five years
in federal prison at Atlanta. Despite appeals, the conviction was upheld.
In 1927 the half-served sentence was commuted by President Coolidge,
but United States immigration laws required that aliens convicted of a
felony be deported. Garvey was taken from his Atlanta penitentiary
cell directly to New Orleans and put on a boat bound for the West Indies.
With his deportation the UNIA movement broke into squabbling fac-
tions.[89]

The black press and leadership throughout the country was ecstatic.[90]
No wonder, for Garvey had been vitriolic in his denunciation of them.
Out "so-called leading men" are servile, he had said.

> The slave instinct has not yet departed from them. They still
> believe that they can only live or exist through the good graces of
> their "masters." . . .
>
> It is the slave spirit of dependence that causes [them] . . . to seek
> the shelter, leadership, protection and patronage of the "master" in
> their organization and so-called advancement work. It is the spirit of
> feeling secured as good servants of the master, rather than as independ-
> ents, why our modern Uncle Toms take pride in laboring under alien
> leadership and becoming surprised at the audacity of the Universal
> Negro Improvement Association in proclaiming for racial liberty and
> independence.[91]

So the black leaders hated him. W.E.B. DuBois, subject to constant
vilification both personally and as an officer of the NAACP, called Garvey
"a lunatic or a traitor."[92] Charles S. Smith, bishop of the African Methodist Episcopal Church and one of Detroit's Old Guard elite, insisted Garvey "[did] not interpret the thoughts of 1 per cent. of colored Americans" and termed the UNIA "an ephemeral show."[93] And Robert W.
Bagnall, for ten years pastor of St. Matthew's Episcopal Church in
Detroit, and president of the Detroit branch of the NAACP before being
called to New York in 1921 as the association's director of branches,[94]
declared Garvey was a madman and demonstrated his contempt by
painting a verbal portrait of the UNIA leader:

A Jamaican Negro of unmixed stock, squat, stocky, fat and sleek, with protruding jaws, and heavy jowls, small bright pig-like eyes and rather bulldog-like face. Boastful, egotistic, tyrannical, intolerant, cunning, shifty, smooth and suave, avaracious; . . . gifted at self-advertisement, without shame in self-laudation, . . . without regard for veracity, a lover of pomp and tawdry finery and garish display, . . . a sheer opportunist and a demagogic charlatan.[95]

Later, when Garvey's trial seemed to be undergoing interminable delays between arraignment and prosecution, Bagnall would join seven other prominent American blacks in an open letter to the United States attorney general demanding that matters be expedited. Their letter condemned Garveyism for seeking "to arouse ill-feeling between the races," and it attacked Garvey himself as "an unscrupulous demagogue, who has ceaselessly and assiduously sought to spread among Negroes distrust and hatred of all white people."[96]

Garveyism was a program of adjustment for urban blacks, warning them to resist the white man's blandishments and to beware of his agents in dark skin. Its ideology inverted the racial predilection of the host culture and made blackness the test of all things good. It also provided followers with an illusion: that the daily realities of bad housing and job discrimination were impermanent because in the future lay a more congenial homeland—Africa—to which the American black man would return one day soon. Few Garveyites, of course, were prepared actually to go there, but zion's promise presumably made present circumstances more tolerable, not unlike the prospect of hitting a number or even ascending to heaven.

NOTES

1. Eugene Kinckle Jones to John Dancy, October 11, 1944, letter on file in the Detroit Urban League offices, Detroit, Michigan.

2. William J. Norton, "Henry Glover Stevens: Memorial Address," January 6, 1939, transcript in "Henry Glover Stevens" reading room file. BHC; *Detroit Free Press,* February 13, 1934; *Dau's Blue Book for Detroit and Suburban Towns, 1917* (New York: Dau's Blue Books, 1917), p. 121.

3. *Detroit Free Press,* February 13, 1934; *Social Service Directory of Detroit, 1917,* pp. 4, 18, 37.

4. Dancy, *Sand against the Wind,* pp. 93-94.

5. Detroit Urban League Papers, Box 1, MHC; *Social Service Directory of Detroit, 1917,* pp. 18, 37; *Dau's Blue Book for Detroit* (1917), p. 82; Oscar Webber, "J.L. Hudson: The Man and the Store" (Address to the Newcomen Society of North America, Detroit, Michigan, November 8, 1954), reprint in J.L. Hudson Papers, Box 2, BHC; Tom Mahoney and Leonard Sloane, *The Great Merchants* (New York: Harper and Row, 1966), pp. 210-13; *The Genealogical Tree of the Hudson Family,* BHC; *Detroit Saturday Night,* March 23, 1929; *Detroit Free Press,* April 14, 1933; *World Who's Who in Commerce and Industry* (Chicago: Marquis—Who's Who, 1965), pp. 419, 434, 435.

6. Detroit Urban League Papers, Box 1, MHC; *Detroit City Directory, 1917.*

7. Detroit Urban League Papers, Box 1, MHC; *Detroit City Directory, 1917; Dau's Blue Book for Detroit* (1917), p. 79; *Detroit Free Press,* March 2, 1921; *Detroit Saturday Night,* February 20, 1915.

8. Detroit Urban League Papers, Box 1, MHC; *Detroit City Directory, 1917; Social Service Directory of Detroit, 1917,* p. 114; *Community Fund News,* June 1920; *Detroit News,* January 16, 1958.

9. Detroit Urban League Papers, Box 1, MHC; *Social Service Directory of Detroit, 1917,* pp. 37, 73; *Detroit City Directory, 1915; Detroit Journal,* November 12, 1919.

10. Detroit Urban League Papers, Box 1, MHC; *Social Service Directory of Detroit, 1917,* pp. 37, 70; *Detroit City Directory, 1916.*

11. Detroit Urban League Papers, Box 1, MHC; *Detroit City Directory, 1918; Social Service Directory of Detroit, 1917,* pp. 18, 114; *Bulletin of the Detroit Historical Society* 11 (February 1955): 3.

12. Detroit Urban League Papers, Box 1, MHC; *Social Service Directory of Detroit, 1917,* p. 37; *Dau's Blue Book for Detroit* (1917), p. 116; *Detroit News,* January 20, 1910, January 29, 1955; *Detroit Journal,* May 19, 1913, January 4, 1917, p. 8.

The author cannot be sure why the Rev. Eugene Rodman Shippen remained on the Detroit Urban League Board for only little more than a year. What is clear from the Detroit Urban League papers is that Shippen and Chester M. Culver (discussed later in the chapter) never sat on the Board simultaneously. While this is probably coincidental the possibility also exists that Shippen resigned when Culver took a seat on the Board.

13. *Detroit Saturday Night,* August 5, 1922, p. 5.

14. Detroit Urban League Papers, Box 1, MHC; *Social Service Directory of Detroit, 1917,* pp. 18-20, 37; *Detroit City Directories,* 1914-17; *Dau's Blue Book for Detroit* (1917); Burton, *City of Detroit, Michigan, 1701-1922,* vol. 3, p. 921; *Detroit Journal,* November 12, 1919; *Who's Who in Government,* vol. 2 (New York: The Biographical Research Bureau, 1932), p. 1064; Burton, *History of Wayne County and the City of Detroit, Michigan,* vol. 3, p. 585.

15. Detroit Urban League Board, Minutes, February 1924; Detroit Urban League Board, Minutes of a Special Meeting, April 24, 1924; Detroit Urban League Board, Minutes, June 12, 1924. All in Detroit Urban League Papers, Box 1, MHC.

16. Detroit Urban League Papers, Box 1, MHC; *Community Fund News,* June 1920, August 1920, February 15, 1922, January 15, 1923, June 25, 1923; *Detroit Saturday Night,* August 5, 1922.

17. Detroit Urban League Papers, Box 1, MHC; *Community Fund News,* June 1920; *Detroit City Directories,* 1917-19.

18. *Detroit Saturday Night,* August 5, 1922; *Who's Who in America* (1938-39), vol. 20 (Chicago: The A.N. Marquis Co., 1938), p. 1877; *Social Service Directory of Detroit, 1917,* p. 18; *Community Fund News,* August 1920; Detroit Urban League Papers, Box 1, MHC.

19. Fred M. Butzel, "Social Progress in Detroit" (Address delivered at the Annual Meeting of the Detroit Community Union, February 1, 1928), reprint in Detroit Urban League Papers, Box 2, MHC.

20. *Detroit Saturday Night,* August 5, 1922; *Community Fund News,* February 15, 1922, January 15, 1923, February 15, 1924, January 15, 1925.

21. Detroit Urban League Papers, Box 1, MHC; *The Compass Needle* 2 (May 1936): 23-24.

22. Detroit Urban League Papers, Box 1, MHC; *Detroit City Directory, 1918.*

23. See, for example, Urban League Board, Minutes of Special Meeting, November 3, 1919; Report of the Director of the Detroit Urban League, October 14, 1920; Urban League Board Report, July and August 1921; Urban League Board Report, January (dated January 19, 1922); Percival Dodge, acting secretary, Accounting Committee, Detroit Community Union, to John C. Dancy, executive secretary of the Detroit Urban League, August 13, 1924. All in Detroit Urban League Papers, Box 1, MHC.

24. Henry G. Stevens to Henry G. Stevens, August 10, 1920, ibid.

25. Burton, *History of Wayne County and the City of Detroit, Michigan,* vol. 3, pp. 582-85.

26. John D. Green, secretary of the Detroit Stove Works, to the As-

sociated Charities, August 11, 1916; General Manager of the Employers'
Association to Henry G. Stevens, May 8, 1917; Report of a Special Urban
League Board Meeting Held on November 3, 1919 (report dated November 13, 1919); Report of the Detroit Urban League Board for the Months
of July and August 1921. All in Detroit Urban League Papers, Box 1, MHC.
In addition, see Carlson, "The Negro in the Industries of Detroit," pp. 189,
200; Lloyd Bailer, "Negro Labor in the Automobile Industry" (Ph.D. diss.,
University of Michigan, 1943), p. 31; Burton, *History of Wayne County
and the City of Detroit, Michigan,* vol. 3, p. 583.

27. Bailer, "Negro Labor in the Automobile Industry," p. 31. The Louis-
ville and Nashville railroad ran to Cincinnati, and from there migrants
bound for Detroit would take the Michigan Central railroad. Detroit
Bureau of Governmental Research, *The Negro in Detroit,* sect. 2, *Population,* p. 15.

28. Detroit Urban League Papers, Box 1, MHC; *Social Service Directory of Detroit, 1917,* p. 37; *Detroit City Directories,* 1914-18; Arthur Turner and Earl R. Moses, *Colored Detroit* (Detroit, 1924), pp. 49,
81-133; Warren, *Michigan Manual of Freedmen's Progress,* pp. 48,
52-53, 215; Katzman, *Before the Ghetto,* pp. 63, 65, 77, 129, 139, 154,
158, 160; *Detroit News,* October 31, 1927; Dancy, *Sand against the
Wind,* pp. 221-23; *Civic Searchlight,* September 1950.

29. Detroit Urban League Papers, Box 1, MHC; *Social Service Directory of Detroit, 1917,* p. 37; *Detroit Contender,* November 13, 1920;
Detroit Free Press, March 19, 1952; Warren, *Michigan Manual of Freedmen's Progress,* p. 48; *Who's Who in Colored America, 1928-1929,* ed.
Joseph J. Boris, 2d ed. (New York: Who's Who in Colored America Corp.,
1929), p. 237.

30. Detroit Urban League Papers, Box 1, MHC; *Social Service Directory of Detroit, 1917,* p. 37; *Detroit City Directory, 1916; Detroit Contender,* November 13, 1920; *Who's Who in Colored America, 1928-1929,*
p. 316.

31. *Social Service Directory of Detroit, 1917,* p. 37; Turner and Moses,
Colored Detroit, p. 62; Warren, *Michigan Manual of Freedmen's Prog-
ress,* p. 92; Aris A. Mallas, Jr., Rea McCain, and Margaret K. Hedden,
Forty Years in Politics: The Story of Ben Pelham (Detroit: Wayne State
University Press, 1957); interview with Alfred H. Pelham, November 7,
1967; "Benjamin B. Pelham" reading room file, BHC; *Detroit News,*
November 25, 1927, February 8, 1942, October 8, 1948; Katzman, *Be-
fore the Ghetto,* pp. 128-29, 139, 158, 161, 186, 194.

32. Detroit Urban League Papers, Box 1, MHC; *Detroit City Directory,
1917; Who's Who in Colored America,* ed. Thomas Yenser, 5th ed. (Brook-

lyn: Thomas Yenser, 1940), p. 395; tape-recorded interview of William C. Osby by Alex Baskin, Detroit, Michigan, July 27, 1960, MHC, used by permission of Mr. Alex Baskin; Warren, *Michigan Manual of Freedmen's Progress,* pp. 120-21.

33. Benjamin Comfort to William J. Norton, February 7, 1923, Detroit Urban League Papers, Box 1, MHC.

34. George H. Green, quoted in the *Detroit News,* October 31, 1927, p. 14. Green, former postal employee, then undertaker, and Urban League Board member, was the first black nominated to run for the Detroit Common Council. The *Detroit News* article here cited ("Negro Hopes to Aid His Race") appeared during his campaign, which was unsuccessful.

35. Report of the Detroit Urban League Board, February 10, 1921; Detroit Urban League Board, Minutes, February 1921. Both in Detroit Urban League Papers, Box 1, MHC. *Detroit City Directory, 1920-21.*

36. Detroit Urban League Board, Minutes, January 17, 1923, Detroit Urban League Papers, Box 1, MHC.

37. Forrester B. Washington to the Rev. John Meister, superintendent, German Protestant Home for Orphans and Old People, June 9, 1916, ibid. An identical letter was written by Washington to the heads of several agencies, all in June 1916.

38. *Who's Who in Colored America,* 5th ed., p. 542; *Detroit News,* August 27, 1963.

39. George W. Grant, secretary of the Employers' Association of Detroit, to Forrester B. Washington, December 3, 1917, Detroit Urban League Papers, Box 1, MHC.

40. Grant to Washington, March 25, 1918, ibid.

41. Grant to Washington, March 26, 1918, ibid.

42. One need look no further than Booker T. Washington and his autobiography *Up from Slavery* (1901) to find the classic articulation of how success attends hard work, thrift, perseverance, etc., even against incredible odds. Washington, in this and other ways, is as much in the American tradition as Benjamin Franklin, who also explored—for public consumption—the possibilities of right virtue properly cultivated. Washington, who died in 1915, remains the pivotal figure in Afro-American history. He is the man around whom all of the issues still swirl. His supporters (as well as his detractors) have run the gamut from militancy to accommodationism, and they have often been at great pains to disassociate themselves from each other while still laying (or rejecting) claim to the Washington philosophy somehow defined.

Many black intellectuals, of course, have rebelled against the idea that black values are totally derived from white America and have sought, in their art, an expression of the unique features of black life. In the 1920s this literary tradition was particularly rich and, in the Harlem Renaissance, embodied such important figures as Claude McKay, Jean Toomer, Langston Hughes, George S. Schuyler, and Countee Cullen. Leaving aside the question of whether the Harlem Renaissance was a totally separate movement or itself derived at least in part from a general disenchantment among intellectuals with postwar America and middle-class values, the Renaissance literature is interesting for the groping its existence implies. The problem of whether black culture in America is distinct or derivative remains wide open for scholars, but there can be no doubt that for the literati of the 1920s the seeking after cultural uniqueness was a specific, zealous, and often frantic mission.

See Robert Bone, *The Negro Novel in America* (New Haven and London: Yale University Press, 1968), pp. 53-94; also the novels, poems, essays, and recollections of the artists themselves. The bibliography in Bone's study is excellent.

43. Forrester B. Washington, Notes to Speech to the Dress Well Club, Detroit, September 20, 1917, Detroit Urban League Papers, Box 1, MHC. I have corrected some typographical errors in the source for quotation in the text.

44. Dress Well Club brochure, pasted into Washington's notes to the speech to the Dress Well Club, September 20, 1917, ibid. Several obvious printing errors have been corrected. See also Washington's memorandum "For Newspaper," October 9, 1917, ibid.; and *Detroit Times,* October 10, 1917.

45. "Why He Failed" written into Washington's speech notes, "A Program of Work for the Assimilation of Negro Immigrants in Northern Cities," delivered at the Round Table of Negro Migration into Northern Cities at the National Conference of Charities and Corrections, June 13, 1917, Detroit Urban League Papers, Box 1, MHC; the card's message was reprinted (with "behind time" mistakenly changed to "behindhand") in Oscar Leonard and Forrester B. Washington, "Welcoming Southern Negroes: East St. Louis and Detroit—a Contrast," *Survey* 38 (July 14, 1917): 335.

46. Quoted from "Mr. Ford's Page," *Dearborn Independent,* June 17, 1922, p. 5.

47. Carlson, "The Negro in the Industries of Detroit," p. 172; Herbert R. Northrup, *Organized Labor and the Negro* (New York and London: Harper and Brothers, 1944), pp. 186-87; Robert W. Dunn,

Labor and Automobiles (New York: International Publishers Co., 1929), p. 69; Bailer, "Negro Labor in the Automobile Industry," pp. 53-70, 88.

48. Carlson, "The Negro in the Industries of Detroit," chaps. 6 and 7, esp. pp. 97, 102, 105-06, 172; Detroit Bureau of Governmental Research, *The Negro in Detroit*, sect. 3, *Industry,* pp. 8-11; Bailer, "Negro Labor in the Automobile Industry," pp. 53-70; Lloyd Bailer, "The Negro Automobile Worker," *The Journal of Political Economy* 51 (February-December 1943): 417; Dunn, *Labor and Automobiles,* pp. 67-70; Northrup, *Organized Labor and the Negro,* pp. 186-90.

49. Forrester B. Washington, section entitled "The Negro in the Industries of Detroit," in "The Negro in Detroit: A Survey of the Conditions of a Negro Group in a Northern Industrial Center during the War Prosperity Period," (Unpaginated paper written for the Research Bureau of the Associated Charities of Detroit, 1920), copy in DPL; Detroit Bureau of Governmental Research, *The Negro in Detroit*, sect. 3, *Industry,* pp. 14-16. For similar findings see the records of the survey conducted by Boyd Fisher, vice president of the Executives Club of the Detroit Board of Commerce, of fifty-three Detroit manufacturing firms, June 1916, in Detroit Urban League Papers, Box 1, MHC; also Bailer, "Negro Labor in the Automobile Industry," p. 99; and Carlson, "The Negro in the Industries of Detroit," p. 145.

50. Detroit Bureau of Governmental Research, *The Negro in Detroit,* sect. 3, *Industry,* p. 5; Bailer, "Negro Labor in the Automobile Industry," p. 44.

51. Detroit Bureau of Governmental Research, *The Negro in Detroit,* sect. 3, *Industry,* p. 4; Bailer, "Negro Labor in the Automobile Industry." pp. 138-40.

52. Nevins and Hill, *Ford: Expansion and Challenge,* pp. 539-40; Bailer, "The Negro Automobile Worker," pp. 418-19; Bailer, "Negro Labor in the Automobile Industry," pp. 67-70; John C. Dancy to W. C. Donnell, April 1, 1930, Detroit Urban League Papers, Box 2, MHC.

Many people at the time—most of them white trade-unionists—questioned Ford's motivation for hiring blacks in such large numbers and distributing at least a few of them in jobs throughout the plant. The most frequent accusation was that Ford sought insurance against labor unions. This logic went that since blacks presumably were less union-conscious than whites, their token dispersal meant they would be nucleus crews for training new workers in the event white employees struck. Another speculation was that the Ford genius for efficiency saw race rivalry as a means of increasing worker productivity.

What seems clearly to be true is that black employees at Ford directed their loyalty to the company rather than to the unions. Part of this may have stemmed from the semifeudal relationships under which blacks worked in the agricultural South before migrating North. But more substantive motivation must have been operating. Few if any blacks were welcomed into the shaky automobile unions of the 1920s and early 1930s. Ford offered a job; white workers and their unions seemed only to offer resentment. This loyalty to management would continue and would become especially noticeable throughout the industry during the massive organizing drives of the late 1930s. Bailer, "Negro Labor in the Automobile Industry," pp. 90, 97-98, 141,190; Dunn, *Labor and Automobiles,* pp. 67-70; Northrup, *Organized Labor and the Negro,* pp. 186-97; Labor Union Survey, Memorandum No. 4. "For Negro Working Men" (Survey taken September 13-20, 1927), Detroit Urban League Papers, Box 2, MHC; John C. Dancy to Mr. Joseph R. Houchins, September 24, 1929, ibid.; Detroit Bureau of Governmental Research, *The Negro in Detroit,* sect. 3, *Industry,* pp. 22-24.

53. Bailer, "Negro Labor in the Automobile Industry," p. 125.

54. Quoted in Carlson, "The Negro in the Industries of Detroit," pp. 134-35.

55. Ibid., pp. 139-40.

56. Ibid., p. 143.

57. Ibid., p. 142.

58. Ibid., p. 163.

59. Ibid.

60. The Bureau of Business Research of the University of Michigan conducted a survey (ca. 1929) on the power of foremen. Of fifty-nine firms volunteering information, the foremen of fifty-six were empowered to fire men from the gang and from the department; in twenty-one of these fifty-six firms, foremen could discharge men from the company as well, with no other source of appeal open to the worker. Ibid., p. 169.

61. Washington, "The Religious Life of the Negro in Detroit," in "The Negro in Detroit" (1920), DPL; Detroit Bureau of Governmental Research, *The Negro in Detroit,* sect. 10, *Religion,* pp. 1-7; *Detroit Saturday Night,* January 7, 1928; *Detroit Contender,* November 13, 1920.

62. Hartt, "When the Negro Comes North," p. 87.

63. Washington, "The Religious Life of the Negro in Detroit," in "The Negro in Detroit" (1920), DPL; Detroit Bureau of Governmental Research, *The Negro in Detroit,* sect. 10, *Religion,* pp. 17-20.

64. Detroit Bureau of Governmental Research, *The Negro in Detroit,* sect. 10, *Religion,* p. 17.

65. Washington, "The Religious Life of the Negro in Detroit," in "The Negro in Detroit" (1920), DPL.

66. Ibid.

67. Detroit Bureau of Governmental Research, *The Negro in Detroit,* sect. 10, *Religion,* pp. 18-19.

68. Washington, "The Religious Life of the Negro in Detroit," in "The Negro in Detroit" (1920), DPL.

69. Quoted in *Detroit Saturday Night,* January 7, 1928, p. 3.

70. Quoted in ibid.

71. Bailer, "Negro Labor in the Automobile Industry," pp. 154-55.

72. Ibid., pp. 113, 113n, 159-60; Nevins and Hill, *Ford: Expansion and Challenge,* p. 540. The Second Baptist Church (441 Monroe Street, near the corner of Beaubien) increased its membership from 1400 people (1915) to 3100 (1920) to 4000 (1926). It was the largest black church in Detroit. From 1910 to 1920 St. Matthew's Episcopal Church (located at the corner of St. Antoine and Elizabeth streets) grew from 187 members to 600, ranking it eighth in size among black churches in Detroit in 1920. Subsequent to the appointment of the Rev. Robert W. Bagnall as minister (1911-21), pews at St. Matthew's were no longer rented. Rev. Everard W. Daniel succeeded Rev. Bagnall in 1921. Washington, "The Religious Life of the Negro in Detroit," in "The Negro in Detroit" (1920), DPL; Detroit Bureau of Governmental Research, *The Negro in Detroit,* sect. 10, *Religion,* p. 3; Everard W. Daniel, "St. Matthew's Need: A Challenge," *Michigan Churchman* 28 (December 1923): 21-22, 35.

73. Gustav G. Carlson, "Number Gambling: A Study of a Culture Complex" (Ph.D. diss., University of Michigan, 1940), pp. 130, 139-142.

74. Ibid., pp. 131-33.

75. Ibid., pp. 133-35.

76. Quotations from ibid., pp. 144-45.

77. Ibid., pp. 145-49.

78. Editorial on "Business," *Detroit Contender,* November 13, 1920, p. 8. The Rev. Robert L. Bradby, pastor of the Second Baptist Church, echoed these thoughts in his letter to the editor, ibid., p. 4.

79. See, for example, Marcus Garvey, "The True Solution of the Negro Problem" (1922), in *Philosophy and Opinions of Marcus Garvey,* ed. Amy Jacques-Garvey, 2 vols. (New York: Universal Publishing House, 1923-25), 1: 52-53.

80. The standard biographical source on Garvey is Edmund David Cronon, *Black Moses: The Story of Marcus Garvey and the Universal Negro Improvement Association* (Madison, Wis.: The University of Wisconsin Press, 1955).

81. Detroit Bureau of Governmental Research, *The Negro in Detroit,* sect. 11, *Community Organization,* pp. 6-7.

Cronon estimates the Detroit membership in 1924 to have been 4000. Cronon, *Black Moses,* p. 206.

82. All quoted in Cronon, *Black Moses,* pp. 191-95.

83. Garvey, *Philosophy and Opinions,* 2: 3.

84. Mrs. Josephine Dunkrett, Detroit, to the editors, *The Negro World* (New York), September 10, 1927, p. 8.

85. Ibid., July 24, August 21, August 28, and September 4, 1926.

86. List of contributors and amount of contribution to "Rehabilitation and Expansion Fund," ibid., July 3 and September 4, 1926. These names were checked for occupation and place of residence in the *Detroit City Directory, 1925-26.*

87. *The Owl* (Detroit), January 21, 1927, p. 2; Cronon, *Black Moses,* p. 139; *Detroit Free Press,* June 23, 1962; *Detroit News,* June 23, 1962.

88. See, for example, the attack on racial extremists of either stripe in "Negro 'Coming,' on a Hard Road," *Detroit Saturday Night,* January 21, 1928. The editor of this weekly newspaper, H. M. Nimmo, sat on the executive board of the Employers' Association of Detroit.

89. Cronon, *Black Moses,* esp. pp. 50-169.

90. Ibid., pp. 135-36.

91. Garvey, *Philosophy and Opinions,* 2: 24-25.

92. DuBois editorial, "A Lunatic or a Traitor," *Crisis* 28 (May 1924): 8-9. Wrote DuBois: "Not even Tom Dixon or Ben Tillman or the hatefulest enemies of the Negro have ever stooped to a more vicious campaign than Marcus Garvey, sane or insane, is carrying on. He is not attacking white prejudice, he is grovelling before it and applauding it; his only attack is on men of his own race who are striving for freedom; his only contempt is for Negroes; his only threats are for black blood."

93. C. S. Smith, Detroit, to the editors, *World's Work* 41 (March 1921): 435-36; Katzman, *Before the Ghetto,* pp. 77, 160.

94. *Michigan State News* (Grand Rapids), February 8, 1921; *Detroit News,* February 27, 1919; Katzman, *Before the Ghetto,* pp. 137-39.

95. Robert W. Bagnall, "The Madness of Marcus Garvey," *Messenger* 5 (March 1923): 638.

96. Quoted in Garvey, *Philosophy and Opinions,* 2: 295. The other members of the "Committee of Eight" were Dr. Julia P. Coleman, president of the Hair-Vim Chemical Co.; Robert S. Abbott, founder and publisher of the *Chicago Defender;* Harry H. Pace, insurance company executive, music publisher, and lawyer; John E. Nail, pioneer in Harlem real

estate and brother-in-law of James Weldon Johnson; George W. Harris, editor and publisher of the *New York News* and New York City Alderman from 1920 to 1924; Chandler Owen, socialist, intellectual, and co-editor of the journal *Messenger;* and William Pickens, educator, author, and field secretary of the NAACP.

chapter FOUR

Forebodings:
The Housing Crush
and Rising Hatreds

I

In 1918 John C. Dancy succeeded Forrester B. Washington as executive director of the Detroit Urban League. Like his predecessor, who went to work for the U.S. Department of Labor before returning to Detroit and the Associated Charities, Dancy was also a young man, barely thirty years old. He had been born in Salisbury, North Carolina, the son of free parents and grandparents. From his earliest childhood he was made aware of books and learning and race progress. Dancy's father, John, Sr., was a skilled typesetter who, after saving enough money as an apprentice in a printing office, had attended Howard University, then worked for a while in the United States Treasury Department, and at the time of his son's birth was teaching printing and publishing at Livingstone College in Salisbury. Family friends included Booker T. Washington, Robert H. Terrell, and P. B. S. Pinchback.[1]

Until he was sixteen years old John Dancy attended the elementary and secondary school classes run by Livingstone. Then his father decided it was time for him to go to school with whites, and young John was enrolled at the Phillips Exeter Academy in Exeter, New Hampshire, an elite preparatory school. Although planters from the West Indies had been sending their sons to the school for years, John Dancy was perhaps the first American black to attend.[2]

His aspirations heightened with his experience in New Hampshire. Young men graduating from Exeter usually matriculated at Ivy League universities, and John Dancy was no exception. He chose the University of Pennsylvania, and there he participated in track and boxing. But his main energies were directed toward the classroom. He concentrated in sociology, for he had long since decided that he wanted to do something—perhaps as a teacher—"to help improve the condition of Negroes."[3]

The year before coming to Detroit, Dancy worked for the Urban League in New York. His responsibility as industrial secretary was to find jobs for blacks coming into the city. Here was his first confrontation with the realities of northern employment patterns. It was easy enough, he found, to secure jobs for blacks in menial service, but for black men with special skills there were no openings. Soon he begun to realize that if any progress at all was to be made for blacks of ability, it would have to come as a result of contacts established with a sympathetic white community.[4]

In New York he courted childhood sweetheart Maude Bulkley, the daughter of the city's first black school principal. The austere Dr. William Lewis Bulkley, a founder of the National Urban League, had risen from slavery to Wesleyan University to study in France and Germany to a doctorate in ancient languages and literature from Syracuse University; he was not enthusiastic at the prospect of an American, still less a black, for a son-in-law. He had been careful to educate his daughters in Europe (Maude in Switzerland), where, he felt, they would be free from the indignities of life in the United States. He spent his summer vacations abroad with them, traveling the Continent so they could become thoroughly familiar—and, hopefully, enamored—with the languages and culture of the French, Italians, and Germans. The guns of war cancelled his plans to find the young women a permanent home overseas and forced the Bulkleys to return together to the United States. Despite her father's misgivings, Maude Bulkley soon married John Dancy. The marriage was a happy one for the dozen years until her death. She seemed to like Detroit and would enjoy walking through the markets of the foreign neighborhoods and talking with the merchants in their own languages. Dancy was very proud of her and of the glory she reflected on him. "I have always felt honored," he said years later, "that she chose to cast her lot with me rather than marry white as did two of her sisters."[5]

The change of nominal leaders had no effect on the broad outlines of Urban League policy. The league continued to place thousands of blacks in jobs through its employment bureau; and powerful white men tried to channel the newcomers into pursuits where their labor would be the most useful. In January 1922 Chester Culver suggested the Urban League establish a program of instruction in housework for black women, with jobs as domestics available through the league employment bureau for those who completed the course.[6] Here Culver was acceding to a trend which was clearly discernible by 1922—the dramatic increase in the percentage of Detroit female servants who were black. In 1910 the figure was 6.1 percent; by 1920 it had risen to 23.1 percent.[7]

It is a fact that the Detroit Urban League employment bureau rarely had difficulty placing women as domestics. The demand was great ("We have not enough applying to fill all of the calls," said Dancy in June 1922[8]), and many white women in Detroit complained of the scarcity of competent black domestic help.[9] But what is also true is that black women were usually limited to service as domestics in their employment possibilities. "We are finding it increasingly difficult," said Dancy in September 1922, "to find jobs for women other than those doing domestic work—those with training, graduates of high schools, training schools and colleges."[10]

As difficult as employment problems were for black women, they were much worse for black men. Some placement for women was almost always possible because the availability of domestic jobs rarely fluctuated with the business cycle. For men, however, the business cycle was much the determining factor. In the depression year of 1921 the Urban League had 11,336 applications for employment. From these, 2604 people were placed—284 men and 2320 women.[11] In the prosperous year of 1925 women were still more easily placed, the difference being only one of degree: of the 5036 persons for whom the Urban League found jobs, 1465 were men and 3571 were women.[12]

Another Urban League policy unaffected by the transition in executive directors was the league's preoccupation with the moral fiber of the black ghetto. The Urban League noticed some "indecency" appearing in the shows of the St. Antoine Street neighborhood theatres. "This has become so obvious of late," said Dancy in his report to the board in March 1921, "that the matter was taken up with the recreation commission and they have agreed to call a halt of such practices with the owners of these theatres."[13] Detroit's commissioner of recreation was Clarence E. Brewer. Within two years Brewer would be a member of the Detroit Urban League Board.[14]

Similarly, there was continuity in Dancy's recommendation (1922) that "in order to make as much sentiment as possible in favor of Negroes" the Dress Well brochure to newcomers be redistributed.[15] Also there was Dancy enjoining Detroit blacks to give to the Community Fund.[16] And there were the quiet mutterings at Garvey fantasies and UNIA regalia.[17]

For John Dancy, even with the energy of youth, the job to be done seemed enormous. Every week hundreds of migrants were arriving, the preponderance from the South, a few from northern cities whose industrial opportunities lagged behind Detroit's. Dancy estimated that there were 3500 newcomers in July 1922 alone, and another 3500 in August.[18] He got into the habit of meeting the trains each day—the Wabash from St. Louis, the Michigan Central from Cincinnati, where the Urban League agent was stationed. Often he would bring men directly to the Urban League office and, when times were good, immediately send them out to a job on the company trucks that transported workers from the door of the league's employment bureau. He would try to tell newcomers not to be deceived by the seeming riches of their weekly wages, amounts of money they had likely never seen at one time before. The cost of living in Detroit would eat into money quickly, he said. There was food to buy, and housing, and warm clothing, and all of these things were expensive, and money would never last if it were spent foolishly.[19] But for many the realization came only with experience, and for more than a few the learning was painful.[20]

The prevalence of disease in the ghetto was of constant concern to the Urban League and to Dancy. It took no particular statistical skill to see that the incidence of tuberculosis, influenza, pneumonia, and smallpox among Detroit blacks was far above the corresponding rates for the city's white population.[21] The situation in Detroit reflected a national condition. The life expectancy of blacks was almost ten years below that of whites; death rates were 40 percent higher.[22] One possible course of action was to demand a total reconstruction of the society which, in the jobs and housing it offered black men, put the cheapest possible price on their lives.[23] But National Urban League leaders did not think in terms of social upheaval. Their response called for the observance of a National Negro Health Week. During this time the various branches, in cooperation with local physicians, would try to explain through mass meetings and lectures some rudimentary health and sanitation procedures to the uninformed black newcomers. The week became an annual event in Detroit.[24]

The Detroit Urban League knew it could not limit its education in health to one week a year. "Half the serious illnesses that overtakes [sic] colored people," wrote Dancy, "could be avoided if they would only pay some attention to general cleanliness around their homes. Small pox, typhoid fever, and tuberculosis are always found lurking about in filthy homes where unsanitary conditions prevail."[25] A more concerted effort was thus called for, and in 1918 the league assigned a social worker to visit the home of every black newcomer to the city. Her function was to persuade the migrants to become vaccinated against smallpox and to instruct them in proper diet and clothing.[26] But the job obviously was too great for one person. It became clear—especially with the onset of an influenza epidemic in 1919—that a more centralized educational device was needed. The solution was the baby clinic, established in 1919 with the cooperation of the Board of Health and housed in the Urban League Community Center. The clinic was staffed by a doctor and three nurses, and ghetto mothers were encouraged to attend periodic instruction in child care and to bring their sick babies for free medical treatment.[27] Hundreds of people a month used the clinic.[28] For many of the women it was their first experience with trained medical personnel, and sometimes the folkways of the Deep South clashed with the predilections of the doctors. Sick children were brought to the clinic with asafoetida bags or dimes hung from their necks because of the presumed healing properties of such fetishes. The doctors did their best to explain that asafoetida was useless and that dimes were best spent for milk.[29]

On at least one occasion, however, a seemingly innocent Urban

League activity in the name of health and recreation became wickedly perverse, and the old self-hatred derived from the dominant culture was again nourished. Dancy had scheduled the girl's basketball team of the league's Community Center to play a game against the girls of the Grosse Pointe Neighborhood Club on the white team's home court. Grosse Pointe, on the eastern boundary of Detroit, was the acknowledged quintessence of white suburban living, and the black children were dazzled at the prospect of playing there. They had been learning from the nurses at the clinic all the details of personal hygiene, and they had long since come to accept the white judgment that blacks had an odor peculiarly different from other people. As a result they were firmly resolved that they would not offend, that they would not leave any foreign and objectionable smell in the Grosse Pointe gymnasium. So just before they were to go out onto the floor to play their game, all the girls bathed and showered. John Dancy knew this was against sensible athletic custom, but he also felt that making a good impression was far more important than winning a basketball game. "This was in line with the lesson I was always trying to teach," he recalled. "'Demean yourselves always so that you make friends; strive to be assets rather than liabilities to your community.' " "It was a great experience," he went on,

> for these girls to be invited to Grosse Pointe, which to them represented the ultima thule in wealth and position. I am sure none of them ever forgot it. Whenever things looked discouraging they could say, "Everybody isn't drawing the line against us. We've been to Grosse Pointe!"[30]

For John Dancy there must have been many satisfactions derived from his job. There was the satisfaction of setting up night schools for Detroit blacks who did not know how to read or write,[31] the accomplishment being one aspect of what he would call some years later "the Detroitization of these people."[32] There was the satisfaction of telling the commissioner of police that the abusive manner of officers when dealing with blacks accounted in large part for the high crime rate among Detroit black men, and receiving a short time thereafter from the commissioner's office a copy of a memorandum sent to all members of the department deploring the use of coarse and insulting language.[33] And above all, there was for Dancy the satisfaction of his association with the white leaders. "I was close to all of them," he would say proudly, "and I had to depend on them for so much."[34] He could never really get over his amazement at the camaraderie that existed between himself, a black man, and these powers of Detroit civic and social life. "They were all so down to earth," he recalled. "They didn't put on any lugs."[35] So Dancy would repay them—by working hard at the job they gave him and by telling them what they wanted to hear. He would report to the leaders in his monthly summaries about the happy adjustments migrant families were making in Detroit after rocky beginnings.[36] He would poke mild fun at one of the black members of the Urban League board who persisted in calling a bulletin board a "bulleting board."[37] And he would assure them "there appears to be the friendliest sort of attitude" with "the Jewish, Italian and Greek neighbors which we live among,"[38] even though he must have known of tense relations and the potential for flare-up.[39]

It was the contagion of being near power and of feeling an integral part of it that made playing the game worth the price of quietly looking at your hands and knowing. It was a game Dancy had in a real sense almost been born into. Perhaps it is impossible for a man of comfortable salary, brought up among books and learning and educated in an university, to understand viscerally the hopes and despairs of people who are swept from day to day. But John Dancy could not allow himself to reflect on the contingency, for to do so would have been to eliminate the one meaningful reason for living on the jagged boundary between black and white. So he remained convinced that it was precisely his understanding of the reality of things that made him the hero, for example, of an incident in the St. Antoine Street ghetto. ("My understanding of the neighborhood came in handy one day when I encountered a lady in distress.") The chauffeur-driven limousine of a philanthropic society matron had slammed into a black man's jalopy, and Dancy, coming out of a barber shop, calmed the unruly crowd by pointing out that the frightened white woman was the mother of the man who owned a particular race horse.[40]

But could Dancy know who the heroes of the black man of the ghetto were? "Negroes like to have some incentive," he said, "somebody in a top spot that they can point to with pride, an example to inspire our young people."[41] He was referring to Mayor James Couzens' appointment of black attorney Charles Mahoney to the city plan commission. But did the man on the streets of Detroit's black ghetto identify with a member of the city plan commission? Perhaps Dancy was right in embracing as heroes for blacks those men who received gratuities from the white community. Couzens appointed Dancy himself to a committee welcoming soldiers home from the war. ("It was amazing how much excitement this stirred," Dancy said, "when Negroes saw my name in the paper. This was something new. I can remember ministers and other community leaders calling me up to talk about it."[42]) But perhaps, too, the hero was the small black grocer on the corner who managed to keep ahead and set things right in small ways. Or perhaps it was the man who sold numbers for the syndicate; or perhaps, the man who turned his rage to violence and shot a policeman.

The game in the North was more complex than the cotton-patch style of simply accepting the white man's petty dispensations and being grateful. The new rules held that when ritualistic offerings were made by the white man, the gifts were still to be gratefully accepted, but now with a semblance of dignity. Otherwise you got what you deserved.

For several years the Detroit Urban League had enjoyed a working agreement with Charles Winegar, superintendent of labor at Dodge. When there were jobs available for blacks at the company, Winegar would let the league know, and the employment bureau would dispatch men to fill them. Eventually enough blacks were employed by Dodge for Dancy to make a suggestion. Why not hire a black man in a liaison capacity between Winegar and the black employees? A welfare worker advising black laborers "how they can best serve the company's interest" might increase productivity, Dancy said. Winegar agreed that it was a useful idea, and all the details were worked out between the two men, including the position's salary, which was to be $2400 a year. Dancy then looked for a person to fill the job. He selected James Bailey, a Tuskegee graduate, and carefully instructed him about the prearranged details. "Now when you go out there," Dancy told him, "remember the salary is all set." Bailey simply had to follow the charade. But when Winegar asked him, "How much salary do you expect to receive?" Bailey lacked the temerity to carry it through.

"Well, you know, I've been interested in doing something to help my people, and so I'm willing to make any concessions."

"How about $1800 a year?" asked Winegar.

"That will be fine," said Bailey.

When Dancy heard what had happened he became livid. He was convinced Winegar, "one of the finest friends the Detroit Urban League ever had," was merely acting "as a matter of form." The villain was Bailey, "one of those altruistic people who think they must do something for their folks" and thereby dissolve their self-respect in the process.[43]

Bailey stayed on at Dodge for some time and performed his job well, but he never received more than $1800 a year. Dancy could acknowledge that the man "did a good job for Dodge, and for the Negroes of Detroit," and that "he was a fine man, and the community was very fortunate to have him." And Dancy could admire the way Bailey and three fellow alumni from Tuskegee sang spirituals and folk music, once in Cadillac Square before thousands of people at a liberty bond rally. ("They could really sway an audience.") But he could never quite respect a man who did not understand the rules of the game—"you must not grovel"—a man who could not understand that though you were worth $2400 a year you had to ask for it, even if it were prearranged.[44]

The game of moral guardianship was above all limited in its players. Qualifications for leaders were strictly defined, and any outsider who attempted to assume the function of leadership was immediately identified as a menace. When the dissidents were ghetto blacks, the situation was particularly threatening. In February 1918 an organization called the Good Citizenship League was incorporated. It advertised itself in its solicitations as "not the same as the URBAN LEAGUE. THE URBAN LEAGUE is a negro employment bureau. THE GOOD CITIZENSHIP LEAGUE is the only INCORPORATED organization doing welfare work among negroes in this city."[45] It dared to address itself directly to the recognizable white leaders of the city. To the officers of the Detroit Board of Commerce it wrote: "We feel that your Board and all the Civic and social organizations in the city are either misled, badly advised, or else are not the least interested in the Negroes' problems in this city."[46] The Urban League had been established, the Good Citizenship League went on, for precisely the purpose of preventing any real action being taken with regard to the problems of blacks:

Negro ministers, and other worthy citizens can't reach the Civic
Boards now on account of the Urban League, being the accepted
channel through which all matters pertaining to Negro welfare must
pass. As far as we have been able to learn, every application for aid
of any kind, worthy or unworthy, that has been presented to the
Board of Charity, during the last year or more, has died in the office
of the Urban League, the application seldom receiving a reply.[47]

What has the Urban League done? the dissidents asked rhetorically.
"It has blocked every worthy move for bettering conditions, shut up
every Negro ministers' mouth in this city, on Buffet flats, gambling
dens, and street women." If anyone did say anything or try to bring
about a change in conditions, the white leaders merely claimed that
"such a person is 'hunting a job', that they should let it alone, that . . .
the white Urban League [is] looking after conditions among
Negroes."[48]

When the Good Citizenship League published a pamphlet two years
later, many of the charges made to the board of commerce in private
correspondence were restated publicly. But now there was a new
thrust to the attack, one which had only been hinted at earlier. It was
the theme of the corruption of black leadership. "We are tired of picked
leaders," said the dissidents. "We haven't a man in Detroit that the
masses of colored people can point to and really trust as a leader." As
for the cause of the corruption the dissidents understood that everyone
was to blame: the whites—i.e., the Community Fund (referred to constantly as "the Board of Charity"); the Urban League; and the "picked
advisers" themselves, particularly the Reverend Robert L. Bradby of
the Second Baptist Church and John Dancy. There seemed to the Good
Citizenship League to be only one way for black leaders to avoid the
temptations of treason, and that was for their selection and control to
rest exclusively in black hands. "We reserve the right," said the league,
"to pick our own leaders, and when they don't suit us we have the power
to move them. We know who is best fitted for leadership among us."[49]

Although this concept was traditional democratic piety, it sounded
to progressive whites like the crack of doom. "Detroit's Negro colony
has among its members an element of crabby, muddle-headed near-reds
whose idea of progress is apparently to foment race-hatred," thundered

an editorial in *Detroit Saturday Night*, a weekly journal whose editor-in-chief sat on the executive board of the Employers' Association. Why didn't the Good Citizenship League acknowledge "the very considerable welfare work done among Detroit Negroes by many Protestant denominations and by Community Fund organizations?" the *Saturday Night* asked. "There is nothing constructive about this so-called 'report' " it decided. "It reads like the production of a disgruntled smart-aleck who wants to kick, and is not sure what to kick about. We call attention to it only because it is capable of making mischief, and therefore merits exposure."[50] The leaders at the Urban League agreed. Nothing could be gained from prosecuting, Fred Butzel advised, except notoriety, and that is what they want. Only one gesture seemed to be called for, and Dancy made it. He wrote to the *Saturday Night* thanking the editors for the exposure and assuring them they had made no mistake in their evaluation.[51]

The Good Citizenship League surfaced for the last time in June 1929. Police carrying a search warrant raided a ramshackle one-story house on South Junction Avenue, south of West Fort Street and near the river. The building was the residence of Sarah Bannister, league secretary; it also was league headquarters and a home for black children. In the house police found what they were looking for—a quantity of pamphlets characterized as violent and inflammatory by the assistant prosecuting attorney on the scene. Bannister, J. Henry Porter, league president, and Mary E. Jones, treasurer, were arrested and charged with criminal syndicalism. Police also found six children, including one white baby, in the home and delivered them to Children's Hospital for observation.[52]

II

An urban rot accompanied Detroit's economic progress. As the city pushed outward and conquered the countryside, the business center was also expanding. Where there had once been rich private homes—on Washington Boulevard and Elizabeth and lower Jefferson and Woodward—now the stone buildings of commerce and industry began to appear. Land values crept upward in anticipation of a proliferating commercial usage, and the area's residential attractiveness began to decline.[53]

Downtown land values reflected Detroit's boom spirit. Local real-

estate men, convinced that the city's economic growth would continue
far into the future ("The growth of the past twenty years should be in-
significant as compared with the growth of the next twenty years"),
boasted of the impossibility of buying an acre of land in the central
business area—bounded by Woodward, Michigan, Washington Boulevard,
and Grand Circus Park—or on contiguous streets, for less than $5 million.
If acreage in an expanded downtown was worth millions, old residential
structures there were doomed. Although unfortunate, no doubt, for
those who were nostalgic for the old homes, for others it meant opportunity for profit. People who owned property in the area of expansion
could sell at a good price and move to the open spaces on the city's
periphery or to Grosse Pointe, now making the transition from resort
to exclusive suburb.[54]

But for black people in the St. Antoine Street ghetto, prospects for a
downtown expansion only aggravated problems they already had. The
basic difficulty—the housing shortage—was unchanged. Ghetto blacks
had no choice but to stay where they were, since there was little housing
available for them anywhere else. But because the ghetto was just a few
blocks east of downtown, bordering on the main commercial area of the
city, its potential land value was enormous, far out of proportion to the
value of the structures then on it. For the realtors' visions of an expanded
business center to come true, ramshackle dwellings housing blacks would
have to be torn down. Already, manufacturing and commercial ventures
were finding their way in. What incentive could there be, then, for landlords—most of them white men, some of them black—to spend money
maintaining residential property already nearing the end of its lifetime,
particularly if the income being derived with minimum maintenance was
enormous?[55]

So the general conditions of overcrowding, compounded by
accelerated blight, created for ghetto blacks a housing crush of frightful
magnitude. Soon after the onset of the migration there was not a vacant
house or tenement in the black section of the city. Three or four families crowded into nearly every apartment. Fourteen people lived in the
attic of a house on Napoleon Street. Housing with no indoor bathroom facilities, no electric lights, and leaking water pipes was common-
place.[56]

Rents soared. In July 1916 the average price paid per unfurnished
room by 500 selected black families in Detroit had been $4.60 a month.

By January 1920 it was $7.72. Seven months later it was $9.27.[57] Blacks were forced to spend at least 30 percent, perhaps 40 or even 50 percent, of their monthly wages just for someplace to live. The people who could find an apartment or room of any sort were lucky. Many paid for the chance to sleep on a pool table or in a parked automobile.[58]

John Dancy put the matter succinctly in his report to the Detroit Urban League Board, May 1920:

> At this particular time there is nothing new in the housing situation except possibly the tendency on the part of landlords in this vicinity to raise even higher the present high rentals. In this neighborhood houses that in 1915 rented for $20.00 per month are now renting from $75 to $100, an increase of 300 or more percent. Of course all these houses are filled with roomers who pay from $4.00 to $6.00 a week per person. I venture the assertion that in this district there is no house no matter how lacking in conveniences it might be that rents for under $60.00 per month.[59]

The housing shortage benefited a few people of both races: the landlords and individuals who perceived a fertile field for exploitation. In May 1920 a white man entered a black's house on Benton Street. He informed him that he was the new landlord and that he had come to serve notice on the tenant to vacate. The black began to protest that he had just paid his rent. The fake landlord replied he would be as considerate as possible and would allow him fifteen days to get out. Then he left. The imposter's next step was to find someone who was in search of a house, which was not difficult. Accompanied by the second victim, also black, the imposter returned to the place on Benton Street. By the time he left he had received a generous fee from the second man for finding him a home and also a deposit from the legal tenant on another (nonexistent) house. Both blacks felt the white man had done them a favor.[60]

And some black men were just as eager to profit from the congestion of the ghetto. In the first six months of 1920 the county prosecutor initiated proceedings against seven black real-estate agents for rent profiteering. One black real-estate man pretended to rent his own home five times within a few days, collecting from each of the grateful families a sizeable deposit. Black businessmen who had never before speculated in real estate began to invest in the housing market. In April

1920, for example, one businessman leased a number of houses in the vicinity of Russell Street. Each of them had been renting for $25 a month. He immediately raised the rent to $60 and evicted several black families who were unable to pay.[61]

Even the aged and the infirm joined the search for sudden wealth. An old, barely literate black woman who herself lived in a dilapidated frame house on Winder Street decided to pose as a real-estate agent. She claimed to be the representative of Jews in her neighborhood who were building two apartment houses and was able to convince blacks that the renting of apartments in these partially completed buildings had been consigned to her. By the time a warrant was sworn out for her arrest, she had collected at least $5000 in advance rentals on property with which she had no connection.[62]

There seemed little that organized authority could do. The Detroit Board of Commerce's Americanization Committee met with John Dancy in December 1919 to get some "direct information" on the housing situation "from one who knew conditions thoroughly." After their meeting there was a tour of the ghetto. The Urban League's director led the white men through the city's most congested area—the area bounded by Beaubien, Lafayette, Hastings, and Winder. The men from the board of commerce were startled at what they saw: the overcrowding, the lack of sanitation facilities, the exorbitant rents. When they reported back to their directors, they recommended that a special committee be appointed immediately "to delve further into the conditions" and to "suggest a program of activity which at least in part would relieve this blot in the city's boundaries." Our group became involved, explained the Americanization Committee, "because the Negroes are all native-born, full American citizens, whose entire culture is derived in America and it was not deemed proper to imply in any degree that the Negroes were not all Americans."[63]

For some time thereafter Dancy was enthusiastic about the possibilities for action. "What we consider the biggest forward step yet taken with regard to our housing situation," he wrote in his monthly report to the Urban League board,

> was a meeting which we attended as the guest of the Americanization Committee of the Board of Commerce . . . with a view to getting some facts and figures which might be used by the Board of Com-

merce in getting something done about our housing situation. . . . In
a letter to this office by the secretary of the Americanization Committee which has handled the situation up to this time, we have been
advised that a very strong committee from the Board of Commerce
has been formed to go further into this matter.[64]

But as the months passed there was no action forthcoming, and Dancy
realized that the Urban League would be left to its own devices.[65]

The league maintained a listing of available rooms and houses, but
this was just a symbolic service. The demand for living space always
overwhelmed the supply.[66] More than once someone in league board
meetings suggested that tent colonies be built to house the homeless.
The inconveniences of living in a tent, the argument went, could hardly
be greater than those people were already experiencing.[67] During the
depression of 1920/21, when many blacks were jobless as well as homeless, the league discussed the possibility of placing black men on farms
throughout Michigan.[68] Such proposals only suggest the futility the
leaders must have felt in dealing with the most crushing of all urban
dilemmas. "Like the poor," the problem of housing "is always with
us," Dancy lamented in 1922. "It is the one problem we seemingly
have no effort to combat."[69]

But sometimes Dancy had to wonder whether at least a few of his
colleagues on the Urban League board really understood the realities of
the situation. One night the league listened to an address by a visiting
settlement house director, who used lantern slides of housing conditions
in London to illustrate her talk. When the visual images flashed on the
screen, Dancy heard sobs of sorrow coming from some in the gathering.
He could hardly believe it. The situation in this very neighborhood is so
much worse, he thought, that those houses on the screen look like
castles by comparison.[70]

The only solution was a frenzy of homebuilding, as Detroit real-estate
developers, now cognizant of the market need, raced to make up for lost
time. In their activity there was a conceptual approach which with varia-
tions was repeated throughout the period of the Great Migration. It was
the conscious policy—born of custom, with sanction by the courts—of
building widely separate, completely segregated housing on the urban
fringe.

Henry Stevens owned a considerable amount of land beyond the city limits, north of Eight Mile Road between Livernois and Wyoming. In 1921 he sold a part of this property to real-estate developers, who subdivided it and offered it for sale to blacks for home sites. Soon a hundred black families were living in the area.[71] A number of difficulties confronted these new suburban pioneers. Because the subdivision was beyond the city limits, there was no municipal water service or sewerage available. Families had to walk a quarter of a mile to reach the nearest water.[72] Also the problems of building a house were considerable. Private contractors invariably charged blacks higher than normal interest rates because the discount available to professional builders through the banks was always much less attractive on jobs being done for black men than on those being done for whites.[73] Few of the black men in Eight Mile Road were skilled enough at carpentry to do a proper job themselves. As a result many just built a floor and on it erected a tent to live in until they could somehow afford the cost of constructing a home. Others fabricated shacks, supposedly temporary but having a way of becoming permanent. And some paid the contractor's price.[74]

The suburbanites became squatters on the land. Many raised chickens to supplement family income; others raised hogs.[75] The spectacle horrified at least one black welfare worker:

> The subdivisions idea on the whole is not a good one because few of the better Negroes invest in subdivisions and live in them. Living in subdivisions aggravates the health problem and people who adopt it slip into the old southern rural way of doing things. If they lived in better communities suggestion and public opinion would force them to keep [up] their property and maintain a higher standard of conduct. If there are high grade reservations in the subdivision, it may turn out all right. When there is a large isolated Negro group in any area there is apt to be neglect both on the part of the inhabitants and on the part of the municipal authorities.[76]

By 1926 there were 4000 blacks in the Eight Mile Road subdivision. Bounded now by Greenlawn (east), Northend (north), and Wyoming (west), it had spread south to Pembroke and thus back across the city limits, so that 1085 of its inhabitants were officially Detroiters.[77]

Another 2000 blacks lived in Inkster, a place which a few years earlier had been an empty 20-acre tract 14 miles west of Detroit City Hall. As in the Eight Mile Road subdivision, problems of sewerage and water supply existed at the outset, but in Inkster the white developer himself was building the houses, four-room cottages to sell for $2600-$3000, with a $350 down payment. Because the new settlement was just beyond Dearborn, it was especially attractive to black workers employed by Ford. The area would continue to grow.[78]

But white real-estate men were more concerned with sanctifying the subdivisions of their own race against black encroachment than with creating isolated suburban settlements for blacks. The method they used was the restrictive covenant—a contractual agreement between two or more parties restricting the use of property to particular tenancies. Before 1910 no race restrictions were written into deeds of new property in Detroit. Gradually thereafter they began to appear, and by the 1920s—the peak years of the migration and of the subdividing and house-building—racial covenants restricting ownership of property to Caucasians only characterized nearly every new housing development begun in Detroit.[79]

It was true of Russel Woods. A tract 7 miles northwest of downtown Detroit bounded by Livernois on the west and Dexter on the east, the area was forest when platted in 1916. Construction began early in the 1920s. The developers concentrated on the western half of the site, building homes valued then at $7000-$10,000 on 40-x-160-foot lots, which were often sold in pairs. Front lawns were spacious, and the old trees, which had been allowed to stand, contributed to a parklike effect. The houses were basically of the same design—three floors, with a living room, dining room, den, kitchen, breakfast nook, and small lavatory on the first floor, three or four bedrooms and a bath on the second floor, and a third floor or attic sometimes made over into maid's quarters. The new owners were almost without exception Protestant or Catholic. They were successful business and professional men—executives in Detroit companies, owners of small businesses, doctors, lawyers, accountants. Their new neighborhood was fashionable and comfortable.[80] And written into the deed of property by the original subdivider was their guarantee of sanctuary from the forbidden neighbors: "The sale of intoxicating liquors in any form shall not be permitted in any lot in this subdivision except that a druggist may sell the same for medicinal purposes in buildings constructed on Livernois Road. No lot shall be sold, leased or occupied by any person other than one of Caucasian race."[81]

The white realtors, whatever their individual, visceral feelings about black men, were generally agreed as a group that black movement into a white neighborhood invariably occasioned a precipitous decline in property values.[82] As a result, no member of the Detroit Real Estate Board—all of whom were white—was allowed to sell a home to a black in a strictly white neighborhood.[83] All subscribed to Article 34 of the Code of Ethics of the National Association of Real Estate Boards. "A Realtor should never be instrumental in introducing into a neighborhood a character of property or occupancy, members of any race or nationality, or any individuals whose presence will clearly be detrimental to property values in that neighborhood."[84]

The policy was consistent with the judicial opinion of the day. Early in the 1920s a piece of property in Pontiac was subdivided and sold under a contract containing the following restriction: "No building shall be built within twenty feet of the front line of the lot. Said lot shall not be occupied by a colored person, nor for the purpose of doing a liquor business thereon." One of the lots was sold to blacks, and the purchaser of another lot obtained an injunction, by reason of the restriction, to keep them from occupying the property. Litigation followed, with the black defendants claiming the restriction violated the Thirteenth and Fourteenth amendments to the Constitution. In 1922 the Supreme Court of the State of Michigan held the restriction free from objection on either ground and sustained the injunction issued by the lower court. The high court said that the Thirteenth and Fourteenth amendments referred only to legislative action and not to the action of individuals, and it added:

> Suppose the situation was reversed, and some negro who had a tract of land platted it and stated in the recorded plat that no lot should be occupied by a Caucasian and that the deeds which were afterwards executed contained a like restriction, would any one think that dire results to the white race would follow an enforcement of the restrictions? . . . He [Charles Morris, the black defendant] did not have to buy the land and he should not have bought it unless

willing to observe the restrictions it contained.

The issue involved in the instant case is a simple one, *i.e.*, shall the law applicable to restrictions as to occupancy contained in deeds to real estate be enforced or shall one be absolved from the provisions of the law simply because he is a negro?[85]

III

Politics, by design, distorts individual expression. As an organizational framework its function is to absorb or deflect those who might become passionate in more dangerous places. The ward-heeling big city political machines did that very well, dispensing rewards to the faithful so as to leave the fabric of society basically untouched. Progressive men and women around the country, however, saw only the price tag: unscrupulous demagogues leading "ignorant" masses, corrupt functionaries, inefficient governmental operation. So, in many cities progressives battled the machines, most often with marginal success, until Franklin Roosevelt defeated them both in an instant and removed hostilities to Washington.

In Detroit, however, the progressives achieved absolute victory. Because the economic stakes in Detroit before 1900 were not high enough to have produced a battle-hardened political organization, the city presented no firmly entrenched opposition to its twentieth-century reformers. So the old structure was overturned rather easily, and the new political machinery came to be dominated by proponents of civic progress. Inner-city voices who might have found some solace in political forms as they used to be were virtually excluded. Outside now, allowed no institutional outlet for their discontents, the overcrowded and the fearful could only carry their passions to the street.

Detroit city government never enjoyed the wrath of the muckraker's exposé. The political machinery of St. Louis, Minneapolis, Pittsburgh, Philadelphia, Chicago, and New York City was treated each in its turn by journalist Lincoln Steffens in *McClure's Magazine* in 1902 and 1903; but Detroit then—its population burst and economic modernity still ahead—produced no great story because it did not yet have the energy of an important city. There was, of course, corruption in Detroit—municipal machines rarely run without extralegal lubricant—but the corruption was petty. The most notorious episode was the Glinnan scandal of 1912, breaking at the disclosure that some members of the common council had presumably accepted bribes for votes favorable to the Wabash Railroad. At issue was a franchise to build a warehouse on city property, Seventh Street. Less than $4000 in payoffs was involved; by the standards of the day this was miniscule.[86]

No one at the turn of the century claimed that Detroit was blessed with administrative efficiency. The city was run on a charter given it by the Michigan legislature in 1883; subsequent editions of the document, along with enabling legislation, covered almost 600 pages. The mayor was weak. The common council—two men from each of the city's wards, elected by partisan ballot to two-year terms—controlled election machinery. Taxing power rested with a ward-elected board of estimates.[87]

The influence of the saloon was pervasive in those years before reform. In some common councils as many as one-third of the members were saloon keepers or bartenders. Many of the city's voting districts—inner-city and particularly river precincts—were controlled by saloon keepers. The organization which unified the liquor interest and controlled elections was the Royal Ark. It appointed ward captains and endorsed candidates. Few politicians cared to oppose it.[88]

Twentieth century reformers were horrified. The liquor interests were stuffing ballot boxes, padding registration rolls, and controlling the council. The foreign voters living in the inner city were seemingly being corrupted by liquor, and the vision of democracy prostituted.[89] And apparently nothing could be done within the system. Since the common council alone was empowered to investigate voting irregularities, abuses invariably went unchecked. Complaints were referred to a committee, and there they would be buried forever.[90]

The reformers' dissatisfaction led to the formation in 1907 of the Detroit Municipal League. It was ineffective.[91] Five years later the reformers tried again. In the glare of the Glinnan scandal the Detroit Citizens League was formed, with the avowed purpose to "seek to preserve the purity of elections, guard against the abuse of the elective franchise, to publish information regarding public affairs, and to promote governmental efficiency in the City of Detroit."[92] The Citizens League was anything but democratic. Though membership was open to any person who would pay the $1 annual dues, participation in policy making was rigidly controlled. Power was vested in an executive board of nine persons, elected to three-year staggered terms. Candidates for the board were selected by a committee appointed by the president. No additional nominations by the general membership were allowed. When the list of nominees was drawn up, the membership was permitted to elect them. All committee work was done under the supervision of the officers. Members were allowed to sit on committees as a privilege.[93]

The rank and file of the league was largely middle-class. The governors were the wealthy and powerful of Detroit. In 1917 the league's president was its principal financial backer, Henry M. Leland, president of the Cadillac Motor Car Company and a founding father of the Employers' Association of Detroit. His colleagues included corporation executives, lawyers, a bank executive, and a builder and land speculator. All lived on the city's periphery.[94]

The Citizens League was the prime mover in the drive to reform Detroit city government. Inextricably bound up in the movement was the campaign for stringent liquor control.[95] It was his dissatisfaction with the enforcement of the liquor laws which originally brought Henry Leland into the organization. Both William P. Lovett and attorney Pliny W. Marsh, who began administering league activities in 1915, were actively involved with the Anti-Saloon League previous to their affiliation with the Citizens League.[96]

The malign influences had been identified: they were liquor and its corruptive effect on the city's democracy. Control had to be taken from the hands of the Royal Ark and the ward and precinct bosses and invested in the hands of the progressives. With the complete cooperation of the Detroit Council of Churches, the Citizens League began its campaign. In 1915, with the aid of some outstate groups, it secured the passage in Lansing of the Scott-Flowers Act to regulate voting. The new state law barred officeholders from serving on election boards, prevented voters from being offered assistance in marking ballots except in full view of the occupants of the polling place, required that all ballots be numbered, and imposed penalties for the alteration of election records. Legislation passed at the same time gave the governor the power to remove dishonest election officials and provided for court investigation of the conduct of elections. When the Detroit Common Council chal-

lenged the constitutionality of the Scott-Flowers Act, the Citizens
League initiated proposals to amend the city charter with a virtual
restatement of the law. The proposals were adopted at a municipal
election in August 1916.[97]

The biggest hurdle to reform was cleared in November 1916, when
Michigan enacted prohibition, abstinence to begin on the first of May,
1918. The total vote in Detroit went against the proposition, but local
option was not available, and the city was legally bound to obey.[98]
With Detroit the first urban area of nearly a million people to be voted
dry, the reform campaign sped ahead. In 1917 an amendment to the
city charter separating municipal elections from those of the state and
nation was adopted. The same year the state legislature passed a law
permitting the election of charter commissioners on a nonpartisan
ballot.[99] Then the Citizens League initiated a proposal for a complete
charter revision, giving particular emphasis to the need for nonpartisan
elections and a small common council chosen at large. The campaign
received front-page support in all the major Detroit newspapers.[100]

In the election of November 1917 the proposal for charter revision
was adopted, and the charter commission—composed of lawyers and
business executives whose job it was to write a new organic document
subject to the voters' approval—went to work.[101] To the men of the
Detroit Real Estate Board, represented on the charter commission by
their former president Edward C. Van Husan, the need for basic change
in the leadership of government was clear. "Men with more brains than
the average peanut politician are absolutely necessary in our city
government," they said.[102]

The charter the commissioners wrote created a structure for such
change. The ward was eliminated as a factor in politics. It was retained
for the purpose of electing constables, for jury selection, for property
assessments, and for election administration. But as a significant
political subdivision it was done. So too were political parties, now
barred from formal participation in both primaries and election. Municipal elections were scheduled for years in which there would be no
county, state, or national contests. And, the most fundamental change
of all, replacing the old forty-two-man council was a nine-man council
whose members were to be elected at large.[103]

The charter ratification campaign could not help but succeed: there was barely any opposition. The Royal Ark was dead, as was its ward and precinct organization. Prohibition, now in effect, had driven the liquor interests underground, and the reformed voting system had made the manufacturing of votes all but impossible. And the Citizens League, for the purposes of the campaign, had adopted the old methods of the enemy. It appointed 21 ward majors, 250 precinct captains, and several hundred block lieutenants, who personally visited 80 percent of the homes in Detroit. To supplement the almost daily contributions of the press, the league also issued 190,000 pieces of printed material. The ratification election in June 1918 was hardly a contest. The new charter carried by a margin of more than seven to one.[104]

It seemed as if the Citizens League and other representatives of efficiency and progress had succeeded in placing themselves in unchallengeable control of the city's government. In 1919 there were five realtors on the new nine-man council; in 1922, four; in 1924; three; in 1926, four again. From 1919 to 1940, 38 percent of the membership of the council would be in some principal way concerned with the real-estate business.[105]

A smaller council enhanced progressive authority within it. Fewer seats also kept some undesirables out. With council size reduced from forty-two members to nine, labor was virtually unable to secure representation. In the first twenty-two years of government under the new charter just three councilmen were union officials. These were Robert Ewald, Fred Castator, and George Edwards; and their politics were not devoted exclusively to the interests of the laboring man. In their campaigns all three generally received the support of both the labor-hating Citizens League and the Detroit Board of Commerce.[106]

But into the restructured political arena there came a new force that challenged the progressives' right to govern. It was the Ku Klux Klan.

The Klan of the 1920s was predominantly an urban institution.[107] Its greatest strength was in Indianapolis, but its spirit was widespread, rooted in men's fears as they confronted the polyglot intensity of many American cities. Detroit was one such place. The Klansmen of the city would drive to the surrounding countryside and there hold the torch-light ceremonies of initiation for new celebrants. Hundreds, sometimes thousands, of people would take the solemn oaths of allegiance to the Invisible Empire.[108] The entire ritual was carefully worded to exclude all who were alien: "Only native-born, white American citizens, who believe in the tenets of the Christian religion, and who owe no allegiance of any degree or nature to any foreign government or institution, religious or political, or to any sect, people, or persons, are eligible for membership."[109]

Membership in the Detroit-area Klan grew from 3000 in the autumn of 1921 to 22,000 eighteen months later.[110] The apostles of "one hundred per cent Americanism" were always fearful of Catholics, but in Detroit an additional object of concern was the black. "Nigger!" the Klan wrote to a school teacher in 1923, "You are being watched very closely at present. You are too versatile [sic] with the White Students. If you value your hide, you will be more discrete [sic] and KNOW YOUR PLACE in the future. This applies in the class-room as well as other places. Speak when spoken to and not OTHERWISE. You may be in the north, but there are still tar and feathers up here."[111]

With the confidence gained from increasing numbers Detroit Klansmen began in 1923 to burn crosses near public buildings.[112] The night of the municipal election in November, a cross was set ablaze on the front lawn of city hall just as officials were preparing to count ballots.[113] On Christmas Eve a six-foot oil-soaked cross was ignited on the steps of the county building, an event which was immediately followed by a prearranged rally in Cadillac Square, where a masked Santa Claus led a huge crowd—estimated by the *Detroit News* at 4000 and by the Klan at 25,000—in the Lord's Prayer. Police riot squads interrupted any further proceedings by dispersing the assemblage with drawn weapons.[114]

The Klan decided to use the strength of its membership in 1924 to enter politics. On the state level Klansmen tried to elect a sympathizer to the governorship and to secure enactment of a law abolishing parochial schools. They were unsuccessful. But in the more concentrated political arena of Detroit, the Klan almost accomplished a miracle.

On September 9, 1924, a primary election was held to determine candidates for the remaining one year of the term of Mayor Frank E. Doremus, who had become seriously ill and could not continue in office. Leading the voting and thereby certified for the runoff election in November were John W. Smith and Joseph A. Martin. Smith, a Catholic, received most of his support from Catholics, blacks, and recent immigrants. Martin was the businessman's candidate, and his call for clean government appealed to the upper-income wards. But the third-place finisher also decided to run. He was Charles Bowles, attorney, and his plan was to disregard the primary election and compete as a write-in candidate against the two endorsed men. It was a daring move, but made with the active support of the Klan.[115]

Bowles had been born in rural Yale, Michigan, in 1884 and had received his undergraduate training at Ferris Institute in Big Rapids. He came to Detroit as a twenty-year-old in 1904 and subsequently matriculated at the University of Michigan law school in Ann Arbor, receiving his degree in 1909. In his law practice he specialized in divorce. The mysteries of ritualistic brotherhood always attracted him. He was prominent in Masonic organizations—a past high priest of the Monroe chapter, a master of Waverly Lodge, and a member of the Damascus Commandery. He was also the first president of the junior Masonic Order of DeMolay in Detroit.[116]

Bowles' platform emphasized municipal improvements, economy and cleanliness in government, and strict law enforcement.[117] His support by the Ku Klux Klan was evident. On October 21, an anti-Klan rally was scheduled at Arena Gardens. Hours before the event was to begin, a crowd of some 6000 people gathered at the entrance to block the box offices from potential ticket buyers. Police were unable to disperse the militants. The mob then formed a rough column, three abreast and several blocks long, and marched up and down Woodward Avenue shouting "Bowles, Bowles, Bowles." Several hundred massed opposite the public library and pasted Bowles stickers onto the windows of passing cars as they were forced to slow down.

The police regrouped. Reinforced by four riot squads of fifty men each they formed flying wedges and drove the mob in both directions on Woodward. Tear gas speeded up the crowd's retreat. The police then lined both sides of the street at Arena Gardens to allow 4500 people to purchase tickets to the rally.[118]

Neither of Bowles' opponents chose to disregard the evidence of Klan support. "Last Tuesday night Mr. Bowles' mask was torn from him," said Joseph A. Martin.

In an orgy of un-Americanism the Ku Klux Klan accidentally tore the night shirt and pillow case from its hero and revealed to Detroit's entire citizenship the Ku Klux candidate for Mayor and general manager of Detroit—Charles Bowles, the divorce lawyer. In a riotous demonstration to prevent an anti-Klan lecture, the Ku Klux Klan of Detroit pasted the symbols of the Klan and the symbols of the Bowles campaign side by side the length and breadth of Woodward avenue from Antoinette street to Palmer avenue.[119]

The Bowles stickers had borne the image of a little red school house, a symbol of a more comprehensible America. To John Smith, whose political career was based largely on the support of people who contributed to the complexity, the Bowles-Klan campaign was menacing. Two days before the election he appeared at St. Stanislaus Roman Catholic Church and told the gathering that Klansmen "have robbed Catholic churches and have attempted to burn them. They have tortured and slain Negroes and Jews."[120] The next day he was at St. Hedwig Roman Catholic Church, on the city's west side. "There has been brought here from the South an ugly monster known as the Ku Klux Klan," he said, "which is going to the polls tomorrow to put over the parochial school amendment and its candidate for Mayor. God forbid that they succeed; and God forbid that they make even a respectable showing."[121] To the ethnic and black working-class audiences who constituted the principal focus of his campaign Smith told stories of atrocities and denounced southern whites as "ignorant hillbillies."[122] To the more comfortable voters on the urban periphery he stressed law and order. "If I am elected Mayor," he told a gathering, "and the Ku Klux Klan ever tries to stop peaceful assemblage in the City of Detroit, they are not going to be chased out of the hall with gas bombs. They are going to be put in jail and punished."[123]

To all charges of Klan support and manipulation Bowles remained discreetly silent.[124] Early in the campaign, however, he had anticipated a major problem. "My difficulty," he told a group at Elks Temple on October 22, "is to educate the voters how to make out a ballot properly, as the slightest error may invalidate the vote."[125] The problem was crucial to a write-in candidate. Any deviation from the designation "Charles Bowles" might void the ballot.

On the Saturday night before the election the largest gathering of Klansmen in Detroit history—estimates of the size of the crowd ranged from 25,000 to 50,000—met on a field in Dearborn Township. The area was lighted by a huge flaming cross and by the headlamps of thousands of automobiles. Bowles' name was everywhere. Most of the automobiles were plastered with his campaign stickers and with instructions on how to vote for the write-in candidate. Since only Klansmen were permitted onto the grounds, Bowles' attendance was not officially recorded. He might well have been present, however.[126]

The vote for mayor was the heaviest in Detroit history. When the returns began to come in, it was clear that Bowles had cut deeply into Martin's strength. In most of the precincts where Smith was strong, Bowles and Martin were both weak. But in districts where Martin was strong Bowles was also strong, and the Smith vote was light. Only in those parts of the city housing the securest of the respectables was Martin's margin comfortable. In the lower-middle-class Protestant precincts Bowles did much the better of the two. It is therefore likely, as Martin supporters claimed, that had Bowles accepted his primary defeat and stayed out of the general election, Martin would have won a convincing victory.[127]

When all the votes were in, John Smith seemed to be the winner. He had accumulated 116,807 votes to Bowles' 106,679 and Martin's 84,929. Smith piled up big majorities in the east side's Third, Fifth, Seventh, Ninth, Eleventh, and Thirteenth wards. His greatest strength, predictably, was on the lower east side, where the predominantly black and Catholic working-class precincts returned majorities for him of over 90 percent. Anti-Klan sentiment was overwhelming in the St. Antoine Street ghetto precincts. In the Third Ward, fourth precinct, the vote for Smith against Bowles was 699 to 0. In the Fifth Ward, third precinct, the vote was 792 to 1; in the fourth precinct, 806 to 1; in the fifth precinct, 718 to 2. In the Seventh Ward, second precinct, it was 762 to 3; in the Ninth Ward, eleventh precinct, 578 to 0.[128]

Bowles, however, carried twice as many wards as Smith. His greatest support came from the triangular area bounded roughly by Grand River Avenue, West Philadelphia Avenue, and Fifth Street, an area scarcely ten blocks west of the teeming black ghetto. Additional Bowles strength lay in the precincts bordering east of Woodward north of Grand Boulevard, the area where Arthur Palmer's family had been pioneers and where further black settlement now seemed a great likelihood. Bowles also showed strength on the northwest side of the city, in districts newer than the crowded west side but still close to the Polish, Slavic, and Italian working-class neighborhoods where St. Hedwig Church was located.[129]

Had all of the votes been counted as they were cast, Charles Bowles would have won the election. But while 325,678 votes had been cast, only 308,415 ballots were counted. Election officials discarded 17,263 votes, and most of these were for the write-in candidate. Any ballot not marked "Charles Bowles," "Chas. Bowles," or "Charley Bowles" was voided, as were all ballots however marked or with sticker affixed where the voter failed to place an X beside the candidate's name.[130] Voters had marked Bowles ballots 120 different ways, 117 of which were judged invalid. These included

Charles Boles	Charles Bowels
Charles Bowls	Charles Bouls
Charles E. Bowles	Cha. Bowles
Charles S. Bowles	Ch. Bowles
Bowles	Bowls[131]

Bowles asked for a recount. "Irrespective of my personal views," he said, "I feel it is my duty and moral obligation to ask for a recount, since unquestionably more persons attempted to vote for me than either of the other candidates."[132] His attorney claimed there were many precedents demonstrating that absolutely correct spelling was neither essential nor necessary, and that the presumptive intent of the elector was shown in many instances where the ballot was thrown out.[133]

The request for a recount was granted, but the election commission simply followed its original procedure and discarded all votes not judged absolutely perfect. Bowles' supporters claimed that 15,545 disputed ballots should have given him victory, but the Board of Canvassers, sustained by the Circuit Court, declared John Smith mayor. Because the litigation necessary to get the case before the Michigan Supreme Court would have taken at least a year and there was only one year remaining on the mayoral term being contested, Bowles reluctantly withdrew.[134]

With the defeat of the write-in candidate a challenge to progressive leadership was thwarted.[135] But the rumblings in the neighborhoods could not be stilled by electoral manipulations. Sounds which bespoke a more primitive dimension to a now partisan battlefield would yet be heard.

NOTES

1. Dancy, *Sand against the Wind,* esp. pp. 62-64, 74-75.

2. Ibid., pp. 72-73.

3. Ibid., p. 76.

4. Ibid., pp. 87-89.

5. Ibid., pp. 82-84, 166-67; Gilbert Osofsky, *Harlem: The Making of a Ghetto* (New York: Harper Torchbooks, 1966), pp. 63-66. The husbands of Maude Bulkley's sisters never knew their wives were black. Dancy, *Sand against the Wind,* p. 84.

6. Urban League Board, Minutes, January 19, 1922, Detroit Urban League Papers, Box 1, MHC; Dancy, *Sand against the Wind,* pp. 100-101; also *Detroit News,* April 2, 1918, on some earlier Urban League training of female migrants as domestics.

7. Joseph A. Hill, "Recent Northward Migration of the Negro," *Monthly Labor Review* 18 (March 1924): 486.

8. Report of the Director of the Detroit Urban League, June 8, 1922, Detroit Urban League Papers, Box 1, MHC.

9. Detroit Bureau of Governmental Research, *The Negro in Detroit,* sect. 3, *Industry,* pp. 27-28.

10. Report to the Board of the Detroit Urban League, September 14, 1922, Detroit Urban League Papers, Box 1, MHC.

11. Report of the Director to the Urban League Board, January 19, 1922, ibid.

12. Annual Report of the Detroit Urban League (for 1925), March 1, 1926, ibid.

13. Report of the Director to the Urban League, March 10, 1921, ibid.

14. C.E. Brewer to William J. Norton, February 7, 1923, ibid.

15. Urban League Director's Report for May 1922, ibid; also Dancy, *Sand against the Wind,* pp. 155-56.

16. Memorandum of John C. Dancy, "What the Community Fund Means to the Negroes of Detroit," for the *Detroit Contender* Fund Drive, 1920, Detroit Urban League Papers, Box 1, MHC. In the autumn of 1920, when many black men were out of work and rents were as high as ever, the black citizens of Detroit contributed $6500 to the Community Fund Drive. Memorandum of Forrester B. Washington to black newspapers, November 1920, ibid. With the return of prosperity, contributions from blacks increased: they gave more than $8300 in 1922 and more than $7600 in 1924. Urban League Board Report for November 1922, ibid.; Report of the Director for September and October 1924, ibid.

17. Dancy, *Sand against the Wind,* pp. 167-68.

18. Urban League Director's Report for April 1923, Detroit Urban League Papers, Box 1, MHC; Urban League Director's Report, June 8, 1922, ibid.; Report of the Director to the Urban League Board, September 14, 1922, ibid.; Dancy, *Sand against the Wind,* pp. 54-55. The year of heaviest black migration to Detroit was 1923, when, according to Dancy, approximately 14,000 newcomers arrived. John C. Dancy to E. A. Carter of the Minneapolis Urban League, July 12, 1927, Detroit Urban League Papers, Box 2, MHC.

19. Dancy, *Sand against the Wind,* pp. 52-56.

20. The depression of 1920/21 in Detroit severely tested all those who had not saved conscientiously. See Dancy's Report to the Urban League Board, January 13, 1921, Detroit Urban League Papers, Box 1, MHC.

21. Detroit Bureau of Governmental Research, *The Negro in Detroit,* sect. 6, *Health,* pp. 3-4; Urban League Director's Report for April 8, 1920, Detroit Urban League Papers, Box 1, MHC; Urban League Director's Report for May 1922, ibid.; Urban League Board Meeting Report, May 13, 1920, ibid.

22. In 1920, for the United States as a whole the combined life expectancy at birth for whites of both sexes was 54.9 years; for blacks it was 45.3 years. Also in 1920, the death rate for whites was 12.6 per one thousand population; for blacks it was 17.7. U.S., Department of Commerce, Bureau of the Census, *Historical Statistics of the United States,* pp. 25, 27.

23. The idea of a total reconstruction of society was hardly distasteful to a number of black intellectuals in the 1920s. Most prominent among these were A. Philip Randolph and Chandler Owen, editors of the *Messenger,* "the only Radical Negro magazine in America." The journal, founded in Harlem in 1917, took as its vision a "new social order," and Randolph and Owen in their early editorials openly preached social revolution. They called on blacks to resist an oppressive society by whatever means appropriate, and suggested boycott and violence as two effective tools of revolution. They constantly criticized an exploitative capitalism, proposed socialism as a more equitable way of distributing wealth, and called for solidarity among black and white workers to better confront the employer enemy.

There were others in Harlem in those years writing and pursuing radical causes and squabbling among themselves. They included Lovett Fort-Whiteman, W. A. Domingo, Hubert H. Harrison, Richard B. Moore, Otto Huiswoud, Grace Campbell, Cyril V. Briggs, and Frank Crosswaith. DuBois too was working toward a kind of socialism, though he was not in favor with the new wave socialists of the *Messenger.* There were also the communists of the African Blood Brotherhood.

For the most cogent, though sometimes polemical, discussion of black radicalism from its origins to the 1960s, see Harold Cruse, *The Crisis of the Negro Intellectual* (New York: William Morrow and Company, 1967).

24. Dancy, *Sand against the Wind,* p. 144; Notice of Health Meeting, Urban League, November 7, 1920, Detroit Urban League Papers, Box 1, MHC.

25. Memorandum by Dancy, "Health Week and Clean Up and Paint Up Campaign Started" [November 1925?], Detroit Urban League Papers, Box 1, MHC.

26. Dancy, Memorandum on Health [1918], ibid.

27. Dancy, *Sand against the Wind,* pp. 144-45.

28. See the numerous Reports of the Director (Dancy) to the Community Center Settlement House Committee in the Detroit Urban League Papers, Box 1, MHC. The reports include detailed accounts of the activities of the baby clinic.

29. Dancy, *Sand against the Wind,* pp. 144-45.

30. Ibid., pp. 156-57.

31. John C. Dancy to "My dear Sir," November 12, 1918, Detroit Urban League Papers, Box 1, MHC. Copies of this letter were distributed throughout the neighborhood.

The schools were advertised with the cooperation of the clergy. See Dancy to the Rev. Robert W. Bagnall, November 14, 1918, ibid.

32. Annual Urban League Report by the Director (for 1923), January 10, 1924, ibid.

33. John C. Dancy to Dr. James W. Inches, commissioner of police, November 27, 1920, ibid.; Ford Ballard, secretary to the commissioner, to John C. Dancy, December 30, 1920, with attached memorandum dated December 16, 1920, ibid.

34. Interview with John C. Dancy, April 13, 1967.

35. Ibid.

36. See, for example, Dancy's Urban League Board Report for September 13, 1923; Report of Director for May 1924; and Director's Report for June 12, 1924, all in Detroit Urban League Papers, Box 1, MHC.

37. Urban League Board, Minutes, September 22, 1921, ibid.

38. Report of the Director of the Urban League, August 14, 1919, ibid.

39. A single issue—one of the few extant—of the black newspaper the *Detroit Contender,* November 13, 1920, carried two long items,

unrelated in their specifics, testifying to the discord between blacks and Greeks (" 'Fat' Greek Restaurants versus 'Lean' Colored Restaurants, and Why?"; "Greeks Up For Trial"). A major reason for this feeling, very probably, was proximity. "Greek town" bordered and overlapped the St. Antoine-Hastings-Macomb black ghetto, so animosities were likely stirred by daily contact.

For relevant population data by ward, see the *Fourteenth Census* (1920), vol. 3, *Population,* pp. 496-97.

40. Dancy, *Sand against the Wind,* pp. 112-13; interview with John C. Dancy, April 13, 1967.

41. Dancy, *Sand against the Wind,* p. 105.

42. Ibid., p. 106.

43. Ibid., pp. 129-31; also see Dancy's memorandum "Plans for Colored Welfare Workers in Industrial Plants," October 26, 1918, and his notes on the employment of the Dodge welfare worker, October 28 and 30, 1918, Detroit Urban League Papers, Box 1, MHC; also Bailer, "Negro Labor in the Automobile Industry," pp. 112-13.

44. Dancy, *Sand against the Wind,* pp. 129-31.

45. The Good Citizenship League card of solicitation [1918], Detroit Urban League Papers, Box 1, MHC.

46. J. H. Porter, chairman, Good Citizenship League, to the officers and members of the Detroit Board of Commerce, March 11, 1918, ibid.

47. Ibid.

48. Ibid. A buffet flat offered gambling, women, and liquor, generally with police protection. George E. Haynes, "Negroes Move North," *Survey* 41 (January 4, 1919): 460.

49. Annual Report of the Good Citizenship League [1920], Detroit Urban League Papers, Box 1, MHC.

50. "Mischievous Negroes" (editorial), *Detroit Saturday Night,* January 8, 1921, p. 9.

51. Urban League Board, Minutes, January 13, 1921 (minutes dated February 10, 1921), Detroit Urban League Papers, Box 1, MHC; John C. Dancy to *Detroit Saturday Night,* January 20, 1921, ibid.

52. *Detroit Free Press,* June 12, 1929; *Detroit City Directory, 1929-30.* The city directories list no occupations for Porter, Jones, or Bannister other than their Good Citizenship League offices. Forrester B. Washington in 1917 referred to Sarah Bannister as "a day worker in private families in this city." Washington to Byres H. Gitchell, April 13, 1917, Detroit Urban League Papers, Box 1, MHC.

53. Thomas, "The City of Detroit: A Study in Urban Geography," fig. 9, pp. 96-98.

54. Ibid.; Detroit Bureau of Governmental Research, *The Negro in Detroit*, sect. 5, *Housing*, p. 2; *Detroit Realtor* (special edition), May 20-27, 1922, [p. 8] ; *Detroit News Tribune*, April 29, 1917; *Realtor Sales Letter*, January, 1923, in "Realtor Sales Letter" envelope, BHC; *Detroit Free Press*, July 28 and 30, 1927. Also see the *Detroit Free Press*, June 21, 22, and 24, 1925, on the boom spirit occasioned by a national convention of 6000 realtors in Detroit.

55. Detroit Bureau of Governmental Research, *The Negro in Detroit*, sect. 5, *Housing*, pp. 2, 18; Thomas, "The City of Detroit: A Study in Urban Geography," fig. 66, pp. 98-109; Urban League Director's Reports, May 1922, June 8, 1922, Detroit Urban League Papers, Box 1, MHC.

56. Washington, "The Housing of the Negro in Detroit," in "The Negro in Detroit" (1920), DPL; Report to the Urban League Board, October 1922. Detroit Urban League Papers, Box 1, MHC; Report to the Urban League Board, November 1922, ibid.

57. Washington, "The Housing of the Negro in Detroit," in "The Negro in Detroit" (1920), DPL.

Writing in 1924 John Dancy estimated that for the poorest sort of tenement housing, blacks were paying an average of $10-$12 a month per room. He also observed that a black renting a house was frequently required to pay a $200-$300 security, in addition to an advance payment on the first month's rent. John C. Dancy, "A Brief Survey of Negro Life Today in Detroit," in Turner and Moses, *Colored Detroit*, p. 55.

The city tax rate remained quite stable over the two decades from 1911 to 1930, and was especially stable from 1921 to 1930. A rate of $18.15 in 1911 rose to $23.64 in 1915, dipped during the war years, rose to $20.66 in 1920, and from then until 1930 never exceeded $22.56. *Annual Report for the City of Detroit for the Year 1930*, p. 45.

58. Report to the Urban League Board, November 1922, Detroit Urban League Papers, Box 1, MHC; Washington, "The Housing of the Negro in Detroit," in "The Negro in Detroit" (1920), DPL; *The Detroiter*, December 15, 1919, pp. 1-2.

59. Report to the Urban League Board, May 13, 1920, Detroit Urban League Papers, Box 1, MHC; see also memorandum of John C. Dancy, "Cost of Living Report," March 5, 1924, ibid.

60. Washington, "The Housing of the Negro in Detroit," in "The Negro in Detroit" (1920), DPL.

61. Ibid. An interesting question, of course, and one which is nearly impossible to answer, is whether city and county authorities proceeded

more eagerly against whites or against blacks for rent profiteering. There is some evidence that during his term as mayor (1919-22) James Couzens threatened to impose higher taxes on unscrupulous landlords. Dancy, *Sand against the Wind*, pp. 56-57. If any such action was taken—Barnard in his biography of Couzens mentions none—it must have been minimal. The problem clearly continued.

62. Washington, "The Housing of the Negro in Detroit," in "The Negro in Detroit" (1920), DPL.

63. Annual Report of the Americanization Committee for the Year Ending March 31, 1920 (carbon copy), Americanization Committee Papers, MHC; see also *The Detroiter*, December 15, 1919.

64. Report of the Director of the Urban League for November [1919] (dated December 18, 1919), Detroit Urban League Papers, Box 1, MHC.

65. Report of the Urban League Director, April 8, 1920, ibid.

66. For example, see the Reports of the Urban League Director for March 11, 1920, and April 1922, ibid.

67. Urban League Board, Minutes, July 11, 1919, ibid.; Director's Report to the Urban League Board, June 10, 1920, ibid.; Dancy, *Sand against the Wind*, p. 57.

68. Urban League Board, Minutes, May 9, 1921 (dated June 9, 1921), Detroit Urban League Papers, Box 1, MHC; Report of the Urban League Director, May 9, 1921, ibid.

69. Report of the Urban League Director, October 1922, ibid.

70. Report of the Urban League Director, October 14, 1920, ibid.

71. Dancy, *Sand against the Wind*, pp. 57-58; Report of the Urban League Director, March 10, 1921, Detroit Urban League Papers, Box 1, MHC.

72. Dancy, *Sand against the Wind*, pp. 57-58.

73. Detroit Bureau of Governmental Research, *The Negro in Detroit*, sect. 5, *Housing*, pp. 58-59.

74. Dancy, *Sand against the Wind*, p. 57; Harold Black, "Restrictive Covenants in Relation to Segregated Negro Housing in Detroit" (M.A. thesis, Wayne University, 1947), p. 43.

75. Report of the Urban League Director, March 10, 1921, ibid.

76. Detroit Bureau of Governmental Research, *The Negro in Detroit*, sect. 5, *Housing*, p. 59.

77. Ibid., p. 58; ibid., sect. 2, *Population*, pp. 11-12; also John C. Dancy to Eugene Kinckle Jones, November 9, 1926, Detroit Urban League Papers, Box 1, MHC, on league sponsorship in 1926 of a community improvement campaign in Eight Mile Road.

78. Detroit Bureau of Governmental Research, *The Negro in Detroit*,

sect. 5, *Housing*, p. 58; ibid., sect. 2, *Population*, p. 12; Dancy, *Sand against the Wind*, p. 58; Report of the Urban League Director, April 1923, Detroit Urban League Papers, Box 1, MHC.

Inkster became, in effect, a Ford company town. For a discussion of Ford paternalism with regard to that community during the depression of the 1930s, see Bailer, "Negro Labor in the Automobile Industry," pp. 155-57.

There were other black settlements and other problems. In 1926 approximately 500 blacks lived in the Quinn Road subdivision, 9 miles beyond the northern city limit, 19 miles northeast of downtown Detroit. Many of the men worked at a factory located 4 miles west of downtown. They spent five to six hours a day in transit. Report of John C. Dancy, August 3, 1926, Detroit Urban League Papers, Box 1, MHC; Detroit Bureau of Governmental Research, *The Negro in Detroit*, sect. 2, *Population*, p. 13.

79. Real-estate documents on file in the Wayne County Tract Index, City-County Building, Detroit; Black, "Restrictive Covenants," pp. 25-33.

80. Robert Lester Fulton, "Russel Woods: A Study of a Neighborhood's Initial Response to Negro Invasion" (Ph.D. diss., Wayne State University, 1959), pp. 18-21; Albert J. Mayer, "Russel Woods: Change without Conflict; A Case Study of Neighborhood Racial Transition in Detroit," in *Studies in Housing and Minority Groups*, ed. Nathan Glazer and Davis McEntire (Berkeley and Los Angeles: University of California Press, 1960), pp. 200-201.

81. Standard deed issued by the Russel Woods Company, the original subdivider. The deed is on file in the Wayne County Tract Index.

82. Detroit Bureau of Governmental Research, *The Negro in Detroit*, sect. 5, *Housing*, pp. 25-32; Washington, "The Housing of the Negro in Detroit," in "The Negro in Detroit" (1920), DPL.

83. Detroit Bureau of Governmental Research, *The Negro in Detroit*, sect. 5, *Housing*, p. 28; "Why a Realtor is a Dependable Real Estate Man" (Detroit Real Estate Board, 1924), in Detroit Real Estate Board envelope marked "(1924)—miscellaneous material," Box 1, BHC; Turner and Moses, *Colored Detroit*, directory of black real-estate agents, p. 123.

84. "Code of Ethics Adopted by the National Association of Real Estate Boards at its Seventeenth Annual Convention," June 6, 1924, in Detroit Real Estate Board envelope "(1924)—miscellaneous material," Box 1, BHC.

85. Parmalee v. Morris, 218 Mich. 625 (1922). The decision, said

the journal of the Detroit Real Estate Board, is "of very great interest to all persons engaged in subdividing." John R. Rood, "Restriction as to Race and Color," *Detroit Realtor* 4 (July 1922): 2.

86. Maurice M. Ramsey, "Some Aspects of Non-Partisan Government in Detroit, 1918-1940" (Ph.D. diss., University of Michigan, 1944), pp. 16-18, 24, 24n; *Detroit News,* October 25-30, 1937 (a series of articles on the demise of the partisan council and the charter reform). On the Glinnan scandal, see *Detroit News,* July 26, 1912; John P. Scallen, Trial of Thomas E. Glinnan scrapbooks, BHC; and James K. Anderson, "The Rollicking Trial of Detroit's Honest Tom Glinnan," *Detroit News Magazine,* July 30, 1967.

87. Ramsey, "Some Aspects of Non-Partisan Government in Detroit," pp. 3, 24-25; *The Charter of the City of Detroit with Amendments Thereto and the Acts of the Legislature Relating to or Affecting the City of Detroit* (Detroit: Thomas Smith Press, City Printers, 1904). The number of wards in the city increased from seventeen in 1900 to twenty-one in 1916. Hence the membership of the council increased from thirty-four to forty-two. One member of the board of estimates was elected from each ward and five from the city at large. The board was active only in the spring of each year.

88. Ramsey, "Some Aspects of Non-Partisan Government in Detroit," pp. 26-29; Arthur Chester Millspaugh, "Party Organization and Machinery in Michigan since 1890," *Johns Hopkins University Studies in Historical and Political Science,* ser. 35, no. 3 (Baltimore: The Johns Hopkins Press, 1917), pp. 159-64; *Civic Searchlight,* August 1914, September 1914; William P. Lovett, *Detroit Rules Itself* (Boston: Richard G. Badger, 1930), pp. 18-33.

89. Ramsey, "Some Aspects of Non-Partisan Government in Detroit," pp. 27-29; *Civic Searchlight,* September 1914, November 1914, January 1915.

90. Ramsey, "Some Aspects of Non-Partisan Government in Detroit," p. 29; Millspaugh, "Party Organization and Machinery in Michigan since 1890," pp. 159-64.

91. Lovett, *Detroit Rules Itself,* pp. 52-53.

92. "By-Laws of the League," *Civic Searchlight,* July-August 1923, p. 3. The Citizens League solicited its early membership from among some forty Protestant churches in Detroit, before branching out to others who would subscribe to its ideals. The league at the outset made a great effort to explain that it was not itself a church-oriented organization, but that it sought churchgoers as members because it felt that civic

righteousness was likely to be a concomitant of Protestant piety. "Any man whose name appears on a church roll," said its secretary, Pliny W. Marsh, "ought to be a good citizen and at least have a latent interest in improving moral and political conditions of our city." Secretary [Pliny W. Marsh] to Mr. J. M. Crombie, December 23, 1912, Detroit Citizens League Papers, Correspondence Files 1912-45, Box 1, file "1912 Correspondence, A-G," BHC.

93. *Civic Searchlight,* July-August 1923; Ramsey, "Some Aspects of Non-Partisan Government in Detroit," pp. 129-31.

94. *Civic Searchlight,* July-August 1923; *Social Service Directory of Detroit, 1917,* p. 33; *Detroit City Directories,* 1917, 1918; Nevins, *Ford: The Times, The Man, The Company,* p. 377; Ramsey, "Some Aspects of Non-Partisan Government in Detroit," pp. 130,131.

95. As an example of what infuriated the reformers, in February 1913 a resolution was introduced into common council calling for a reduction in the number of saloon licenses granted to one license per 500 inhabitants of the city. The proposal was voted down by the Royal Ark-dominated council, 27 to 7. *Civic Searchlight,* December 1913.

96. Ramsey, "Some Aspects of Non-Partisan Government in Detroit," p. 130; Millspaugh, "Party Organization and Machinery in Michigan since 1890," pp. 159-64; Lovett, *Detroit Rules Itself,* pp. 71-83.

97. Ramsey, "Some Aspects of Non-Partisan Government in Detroit," pp. 31, 129-30; Lovett, *Detroit Rules Itself,* pp. 90-94; *Civic Searchlight,* May 1915, August 1916.

98. *Detroit Free Press,* November 9, 1916.

99. Ramsey, "Some Aspects of Non-Partisan Government in Detroit," p. 32.

100. *Detroit Free Press,* November 1-7, 1917; *Detroit News,* November 1-7, 1917. See also Freeman A. Flynn, "Detroit Voters: A Thirty-Year View" (M.A. thesis, Wayne State University, 1948), pp. 1-10.

101. *Proposed Charter of the City of Detroit* (n.p., 1918); *Detroit City Directories,* 1917, 1918; Ramsey, "Some Aspects of Non-Partisan Government in Detroit," pp. 36-38.

102. Memorandum of Detroit Real Estate Board to members, October 1, 1917, Detroit Real Estate Board, miscellaneous material, envelope "n.d.—1921," Box 1, BHC.

103. "Detroit Adopts a New Charter," *American City* (city edition) 19 (July, 1918): 13; Ramsey, "Some Aspects of Non-Partisan Government in Detroit," pp. 18-19, 40-43.

104. *Detroit News,* June 26, 1918; *Detroit Free Press,* June 28, 1918;

Ramsey, "Some Aspects of Non-Partisan Government in Detroit," pp. 33-36.

105. Ramsey, "Some Aspects of Non-Partisan Government in Detroit," pp. 94-95.

106. Ibid., p. 158 and 158n; also *Detroit Free Press,* November 5, 1973.

107. The most careful study of the Klan as an urban institution is Kenneth T. Jackson, *The Ku Klux Klan in the City* (New York: Oxford University Press, 1967).

108. For initiation ceremonies of the Detroit Klan, see the *Detroit News,* October 21, 1923, and *The Fiery Cross* (Michigan state edition), November 2 and November 30, 1923. At an outdoor muster of the Detroit-area Klan held on an Oakland County farm in June 1923, 11,000 persons by Klan estimate were in attendance, 8,000 according to the *Detroit Free Press. The Fiery Cross,* July 6, 1923; *Detroit Free Press,* June 14, 1923.

109. Jackson, *The Ku Klux Klan in the City,* p. 23.

110. Ibid., p. 129.

111. W. L. P., 1009 Catherine St., Ann Arbor, Michigan, to Mrs. I.G. Postles, 4821 Parker Ave., Detroit, Michigan, postmarked Ann Arbor, Michigan, November 7, 1923, "Negroes in Detroit, Miscellaneous Material: II," BHC.

The letter is in blue mimeograph, which indicates other copies may have been mailed, perhaps to the some twenty-eight other black public school teachers in Detroit at this time.

112. Jackson, *The Ku Klux Klan in the City,* p. 132.

113. *Detroit News,* November 7, 1923.

114. Jackson, *The Ku Klux Klan in the City,* p. 132.

115. Ibid., pp. 134, 135.

116. *Detroit News,* August 31 and October 23, 1924.

117. Jackson, *The Ku Klux Klan in the City,* p. 134; see also "With the Candidates for Mayor," *Detroit News,* October 23, 1924.

118. Jackson, *The Ku Klux Klan in the City,* pp. 134-35; *Detroit News,* October 22, 1924; *Detroit Free Press,* October 22, 1924.

119. *Detroit News,* October 23, 1924, p. 29.

120. Jackson, *The Ku Klux Klan in the City,* p. 135.

121. *Detroit News,* November 4, 1924, p. 21.

122. Jackson, *The Ku Klux Klan in the City,* p. 135.

123. *Detroit News,* November 4, 1924, p. 21.

124. Jackson, *The Ku Klux Klan in the City,* pp. 135-36.

125. *Detroit News,* October 23, 1924, p. 29.

126. Jackson, *The Ku Klux Klan in the City,* p. 136.

127. *Detroit News,* November 5, 1924, p. 23 (chart of returns by precinct); Jackson, *The Ku Klux Klan in the City,* pp. 136-37.

128. *Detroit News,* November 5, 1924, p. 23; ibid., November 8, 1924.

129. Ibid., November 5, 1924, p. 23; Jackson, *The Ku Klux Klan in the City,* p. 137; Adcraft Club, *A Study of the City of Detroit,* maps of population distribution by race and nationality following p. 40.

130. *Detroit News,* November 5, 1924; William P. Lovett, "Detroit's Three-cornered Mayoralty Election," *American City* 32 (January, 1925): 61.

131. *Detroit News,* November 7, 1924, p. 1; also ibid., November 8, 1924.

132. Ibid., November 7, 1924, p. 1.

133. Ibid.

134. *Detroit News,* November 9, 20, and 21, 1924; Lovett, "Detroit's Three-cornered Mayoralty Election," p. 61. The revised totals were Smith, 116, 775; Bowles, 102, 602; and Martin, 84, 462. Had the 15,545 ballots Bowles claimed were rightfully his been added to his total, his margin of victory would have been 1372 votes.

135. The Detroit Citizens League was quietly jubilant. See Lovett, "Detroit's Three-cornered Mayoralty Election," p. 61.

chapter
FIVE

Violence

I

On Thursday, April 9, 1925, a small boy on a bicycle rode furiously to find a policeman. Two stood on the corner of West Warren and McGraw, and he told them there was a huge crowd on Northfield Avenue throwing rocks at a house. The policemen sped the few blocks north and west and found a mob of 5000 people jamming the roadway and spilling onto adjacent avenues. Many were standing on the front lawn of a house, cursing and shouting and threatening to burn the place down. Every window of the house was smashed. "The house is being rented by blacks," someone said. The two policemen decided they could do nothing by themselves and sent for reinforcements. It took hours for the additional police to disperse the crowd. Only at midnight, after the last loiterer had left, did the blacks—a man, his wife, and three boarders—let officers into the house. They said that they had moved in a month before, began receiving warnings to get out of the neighborhood soon afterward, and had no intention of leaving. The police remained on guard throughout the night.[1]

On Tuesday morning, June 23, 1925, there was another incident similarly motivated. Dr. Alexander Turner, a black physician, moved into an expensive brick house on Spokane Avenue, scarcely ten blocks from the Northfield Avenue difficulty. The neighborhood, not far from the city's northwestern boundary, was well established and very exclusive. Houses ranged in value from $13,000 to $25,000. Residents claimed that none of the lots in the original subdivision were sold to blacks, though no one was sure whether the deeds specifically restricted black people.

The house had been left vacant by the previous owner, the president of a beef company, for only five minutes before Turner's van drew up and began to unload furniture. Almost immediately a crowd of whites formed in front of the house. They were mostly women who had seen black people go inside. Black painters were at work on the side of the house, and in their anger the women began to throw potatoes and debris at them. The painters retreated to the rear of the building, but there met another barrage and immediately stopped work.

By noon 200 people stood on the pavement and in the yard in front of the house. Someone hurled a half brick through a front window, and the sound of shattering glass signaled others to begin throwing. Police arrived shortly thereafter and found many windows broken. They arrested one person, a fifteen-year-old boy with a rock in his hand, and took him to the station house. He was soon released.

Hours passed, and the crowd continued to grow, with the police making no attempt to stop it. Early in the evening Dr. Turner appeared on his front porch and talked nervously with some policemen. The crowd grew larger, and by dark the streets and alleys were filled. A police inspector, two lieutenants, and forty additional patrolmen arrived and had difficulty pushing their way through the tightly packed mob. Traffic was hopelessly stalled on Grand River Avenue. There were more than 5000 people surrounding the house.

Turner was petrified and willing to do anything to escape the mob. When two white men entered the house, announced they were representatives of the neighborhood Tireman Avenue Improvement Association, and asked, "Will you sell the property back to us?" Turner replied, "Yes." The group—Turner, his wife and mother, and the two white men—flanked by police then left the house and got into the black man's chauffeur-driven sedan. A volley of bricks and stones came crashing through the car's windows, cutting Turner over the right eye and slightly injuring a policeman. As the sedan pulled from the curb, a truck forced its way through the crowd, and the doctor's furniture was thrown into it.

The men in the car sped to Turner's office on West Warren. There they met Cecil Rowlette, his attorney. "If you do not wish to defend yourself you might as well sell," Rowlette advised. Turner agreed, though for a while his wife refused to sign the papers.[2]

Alexander Turner was a respected member of the Detroit black community, a man who had made good. He was twice a graduate of the University of Michigan, with a Bachelor of Science degree and a degree from the School of Medicine. He was a thoroughly competent surgeon, had a lucrative practice built over more than a decade, treated many white patients, and consulted frequently with white physicians. For a number of years he was the only black doctor in Detroit to enjoy staff privileges at Woman's Hospital and Grace Hospital. He was also a founder and trustee of Dunbar Memorial Hospital and was that institution's chief of surgery. Because of the demands on his time he employed two assistants and a chauffeur, and he often encouraged these men to work hard, it being the only way, he said, to improve and advance. He involved himself in racial uplift work, giving money to worthy black students and taking pleasure in their successes. In 1911 he opened the first of several drug stores in Detroit, which provided employment for black pharmacists. He married a woman who had studied music for six years at Leipzig University in Germany.

Turner owned the comfortable house on West Warren Street in which his office was located. He decided to move his residence when a widening of the street resulted in increased traffic noise. He bought the house on Spokane through a real-estate agent and was crushed at his hostile reception. "I think the whole affair is a disgrace," he lamented. "I don't mind their yelling and their threats, but they have no right to destroy my property. I have lived in a white neighborhood for fifteen years and never had any trouble before. I have operated two drug stores with a white clientele and at present 75 per cent of my practice is white."[3]

Vollington Bristol was no stranger to violence. He was an undertaker; he was also a black man. For many years he had owned a piece of land on American Avenue, just south of Tireman and a few blocks west of Northfield. As the years passed and the city grew outward, the land increased in value, and Bristol decided to build a house on it. He had not planned to live in the house himself, however. He would rent the dwelling to white people. But successive tenants were delinquent

in meeting the rent, and because Britsol could afford neither these
derelictions nor the litigation involved in forcing payment, he decided
to rent the property to blacks. This proved to be impossible. Every
time a black tenant prepared to move into the house, the neighborhood
intimidated the man and forced him to flee. Bristol was confronted with
only two choices: he could either sell the property or he could move into
the house himself. He chose not to truckle.[4]

On Tuesday night, July 7, 1925, only hours after Vollington Bristol
had moved in, gunfire cracked from rifles, shotguns, and revolvers as
several hundred white people, many of them armed, gathered in front
of Bristol's house on American Avenue. The police arrived, and one of
the demonstrators shouted, "Shoot the cops too." But firing stopped.
The police found two rifles and a shotgun lying in the street, these presumably dropped by individuals in the crowd. In all, the authorities
seized thirty-five guns, two knives, and hundreds of rounds of ammunition, and arrested nineteen white men, residents of the immediate neighborhood, and held them for investigation. When the arrests were made,
the crowd dispersed. Police later found eight blacks, several of whom
were armed, in the area and detained them too. A guard was placed on
the house for the remainder of the night.[5]

The next evening, July 8, 1925, a crowd of 2000 people gathered in
front of the Bristol house. A white woman stood on a box and shouted,
"If you call yourselves men and are afraid to move these niggers out, we
women will move them out, you cowards!" Police reinforcements arrived
from nearly every precinct in the city and finally dispersed the gathering.
No shooting occurred, and there were only a few arrests.[6]

Late that night, a white couple began to drive from their home on
Milford Avenue, just south of Tireman, toward Thirtieth Street. As they
slowed down for the intersection, a group of blacks appeared in the
dark, threw rocks through the car windows, and then fled. The man and
woman called for help and were taken to Grace Hospital and treated for
lacerations on the head.[7]

The next day, Thursday, July 9, 1925, a sweltering summer afternoon,
Vollington Bristol finished moving his belongings into the house. Police
remained on guard and told the curious to move on. An armored car
stood prepared and ready.

Downtown, sixteen of the nineteen white men arrested two nights before were released, the charge of carrying concealed deadly weapons dropped. The law states clearly, a lieutenant explained, that concealed weapons must be found on the person. The sixteen men had dropped their guns on the floors of their automobiles or on the ground, and so they could not be held.[8]

That night, a crowd of about 1000 white persons gathered in front of the house on American Avenue. Police closed the street to traffic and scattered the people. There was no violence,[9] and Bristol would stay.

On Friday evening, July 10, 1925, there was another incident, this one north of American Avenue, northwest of Spokane, on Stoepel, near Livernois and Grand River. John Fletcher, a black, had owned a house in the neighborhood for nine days and lived in it for one. The neighborhood was white. As he sat down to dinner with his wife, two children, and two roomers on the evening of the second day, a white woman walked past the house. She looked in and began to yell, "Niggers live in there. Niggers live in there," and repeated it up and down the quiet streets. People began to gather. It was six-thirty. John Fletcher stopped his dinner and called the police. Seven officers arrived. They began to talk with the people in the crowd, too amiably, Fletcher thought. The crowd continued to grow. An hour later Fletcher made another call to the police, and more arrived, bringing the total to fifty. The crowd grew larger, people began to yell, "Lynch him. Lynch him," and the police did nothing. Four thousand persons were now in the streets, and rocks and bricks began to bang against the house. There was five tons of coke in the street, unloaded that afternoon next door. People picked up the black chunks and hurled them at Fletcher's house. A screen ripped, another, a window crashed, another. Inside the house a mirror broke, a chair was smashed. The pile of coal shrank and finally disappeared. All the while the police stood and watched. The yelling grew louder. It was ten o'clock. John Fletcher was terrified. A gun appeared from an upstairs bedroom window, two shots rang out, and a teenage boy in the crowd fell screaming, bullets ripping his thigh. The police then entered the house and arrested the occupants.[10]

On Saturday, July 11, 1925, John Fletcher and his family moved out of the house on Stoepel Avenue. He said he feared for his life. There would be no indictments.[11]

That night, a fiery cross cast a red glare over the darkened countryside. Ten thousand persons were attending a Ku Klux Klan rally on West Fort Street, a mile west of Lincoln Park Village. They heard a speaker call for laws to compel blacks to live only in certain sections of the city.[12]

Far over on the east side of Detroit another white neighborhood was in agitation. It was a working-class neighborhood. Its men labored in the mills, plants, and foundries of the city, and sons could expect to do the same. To these people—a number of them immigrants scarcely two decades before—the prospect of an imminent black invasion was cause for intense concern.

Early in June the threat materialized. A black family was looking at the house at 2905 Garland Avenue, near Charlevoix. During one visit the black man sat on the front porch, in full view of the neighborhood, talking with the owner, a white woman, and her husband, a real-estate dealer. The people of the neighborhood had always been suspicious of the husband, Edward Smith. Rumor had it that he was a black, but no one could ever be sure. But since his skin was light—lighter than many of his neighbors', in fact—the neighborhood left him alone. But now suddenly Edward Smith no longer mattered. The word was out. The black man on the porch had agreed to purchase the house. Now there could be no doubt.[13]

Immediately signs were posted on telephone and electric utility poles throughout the area. There was to be a mass meeting to confront this new threat. We must "maintain the high standard of the residential district between Jefferson and Mack avenues" near Waterworks Park, the advertisements read. Attend the meeting "in self-defense," they urged. "Do you want to maintain the existing good health conditions and environment for your little children? . . . Do you want to see your neighborhood kept up to its present high standard?"[14]

The meeting was held Tuesday night, July 14, 1925, at the Howe school on Charlevoix, diagonally across from the house at 2905 Garland. Community leaders had planned the gathering for the school's auditorium, but an overflow crowd forced the meeting to be relocated in the schoolyard. When proceedings finally got underway, the main speaker was the head of the Tireman Avenue Improvement Association, the group which had organized for the eviction of Dr. Turner. He spoke of technique and successes. The audience listened closely to his advice. Later that night in the schoolyard, the Waterworks Park Improvement Association was born. Its mission was clear.[15]

The man of whom the white people were so afraid was Dr. Ossian (pronounced "ocean") Sweet. A young man barely in his thirties, married, with an infant daughter, he was a physician and surgeon, and specialized in gynecology. He was ambitious. To advance his career he took his wife of less than a year to France in 1923, where he worked for a time under Madame Curie, learning about the effect of radium in the treatment of cancer. Then it was to Vienna for further study in pediatrics and gynecology at the Eiselburg Clinic. Back in Detroit the couple took up residence with the wife's parents.

Ossian Sweet was the oldest of ten children, born in Orlando, Florida, the son of a Methodist preacher. His father tried to supplement the meager family income by raising oranges. Times were frequently hard. Very soon in life, therefore, Ossian Sweet came to see an importance in making money. He also understood at an early age the things white men were capable of doing to blacks. One day near his home he saw a mob of what seemed to him thousands of white people driving a black boy down a dusty road. Ossian hid and watched, and saw the mob pour kerosene over the boy and set fire to the living flesh. He heard the screams of the victim and the howling of the tormentors, and he watched the whites, the victim dead, celebrate the murder by becoming riotously drunk. He saw them laughingly take pictures of the scene and then watched in horror as dozens of whites pulled souvenirs of bones and flesh off the charred remains.

Ossian left home at the age of twelve determined to succeed. He worked as a bellboy, a waiter on steamships and in hotels, a Pullman porter, and a janitor. Finally there was college at Wilberforce University in Ohio and medical school at Howard. Nothing he had experienced assuaged an ever-hardening cynicism. In his profession he was insulted and patronzied because he was black. He was lied to, deceived, robbed, and humiliated. The cynicism deepened—the protection of a sensitive person against an insensitive, now northern world—and his already sharply defined race consciousness grew even more pronounced. Race loyalty became for him a passion.[16]

It was not so with Gladys Sweet, Ossian's wife. She was incapable of wearing her race as a badge. Rather, she was a quiet sort of person, withdrawn and even introverted, one who perhaps bore the lonely realization that there were forces in the world which could easily crush her, the fact that she was black being somehow incidental. When she and her husband were looking for their new home, it was important for her only that the house be attractive, comfortable, and within the limits of their budget. She was not particularly concerned about the neighborhood's racial composition. Whoever my new neighbors were, she said, "I took it for granted that I should have practically nothing to do with them."[17]

Gladys Mitchell Sweet had been born into comfortable surroundings, the only child of a professional musician. She spent her first seven years in Pittsburgh; then her father saw the chance for a better job, and the family moved to Detroit. They bought a house on Cairney, near Gratiot, an area which at the time was close to the city's periphery. The neighborhood, quiet and spacious, was white, but there was never any racial difficulty. Gladys did well in school and enjoyed her studies. It was always understood that she would go on to college; and after graduating from Eastern High School she perfunctorily registered at Detroit Junior College, where she took a premedical course. Then she decided she would become a teacher, enrolled at Detroit Teachers College, and received her degree in 1921. Soon thereafter she met Ossian Sweet, and a year later they were married and off to Europe. She was devoted to her husband, but her duties as wife and mother did not wholly absorb her. She loved literature and enjoyed going to the theater. She was a gently beautiful woman, slender and graceful, with long black hair. Often artists asked if they could paint her. In 1925 she was twenty-three years old.[18]

Ossian Sweet knew of the racial turmoil in the city. He knew of the meeting that had been held in the Howe schoolyard, for light-skinned blacks who had been in the crowd had reported events to him. He knew of the telephone threats received by Marie Smith, the white woman from whom he had purchased the house on Garland, anonymous neighbors promising her death and bombing of the house if Sweet moved in. The doctor was not anxious for a confrontation. He decided to keep his family in the home of his wife's parents for the remainder of the hot summer. It gave him time to think. Should he risk endangering his family by attempting to move into the house on Garland? The possibility

of concerted mob violence was very real. But he had already paid a
$3000 deposit on the $18,500 house, and the deposit would be for-
feited if he reneged. The money had not come easily: it was the sum of
his savings. His family still had to have a home, and there was simply
nothing available in the ghetto. And always there was his race consciousness, the churning racial pride. It pounded through his mind all
that summer: "I could never again respect myself if I allowed a gang of
hoodlums to keep me out."[19]

On Tuesday morning, September 8, 1925, after telling the police of
his intentions, Ossian Sweet moved into the house. There were seven
people making the move with him. They were his wife; Henry Sweet,
his twenty-one-year-old brother, a fourth-year student at Wilberforce
University; Joseph Mack, Ossian Sweet's chauffeur; Dr. Otis Sweet,
another brother, a Detroit dentist; William E. Davis, a friend of Otis',
a pharmacist and a federal narcotics agent; John Latting, a friend of
Henry's, also a student at Wilberforce; and Norris Murray, a chauffeur
and handyman. Both Henry Sweet and John Latting expected to leave
within the week for Wilberforce, for school was scheduled to reopen on
the fifteenth of September. Otis Sweet and William Davis planned to
room with the Sweet family for the winter. With the baby Iva, who had
been left with her grandparents, it was to be household of five.[20]

By moving in with so many people not members of his immediate
family, Ossian Sweet was acting against advice given him by attorney
Cecil Rowlette. On two occasions prior to September 8, Sweet and
several other doctors had met with Rowlette in an office on Vernor
Highway. The first time the conversation focused on the Turner eviction.
The second time it was about Sweet's pending move. On both occasions
Rowlette offered the opinion that though a man had every legal right to
defend his family and his home against a mob, even to the extent of
killing, he had no right to take casual acquaintances into the house for
the purpose of having them intercede for him. If they were there by
accident, and mob violence occurred, they could of course protect themselves, Rowlette said. But if they were there by design, the protection
the law gives a man defending his property is overstepped. Sweet chose
not to act on Rowlette's judgment. But he did remain concerned with
the legal implications of what he was doing. He sought out Julian Perry,
his personal attorney, and asked if Perry would accompany them in the

move. Perry agreed, but on the morning of the eighth, when the time had come to go out to Garland Avenue, the black attorney was nowhere to be seen.[21]

The Sweets did not bring much furniture into the house. Because they had been living with Gladys Sweet's parents, they owned very little and planned to buy new things as soon as they were settled. That morning they did, however, move in a bedroom set, some kitchenware, trunks of clothing, and a substantial amount of food. They also came equipped, in case the requested police protection failed, with seven revolvers and automatic pistols, two rifles, a shotgun, and about 400 rounds of ammunition.[22]

The afternoon was busy. Gladys set Henry and John Latting to work cleaning the house. Otis Sweet and William Davis first attended to their own belongings and then joined in the general effort. Ossian Sweet was pleased that things were going well, felt that he would not be needed for a few hours, and went to his office. Later in the afternoon some dishes the Sweets had purchased were delivered by one of Ossian's colleagues. Five o'clock and the sun still shone brightly. Two young women experienced in interior decorating—Edna Butler and Serena Rochelle—arrived to help Gladys Sweet decide on what sorts of new furniture she should buy. Ossian Sweet returned, and they all sat down to dinner.

Darkness fell, and the night was less happy. Someone inside the house noticed white people moving along the street and sidewalk in more than casual numbers, many stopping to look at the house. The strangers passed, repassed, and passed again. Soon everyone inside was aware of the activity outside. Gladys Sweet watched one woman go back and forth sixteen times. The police had been on the scene all day, and they kept the people moving. But the crowd continued to grow.

The two young women, Miss Butler and Miss Rochelle, were afraid to go out through the crowd and asked Dr. Sweet if they could spend the night. He agreed. Midnight came, and 500 to 800 people still stood outside the house. From time to time, little groups left the general gathering and met in the confectionary store on Charlevoix, next to the corner grocery. Not until three o'clock in the morning did the crowd begin to disperse. By daybreak everyone outside had scattered.[23]

The next morning the street seemed normal. Miss Butler and Miss Rochelle left for work, as did Otis Sweet and William Davis. At noon

Ossian and Gladys Sweet went downtown to look at furniture. It was a successful trip. They bought a walnut dining room set, two new bedroom sets, several armchairs, and a walnut table for the living room, and made arrangements to have the purchases delivered. As usual, Joe Mack was with them, driving the doctor's car. Henry Sweet, John Latting, and Norris Murray remained in the house. They were to continue cleaning.

Late in the afternoon Ossian and Gladys Sweet returned home from shopping. Soon after this, three more men arrived at the house. They were Leonard C. Morse, Charles B. Washington, and Hewitt Watson, all from the Liberty Life Insurance Company office in Detroit. Ossian Sweet often served as a medical examiner for the company. He knew the men casually, he asked them to stay for dinner, and they accepted.

Sweet, Washington, and Morse began to play cards to pass the time before the meal. Watson read a magazine. Norris Murray was finishing his cleaning. Joe Mack was looking after the car. Henry Sweet and John Latting busied themselves in the kitchen trying to help Gladys prepare dinner. From time to time the young woman would glance over to the men playing cards. She needed the table for dinner and wondered when they would be through. It was eight o'clock.

Suddenly, someone cried, "My God, look at the people!"

Resolutely they had come, drawn to the area as if by a prearranged signal. The blacks ran to the windows and looked out. The crowd was growing quickly now, swelled by men returning home from work. People filled the schoolyard and the streets around the corner grocery store. They were in the alleys, on roofs, and on the porches of the neighborhood's two-family frame dwellings. Cars rolled in and parked in every direction and were soon swallowed by the proliferating throng. People were in an ugly-curious mood. Some began to throw stones at the blacks' house, others shouted curses. Seventeen policemen stood within fifty feet of the dwelling; they watched and did nothing.

Ossian Sweet was in a frenzy. He turned out the lights, grabbed a gun, and ran upstairs. He threw himself on his bed, trembling, his mind rolling. A taxi drew up in front of the house. It was Davis and Otis Sweet. They ran toward the house under a barrage of bricks, stones, rocks, and coal. "Niggers! Niggers!" the crowd screamed. "They're niggers. Get them! GET THE NIGGERS!"

Ossian Sweet ran downstairs. He opened the door, and the two men rushed inside. The mob howled in fury. The blacks inside were now in constant motion. They pulled down the blinds, seeking from the half-dark some miraculous benefaction. The barrage of debris continued. Rocks and bricks crashed against the side of the house and banged onto the roof. A window shattered; then another. Almost as one, the blacks sensed what was happening: they were about to be overrun. They scattered to different parts of the house, grabbing for their weapons. Shots came from within the house in answer to the fusillade from without.[24]

Screams arose from the crowd. Women who had taken their children out into the warm evening to witness the festivity suddenly found themselves running in terror, many leaving their children behind. Police moved now to disperse the crowd. Reinforcements arrived. One officer, Inspector Norton Schuknecht of the McClellan Avenue station, pushed his way through the milling throng into the house. He confronted Ossian Sweet. "For Christ sake, what in Hell are you fellows shooting about?" he demanded. "There will be no more shooting," replied the doctor to the white man. Schuknecht turned and went back outside. It was then he discovered that two men had been shot.

Three quarters of an hour passed before the police again entered the house. Led by Schuknecht and Lieutenant Paul Schellenberger, they handcuffed the blacks and began to lead them out the front door. Then another policeman arrived. He was Detective Lieutenant John E. Hayes, a ranking officer of the Black Hand Squad, a special unit which ordinarily dealt with cases involving Italians but lately had been used in episodes of racial conflict. He spoke gently to the Sweets—the only officer who would do so—and he changed the existing procedure to minimize contact with the mob. He ordered a patrol wagon drawn up to the rear of the house and had each prisoner flanked by two policemen as he left the building. Police had their revolvers drawn and warned the crowd that any person attempting to crash into the house would be killed. Hayes got into the patrol wagon with the Sweets.[25]

Downtown on lower Beaubien in the huge new police building of which official Detroit was so proud, the prisoners were told that a man named Leon Breiner had been killed and another, Erick Hougberg, seriously wounded. The blacks asked permission to call a lawyer. The request was denied, and they were separated and questioned alternately from ten o'clock that night to four the next morning. The chief of police asked the first question of Ossian Sweet: "Doctor, what business do you have moving into a white neighborhood where you are not wanted?" In a subsequent interrogation Henry Sweet admitted firing a weapon twice, saying he had shot once into the air and a second time down over the heads of the crowd to frighten it. Early Thursday morning the blacks were told they were all being charged with premeditated murder. Late that afternoon the formal charge was made—conspiracy to murder Leon Breiner and conspiracy to assault with intent to kill Erick Hougberg. Bail was denied.[26]

II

To Mayor John Smith the racial incidents of the spring and summer, culminating in the attempted eviction of the Sweets in September, were abhorrent, both personally and politically. He was at the threshold of a new mayoralty campaign—his partial term expired in November—and he was again relying on black votes. But as a white man and civic official he could not condone the racial violence, and in his mind the blame for it was readily placed. Part of the turmoil was the doing of the Ku Klux Klan, he thought. The group was known to be agitating in white neighborhoods where residents were fearful of black infiltration. But, he was convinced, ultimate responsibility lay with blacks who, by their actions, precipitated violent responses. "I must say that I deprecate most strongly the moving of negroes or other persons into districts in which they know their presence may cause riot or bloodshed," Smith wrote in an open letter to Commissioner of Police Frank Croul on September 13.

> For almost three score years there have lived in Detroit thousands of colored persons, liked, admired and respected by the entire community. In all those years there was no such incident as that which has blackened our city's name within the last few days. These colored men and women, who were long residents of this city, decided their own problems with the realization of their legal rights, modified by their own common sense. It does not always do for any man to demand, to its fullest, the right which the law gives him. Sometimes by doing so he works irremediable harm to himself and his fellows. . . .
> . . . I believe that any colored person who endangers life and prop-

erty, simply to gratify his personal pride, is an enemy of his race as
well as an incitant of riot and murder. . . . I feel that it lies with the
real leaders of the colored race in Detroit to dissipate this murderous
pride. This seems to exist chiefly in a very few colored persons who
are unwilling to live in sections of the city where members of their
race predominate, but who are willing to rely on the natural racial
pride of the rest of their people to protect them when they move into
districts where their presence may be resented.[27]

Three days later Smith created an interracial board with instructions to
study the problem of civil disorder. "Conference, discussion and mutual
understanding" will permit a solution, Smith assured the man he nominated to head the new board, Tracy W. McGregor. McGregor, a white
man, was a professional philanthropist and president of the Detroit Community Union. Joining him on the board were the presidents of the
Detroit Board of Commerce, the Detroit Bar Association, and the Detroit
Citizens League. From the black community came two attorneys, a physician, and Donald Marshall, the Negro-relations executive of the Ford
Motor Company.[28] By creating the board Smith made a political gesture,
a show of activity. But for answers he and the rest of the city were looking toward another arena. Could a black man kill a white man in Detroit
and get away with it? The question bespoke a thousand complexities.

The night of the shooting, William C. Osby, general manager of Dunbar Hospital and member of the Detroit Urban League board, was busy
making final preparations for his morning departure to Denver as a
delegate to the annual convention of the NAACP. Shortly before nine
o'clock his telephone rang. The call was not for him but for attorney
Charles Mahoney, who lived across the street and had no telephone.
Osby was accustomed to taking the lawyer's messages and prepared to
take another. This one, however, was different. There had been a shooting on Garland, and the Sweets had been arrested. Osby hung up the
telephone and hurried across the street to find Mahoney. He knew
Ossian Sweet had planned to move into the house. The two of them had
spoken of it in the hospital lounge only a few weeks before, and Osby
had bravely assured Sweet that in a similar position he would prepare to
defend his home with his life. He rushed into Mahoney's house and
gasped out the news. In a few seconds the lawyer was on his way down-

town. Cecil Rowlette was already there. Osby could do nothing further and left the next morning for Denver.[29]

On Wednesday, September 16, a three-day preliminary hearing was begun in Recorder's Court, the large stone structure on lower St. Antoine Street, directly behind the new police station. Magistrate for the hearing was Judge John Faust. Charles Mahoney, Cecil Rowlette, and Julian Perry appeared for the defense. Wayne County Prosecutor Robert M. Toms and Assistant Prosecutor Lester Moll represented the state. During the hearing several themes emerged which would characterize all subsequent proceedings. One was the denial of white people from the neighborhood that anything unusual took place either before the Sweets' moving in or on the night of the actual shooting. A second was the refusal of the police to admit that there had been any noticeable deviation from normal activity in the neighborhood around Garland and Charlevoix. Nobody threw any stones that I saw, said Inspector Schuknecht. There were hardly more than fifteen or twenty people around on the night of the shooting, testified Ray Dove, who rented a room to the wounded man Erick Hougberg and at whose steps Leon Breiner had fallen dead. I never knew the man who owned the house the Sweets bought was colored, said John R. Getke, a piano tuner who had lived next door to 2905 Garland for ten years. Yes, I shot over the back door when I saw colored men with guns inside, said patrolman Frank Lee Gill, twenty months in Detroit, a migrant from Tennessee. No, there wasn't any meeting at the Howe school that I ever heard of, said Lieutenant Schellenberger. And there wasn't any traffic in the neighborhood the night of the shooting either.[30]

Rowlette, Perry, and Mahoney petitioned the court for a dismissal. There was no evidence produced in the hearing, they said, to indicate which one of the defendants had fired the fatal shot, nor was there any evidence to indicate the existence of a conspiracy to commit murder. Young, liberal Frank Murphy was now sitting on the bench. Under the rotating magistrate system of the Recorder's Court, tenure as presiding judge had passed to him. The presiding judge assigns all cases, and Murphy took this one for himself. He denied the petition of the black attorneys and ordered the defendants bound over for trial. He permitted no bail except for Gladys Sweet, who was released October 5 on $5000 bond.[31]

By this time, the NAACP was seeking more eminent counsel for the Sweet defense. As an organization devoted almost entirely to the legal defense of black men's rights, the NAACP recognized the dramatic significance of the Detroit incident. If the Sweets were convicted, no black's home would be safe from self-appointed segregationists. But if the defendants could be freed, "that would be serving notice on potential mobbists everywhere that only at the peril of their lives could they attempt forcibly to oust peaceable and law-abiding colored citizens from their homes."[32] Clearly, such an important case deserved recognized excellence in counsel.

The man most active in the search for talent was Walter White, a blonde-haired, blue-eyed black who was the assistant secretary of the NAACP. He had been dispatched to Detroit by Executive Secretary James Weldon Johnson to find white attorneys willing to handle the case. He soon discovered, however, that many lawyers refused even to consider it. A few told him frankly that public feeling against the Sweets was so high that they feared the loss of many valuable clients if they accepted. Others demanded outrageously high fees, a less candid way, White suspected, of expressing similar reluctance.

The assistant secretary returned to New York with his discouraging report. The NAACP leadership then decided on a bold move. They would ask Clarence Darrow to defend the blacks. The famed attorney, who had spent the summer in Tennessee defending John Thomas Scopes against the state, agreed to consider the offer. White was confident of Darrow's answer and went to Detroit to continue preparations for the trial, telling everyone involved that Clarence Darrow was to be the attorney. Then he traveled to Chicago to hear the expected decision. He was led into the unkempt office.

"Did the defendants shoot into the mob?" Darrow asked.

White blanched. He was afraid now that if he told the truth Darrow would refuse the case. "I am not sure, particularly as to whether or not one of the defendants fired the shot which killed Leon Breiner, a white man," White mumbled.

Darrow appeared angry. "Don't try to hedge," he said. "I know you were not there. But do you believe the defendants fired?"

White had to give the answer. "I believe they did fire," he said. "And—" He was about to add that he thought they were justified in shooting.

The lawyer interrupted. "Then I'll take the case," he said. "If they had not had the courage to shoot back in defense of their own lives I wouldn't think they were worth defending."[33] Probably he had long since made up his mind.

Clarence Darrow was heretic to the American faith. State the prevailing convictions of American society in 1925—that God's ways rule the world and that they are generally beneficient; that progress is inevitable; that man has free will; that most men typically behave in rational ways; that people who are deeply religious are more likely to be virtuous than atheists or agnostics; that morality and virtue can be defined by a few clear and simple rules; that the United States as a nation, and the people within it as individuals, are better than foreigners who have not enjoyed the countless benefits of the American way of life; that in the United States anybody who is willing to work hard can be a success in life; that the American judicial system produces results which, however roughhewn at times, can still without irony be called justice; that if criminals are punished promptly and efficiently there will be fewer crimes; that blacks are, whether for reason of heredity or birth, inferior to whites—state all of these, and Clarence Darrow dissented from every one.[34] Not simply quiet, polite dissent, but loud, constant, raucous naysaying, wherever he could, day after day, year after year. It was for him in a strange way a religious mission.

Clarence Darrow was born in 1857 in the tiny village of Kinsman in northeastern Ohio. His father was Amirus Darrow, cabinetmaker, undertaker, and freethinker. In his youth Amirus had planned to enter the ministry, but Meadville Theological Seminary ignored the important questions, he thought, and left many others unanswered; and so, soon after completing his studies the young man departed the church for less orthodox creeds. Small midwestern towns did not endure deviants happily, and often there was blatant ostracism, directed mostly against the Darrow children. But Amirus refused to change his views. He made a scanty living for his family, but so long as no one starved it was enough. Otherwise, he was content to remain dreamily indifferent to the doings of the world, happiest when he was lost with his books in the etherea of European philosophy.[35]

The father's disdain for toil of any sort was visited on Clarence. In school the young boy labored over baseball rather than books. And he too loved to lie in the sweet meadows and dream. Once, at his father's urging, he hired out on a farm. The first day he pitched hay and came home exhausted. The second day he was sent out to the fields with a pan of kerosene to kill potato bugs. The bugs were fat and messy. The stooping hurt his back. By noon he had thrown the pan away and walked off the job. It was to be a permanent retreat from labor.[36]

For Clarence Darrow being a lawyer was a virtual guarantee that he could live life pretty much as he pleased. He had talent and knew that the law would earn him a good living. And because there were partners and clerks in Chicago to handle the everyday affairs of the practice, he could leave for weeks or years to work on a case in Idaho, write a novel in Colorado, or inspect at close range the beauteous women of the Holy Land.[37]

Darrow's brilliance as a defense lawyer was as complex and as simple as his genius for biography. He probed deeply into the background of his client's crime. He sifted evidence; he weighed it; he worried over it. In his examination of witnesses he drew out relevant facts, and in his final argument to the jury he pondered the detail. He would talk for hours, now picking up threads, now dropping them, now reexamining them in yet a different light. And gradually, out of the fabric, a pattern would emerge, a rational explanation of behavior for the jury and for himself. Then there could be no room for condemning.

Always there was the underlying premise. Man is a machine. He acts and reacts. His experience is cumulative. His life is a continuum. Each event has its antecedents. Each event has its consequences. Nothing happens without sufficient reason. Causation is always cumulative. "It seems to me to be clear," Darrow wrote, "that there is really no such thing as crime, as the word is generally understood. Every activity of man should came under the head of 'behavior.' . . . Man acts in response to outside stimuli. . . . He does as he must. Therefore, there is no such thing as moral responsibility."[38] Machines might make mistakes, but they certainly cannot be blamed.

When he was first approached by the NAACP in regard to the Sweet case, Darrow suggested that his fee be $50,000. (The father's disdain for money never rubbed off on the son.) The association was stunned. It could not possibly pay that amount, it said, because $50,000 was equal to the total annual budget, and all the money for the trial was going to have to be raised by mass campaigns. Darrow nodded. He would take this into consideration in deciding whether he would accept the case.

In Chicago he gave a relieved Walter White his answer. He would receive a fee of $5000.[39]

Two more attorneys were now hired to defend the Sweets. One was Arthur Garfield Hays, a Jewish lawyer from New York who had worked with Darrow that past summer in Tennessee. Hays, whose huge retainers as counsel for corporate wealth enabled him to accept frequent civil liberties cases, received $3000.[40] The other new attorney was Walter M. Nelson of Detroit, hired because Darrow suggested to the NAACP the advisability of retaining a local attorney who was a white man. Nelson received $2000.[41] Rowlette, Mahoney, and Perry were also kept on.

But Cecil Rowlette was not happy. He was disturbed about the fees. It was typical of the NAACP, he thought, to believe that black attorneys should be willing to receive only a token payment because they were serving on a "colored case." He saw no reason why he, Mahoney, and Perry should be receiving between them little more than Arthur Garfield Hays alone was getting.[42] He was also unhappy that he and his black colleagues were obviously being relegated to the background, and that out-of-state lawyers—"foreign talent"—were being brought in to handle what should have been a local case run by local talent. Juries are antagonized by such practices, he thought, and the members of the jury, even if they are all white men, will be angry that no black attorney is allowed to cross-examine or to argue.[43]

Rowlette and Mahoney were both irked at what they thought was the new counsel's cavalier disregard of their strategy. The three black attorneys had planned to make the prosecution try each of the eleven defendants separately and had filed a petition to this end with Judge Murphy on October 3, four days before Darrow was originally contacted by the NAACP. The three reasoned that if the prosecution tried eleven cases individually, using the same evidence in each one, discrepancies would inevitably arise. Testimony would not jibe, verdicts might differ. Thus there would arise bases for appeal on any convictions the prosecution was able to get, or the prosecution would ultimately tire of the proceedings and quietly drop the charges. But when Darrow entered the case, Rowlette and Mahoney saw what was happening. He was planning to defend all eleven defendants together, "from a sociological standpoint," Rowlette said. They thought this was foolish and expected the worst.[44]

Rowlette also disagreed with the new defense's appraisal of the prosecution. The white attorneys believed—and Darrow would so argue in the case—that had the people in the Sweet house been white and the mob outside black, there would never have been a warrant issued, and that by demanding the documents the prosecutors were simply acquiescing in a prevailing racism.[45] Rowlette demurred. He called the prosecutors, Robert Toms and Lester Moll, his good friends. He was satisfied that Toms was a fair man who was only doing his duty, though many other people familiar with Detroit law enforcement or subsequently connected with the Sweet trial—the latter including Walter White—were convinced that the chief prosecutor was a Klansman.[46] But Rowlette was persuaded by the philosophy of his own advice to Dr. Sweet. He saw Toms acting in a strictly legal role. "You see," Rowlette explained, "if those strangers hadn't gone there for Sweet to protect his home, I would have then censured him [Toms] for issuing the warrant. But since it never was known who fired the shot, and they were there and they had no right to go there for that purpose, the state was perfectly right in issuing that warrant."[47]

The political arena was reflecting the tensions aroused by the case. This time Charles Bowles was a certified candidate, with his name officially on the ballot. Running against a now incumbent Mayor John Smith, Bowles made changes in his campaign strategy. He sought broader electoral support, accepting the Klan endorsement tacitly but vigorously denying membership in the organization to all who would listen. He even actively solicited the vote of blacks and received an enthusiastic response from members of the Universal Negro Improvement Association, whose separatist policy was not incompatible with that of the Klan. To everyone, however, Bowles offered the same message—the need for clean, responsible government, the enforcement of the law, and no special favors for any one group.[48]

The Klan worked hard for success in the election. It brought Kleagle Ira W. Stout to Detroit to direct the campaign. It assessed the Detroit membership $5 a man to finance activities. It appealed to Protestant solidarity. Bowles clubs were formed on many blocks, and thousands of pamphlets and handbills were distributed in the streets.[49]

One factor complicated the strict Klan-anti-Klan polarity. Henry Ford enthusiastically endorsed Mayor Smith four days before the election, and Jews were put in the position of either voting with the Klan or aligning themselves with the country's most renowned anti-Semite.[50]

The election approached, and the campaign boiled. Because issues were defined by the Klan's presence, its hand seemed to be everywhere: in the rotunda of the City Hall, where a 20' x 5' KKK banner was hung; in special church services, where the wife of one Protestant minister declared that any woman not voting for Bowles should be tarred and feathered. In other pulpits Protestant clergymen were horrified and assailed the Klan. One minister, the Reverend Reinhold Niebuhr of Bethel Evangelical Church, denounced the hooded order as "one of the worst specific social phenomena which the religious pride and prejudice of peoples has ever developed."[51]

When the results were in, Bowles had lost, 140,000 to 110,000. He had again made a strong showing in the north and northwest sections of the city, but could not break the incumbent's strength among Catholics, immigrants, and blacks. The Klan did, however, achieve some measure of success. Only one of the five candidates the Klan recommended for common council, incumbent Robert Ewald, refused its endorsement. Four of the five, including Ewald, were elected; and one, Dr. Philip Callahan, was a former Kleagle.[52]

A white Catholic had defeated the Klan's candidate for mayor, and men the hooded order found congenial were voted onto the common council. The mixed results reflected local divisions, and no partisan could derive much satisfaction from the outcome. However, the Sweet trial promised a more definitive statement, and all sides looked to it now with apprehension and with hope.

Darrow and Hays knew the prosecution's case would be difficult to refute. Ten men had gathered at 2905 Garland with provisions, guns, and ammunition enough to withstand a possible siege. Shooting from windows would indicate to the jury a concerted plan. Leon Breiner, the victim, had not been an active member of the mob but had been standing across the street quietly smoking his pipe when the fusillade from the house cut him down. The Sweets had had police protection. And the authorities had taken statements (they were now being called confessions) from each of the defendants.[53]

The white attorneys were further hindered by their clients' reluctance to talk freely with them about events and preparations. The blacks seemed intent on keeping the lawyers from knowing too many possibly damning details, and they persisted for a long time in the stories they had told the police. One after another the black men claimed no knowledge of where anyone else in the house had been, nor any sense of what anyone else in the house had been doing. Darrow and Hays were annoyed. They repeatedly explained that the only defense was for the defendants to admit openly what they had done and then have the attorneys try to justify the action. But the black men remained adamant. Joe Mack, the chauffeur, continued to insist that during the shooting he had been locked in the bathroom taking a bath. Your defense depends upon your attitude of mind, Darrow said to the blacks. What was your state of mind? Weren't any of you afraid? Few would rise to the suggestion and admit they had felt fear. One defendant, Leonard Morse, the insurance agent, made things even more difficult by expressing pride and pleasure in the outcome of the incident. Now the white man has learned a lesson, he said to Darrow, as he had said to the police. Now the white man knows he cannot pick on a black man and get away with it.[54]

III

Two days after the municipal elections the trial began. It had taken five days to fill the jury, finally composed of twelve men, all of them white.[55] Now Prosecutor Robert Toms told the men who would judge why the state believed there had been a conspiracy to commit murder. The defendants had brought a substantial amount of food into the house, he said. There was little furniture. The house was not ready to be lived in. There were ten weapons found in the house, one for each of the men, and only one of the weapons had not been fired. Prior to the shooting the house had been made dark. In front of a number of windows on the second floor there were found chairs, cigar butts, tobacco ashes, burned matches, and comforters or quilts folded for kneeling. Not one of the defendants at the time of the shooting was in danger of his life or of serious bodily harm, Toms said. The property was not being trespassed upon. No damage to the property was imminent. And if damage to the property was imminent, it was not sufficiently serious to justify taking a life. The killing was thus premeditated, he said, because "they went in there with it in mind, and kept it in mind from the time that they went in there armed until the time of the shooting."[56]

Then began the parade of prosecution witnesses—police and people of the neighborhood—all denying there had been any crowds, any rocks thrown, any cause for shooting. They had been coached, and they were obviously lying. Gradually, Darrow drew out the facts. From a member of the Waterworks Park Improvement Association, he got a statement of motivation:

> Q.   Did [news that the Sweets were going to move in] have anything to do with your joining that club?
> A.   Possibly.
> Q.   Did it?
> A.   Yes.
> Q.   You joined that club to aid in keeping that a white district?
> A.   Yes.
> Q.   At that meeting in the school was any reference made to keeping the district free from colored people?
> A.   Yes.
> Q.   How many people were present at that meeting?
> A.   Seven hundred.

From another member came a similar admission:

> Q.   Did you join the organization as a property owner?
> A.   I did.
> Q.   What was your object?
> A.   To keep the neighborhood up to its existing high standard.
> Q.   Your interest was mainly in your property?
> A.   Yes.
> Q.   Your interest was in keeping out negroes to maintain the value of your property?
> A.   Yes.

From Ray Dove, who had told the prosecution in direction examination that there were more women and children around on the night of the shooting than men, Darrow ascertained

> Q.   Did you ever make an estimate of the number of women and children in a crowd before?
> A.   No, I can't say that I have.

"As long as the question was asked by the State you thought you were safe in answering it the way you did?" (A lengthy objection, but the question stood.) "No, not exactly." "Was there a crowd?" "No." "Was there any disturbance?" "No." "When did you hear that Dr. Sweet had bought the place?" "Quite a while before he moved in I heard rumors from the neighbors" "Quite a discussion?" "Yes, I guess so."
"How long before he moved in?" "Six weeks or two months." "You heard it from all the neighbors?" "Yes, two, three or four of them." "You discussed it with your wife?" "Yes." "You didn't want him there?" "I am not prejudiced against them but I don't believe in mixing whites and blacks." "So you did not want him there?" "No, I guess not."

Darrow and Hays were structuring their case on a claim of self-defense—seeking to justify the shooting on the grounds of reasonable apprehension of danger from a mob—and they consistently probed toward a definition of that mob, trying to determine for the jury its size, attitude, and action. Prosecution witnesses vigorously denied that there had been any mob (Schuknecht: "There wasn't anything going on at 6:30 o'clock when I got there; everything was quiet." "Were there people on the streets?" "People were walking up and down, yes." "Were they congregating?" "No, sir."), but this was for the defense a positive advantage. Obvious lying can be exploited by expert cross-examiners; and when the police were consistently unable to explain why reserves had been called in, why traffic had been stopped, why they had ordered people to move on, why they had sent two officers to an apartment house roof across the street, the vapor of doubt began to seep into the minds of the jury.[57]

Darrow was always conscious of his audience, and he played to it. Gestures were studied, demeanor deliberate. While the prosecution was examining the state's witnesses, he would sit slouched in his chair, clothes wrinkled, hair unkempt, busily working on crossword puzzles.[58] Then it was his turn, and he would amble to the witness box and drawl his questions. "What were you doing there?" "I live near by." "What brought you to that corner?" "Curiosity." "About what?" "Nothing in particular." "You knew that colored people had moved into that house?" "Yes." "Did that have anything to do with your curiosity?" "Maybe." "Many people there?" "No." "There were strangers there—people you didn't ordinarily see in the neighborhood?" "Some." "How many?" "Twenty-five or thirty." Then, rapidly, "Did you want the negroes

there?" "Did you belong to the Waterworks Improvement Association?"
"Why?" "Did you attend meetings?" "How many were there?" "What
was said?" "What were you talking about that evening?" And finally a
youngster made a mistake and cracked the charade: "There was a great
crowd—no, I won't say a great crowd, a large crowd—well, there were a
few people there and the officers were keeping them moving." Darrow
was on him instantly. "Have you talked to any one about the case?"
"Lieutenant Johnson [a police detective]." "And when you started to
answer the question you forgot to say a few people, didn't you?" "Yes,
sir."

More breaks came. A prosecution witness admitted hearing sounds
which might have been "pebbles" hitting the house, and he heard the
crash of window glass shattering just before the shooting occurred. What
was the size of the pebbles, he was asked? Perhaps two inches in diameter,
like those on the exhibit table, he replied. (These were stones and chunks
of cement which had been picked from the roof and yard of the Sweet
house the day following the shooting.) Darrow walked over to the table,
picked up a rock, and approached the witness, about to hand it to him.
Then he dropped the rock to the marble floor. The sound cracked
through the courtroom.[59]

Two young boys, also prosecution witnesses, testified seeing a gang
of young toughs throw stones at the Sweet house. One of the boys
offered a detail not yet heard. He had seen a car drive up and two blacks
get out and run into the house. Then he saw rocks hit the house, and
then the breaking of glass. And almost immediately thereafter, he said,
shots were fired.

Eight more prosecution witnesses followed that day, and each of those
told of serenity.[60]

Sometimes, after an exhausting day in court, Darrow would reflect
dispiritedly on what he as a public person was doing. The debate was
wearying, he thought. Perhaps the effort was wasted; perhaps it was even
senseless. This was his mood one night in Detroit when he began to re-
cite to Arthur Garfield Hays his catechism of human benightedness: We
are all creatures of habit, dumbly happy when there are pleasant varia-
tions, dumbly unhappy when there are unpleasant ones. Each of us is
made of chemicals and substances which can be bought in any drugstore
for pennies. So what difference does it make whether or not these people

are convicted? Hays responded with the obvious and the unanswerable:
If it makes no difference, why do you wear yourself out defending them?
Darrow shook his head: "I don't know. I just suppose I'd be uncomfort-
able if I didn't."[61]

So outside the Detroit courtroom Clarence Darrow sought a more
vigorous affirmation of his public being. Without it, there was
nothing for him. He accompanied Prosecutor Toms to lunch at the
Detroit Athletic Club and responded with the familiar, now suddenly
delightful, cynicisms to civic leaders eagerly feeding him questions for
comment.[62] He traveled to Ann Arbor to offer University of Michigan
students and academicians his heresies on crime and criminal behavior,[63] the change in audience again renewing him. He spoke to ghetto
blacks on St. Antoine Street and told them that if the white man went
into the Congo he too would be hated and misunderstood, that without
slavery the black race would never have had its chance for civilization,
that Lincoln's emancipation proclamation was a fraud.[64] He was
nourished by the challenge of the true believers, and he returned to
the battle refreshed.

After a perfunctory request for a directed verdict of not guilty,
which Judge Murphy denied, the defense opened its case. It called two
black men who had been accosted on the outskirts of the mob the night
of September 9. They gave their impressions of the mob, its size, its
density, its ugly temper.[65]

Then the defense called Dr. Ossian Sweet. Under the careful direction
of Arthur Garfield Hays the doctor told of his boyhood in Florida, the
son of a poor minister-farmer, and of the many jobs—porter, bellhop,
waiter, furnace-tender—he had held as he worked his way toward and
through Wilberforce and Howard universities. He told of his travel to
Europe, of study in Vienna and Paris, and of the subsequent purchase
of the house on Garland Avenue because there was no place else to go.
Then Hays shifted the questioning, and Sweet began to explain how fear
had become inculcated into his consciousness as a result of what he had
heard and read and seen in his childhood. He told of his grandfather,
who had been a bondsman, and of the stories the old man used to tell
about the evil of slavery.

Toms was on his feet in objection. "Is everything this man saw as a
child a justification for a crime twenty-five years later?" "Yes," said

Hays. "I might properly bring in the incidents his grandfather had told to him." Darrow approached the bench. "This is the question of the psychology of a race," he said,

> of how everything known to a race affects its actions. What we learn as children we remember—it gets fastened in the mind. I would not claim that the people outside the Sweet home were bad. But they would do to Negroes something they would not do to whites. It's their race psychology. Because this defendant's actions were predicated on the psychology of his past, I ask that this testimony be admitted.

Murphy agreed, his most important single judgment of the trial, and the testimony continued.

Sweet now shifted closer to the present. He told of the Chicago race riots, reciting facts, depicting horrors. Always his voice was low, his words clear. He told of the Tulsa riots in 1921 and of the eminent surgeon who had been killed after having been guaranteed protection by the police. He told of an experience in Washington in which he had seen a black pulled from a streetcar, carried through the streets, and finally beaten to death by a group of white men.

Again he shifted, and now it was the story of Detroit and the racial disturbances. He paused at the recounting of the eviction of Dr. Turner. "Turner," said Sweet, a fine irony now creeping into his voice,

> always had the greatest confidence in the world of white people; he felt that they belonged to a race superior to his own. Consequently, when they wanted to enter his house, to rob him, it wasn't necessary to break down the door. It was far simpler to deceive him. One of the leaders simply knocked, and when Dr. Turner came to the door said, "Open Turner, I'm your friend." Turner believed him and opened the door. The next moment he was dough in the hands of the mob.

Then Sweet spoke of the events immediately preceding his own difficulty. He told of hearing from Mrs. Smith, the white woman who sold him the house, of the threats she had received from her neighbors, white people promising "to get her if they had to follow her to California" and to

"kill the Negro" if he dared to move in. He told of a conversation his
wife's friend Edna Butler, the interior decorator, had overheard on a
streetcar the day before the shooting, in which a woman had remarked
to the motorman that blacks had moved into the neighborhood and that
they would be out by the next night. He admitted he had purchased
many of the firearms found in the house because of fear, and that before
the shooting he had taken the other defendants through the house and
shown them the various rooms, including the closet where the weapons
and ammunition were stored. Then he recited his own impressions of
the events of that night.

"When did you first observe anything outside?" Hays asked.

"We were playing cards. It was about eight o'clock when something
hit the roof of the house."

"What happened after that?"

"Somebody went to the window and I heard them remark, 'People,
the people!' "

"And then?"

"I ran out to the kitchen where my wife was. There were several
lights burning. I turned them out and opened the door. I heard some
one yell, 'Go and raise hell in front; I am going back.' Frightened, and
after getting a gun, I ran upstairs. Stones were hitting the house inter-
mittently. I threw myself on the bed and lay there a short while—perhaps
fifteen or twenty minutes—when a stone came through a window. Part
of the glass hit me."

"What happened next?"

"Pandemonium—I guess that's the best way to describe it—broke
loose. Every one was running from room to room. There was a general
uproar. Somebody yelled, 'There's some one coming.' They said, 'That's
your brother.' A car had pulled up to the curb. My brother and Mr. Davis
got out. The mob yelled, 'Here's niggers, get them! Get them!' As they
rushed in, a mob surged forward, fifteen or twenty feet. It looked like a
human sea. Stones kept coming faster. I was downstairs. Another window
was smashed. Then one shot, then eight or ten from upstairs. Then it was
all over."

"What was your state of mind at the time of the shooting?" Hays
asked.

"When I opened the door and saw the mob, I realized I was facing the same mob that had hounded my people through its entire history. In my mind I was pretty confident of what I was up against. I had my back against the wall. I was filled with a peculiar fear, the fear of one who knows the history of my race. I knew what mobs had done to my people before."[66]

Darrow delivered his final argument in a courtroom packed with spectators. He spoke for two days. Sometimes his theme was guilt. ("I am sick of this talk about an innocent man being killed. There were no innocent men in that bunch, not one.") Sometimes it was the irrationality of the white man's color consciousness. ("Why, I have known people with white blood that were plumb idiots; the more they had of it, the more idiotic they were.") Sometimes it was the arrogance of the race who would judge. ("Do you think that these people, simply because their color is black, are to be forever kept as slaves of the white? Do you think that all the rights which you claim for yourselves are to be denied them? Do you think they should be like the beasts of the field who can do no better than to obey the white man's demands? Who are we anyhow? What is this white race that arrogates all of that authority to itself, what is it? Is it wisdom? Is it knowledge? Is it tolerance? Is it understanding? Or is it pure conceit and force?") Always he kept putting the question to the jury: What would you have done in their place, you who are white and have been taught that it is right to act in your own defense and not to submit? Would you have waited two days to respond if the mob trying to drive you out was black? Would you have waited until the house had fallen down above you, as did Turner, and then sign a document "outraging the rights of an American citizen"? Or would you have waited no more than a minute that first night? "You gentlemen cannot decide this question in cool deliberation as you sit here," Darrow said.

You must imagine yourselves in the position of these eleven over here, with their skins, with the hatred, with the infinite wrongs they have suffered on account of their skin, with the hazards they take every day they live, with the insults that are heaped around them, with the crowd outside, with the knowledge of what that crowd meant, and then ask the question of whether they waited too long or stopped too quick.[67]

Toms followed Darrow. All through the trial the prosecutor had thought to himself, if only the colored people involved were not "so far superior" to our white witnesses "intellectually, in appearance, in culture, and in sympathy-eliciting quality." If only I were not "fighting uphill all the time to get my people to appear to be on a level with the defendants."[68] Now, in his final argument, Toms would try to redress the balance. "I concede the right under the law of any man, black or white, to live where he likes or wherever he can afford to live," he said,

> but we all have many civil rights which we voluntarily waive in the name of public peace, comfort and security, and because we are ashamed to insist upon them. I have a right to be a domineering, arrogant martinet to my subordinates; I have a right to remain seated in a street car while an elderly woman or a mother carrying a child stands; I have a right to keep my hat on in the church or in the theater; I have a right to play the piano or honk my automobile horn when a woman next door is tossing on a sick bed—all these things and many more are civil rights which I may insist upon. But I would be ashamed to insist upon them, and so would you.
>
> But there is one civil right more precious than all the others, which no man surrenders, except at the command of his God or his country, and that is the right to live. When John Hancock and fifty-four others of our forefathers fixed their signatures to the Declaration of Independence, they subscribed, as one of the eternal principles on which our country was founded, to this doctrine: "All men are endowed by their Creator with certain inalienable rights; that among these are life, liberty and the pursuit of happiness." And I have no doubt that in setting forth those inalienable rights our forefathers purposely put the most important of those rights first—the right to live. And right here let us ask ourselves, what has Leon Breiner done to have been deprived of that right?
>
> Has he committed some outrage that his right to live should have been taken away from him, without his having the least chance to

defend it? Did Breiner arm himself to protect his civil rights—his right to live? Which is more important—the right to live where you please, in a certain house on a certain street, or the right to live at all? Certainly the latter. Certainly Breiner, had he been given a chance to speak, would have said, "I'll live anywhere, but let me live."[69]

Cecil Rowlette thought it was one of the most moving appeals he had ever heard.[70]

Judge Murphy was unequivocal in his instructions to the jury. The law holds that a man's home is his castle, he said, and a man has a right to defend his life and property if he has reasonable cause to believe there is danger. The protection the law offers is everyone's. There are no exclusions because of race.

In order to find one or more of the defendants guilty, he continued, you have to be satisfied that there was a criminal intent. The act itself does not make guilt. If the accused believed under the circumstances of the time that danger was actual and imminent, there can be no guilt, even though it might turn out thereafter that he or they were mistaken. It is therefore your province, he instructed, "to consider what were the circumstances which confronted the accused at the time; their situation, race and color, the actions and attitude of those who were outside the Sweet home, all have a bearing on whether or not the sum total of the surrounding circumstances as they appeared to them at the time were such as to induce in a reasonable man the honest belief of danger."[71]

The jury filed out to consider the verdict. The noises of their disagreement cut through the closed door of the jury room. "What's the use of arguing with these fellows." "Two of you had them convicted before you came here." "I'll stay here twenty years if necessary, and I'm younger than any of you." Thanksgiving came, and the holiday dinner served by the state was eaten in sullen silence. The arguing continued, but the deadlock was apparent. After forty-six hours the jurors filed back into the courtroom. They could reach no verdict. Seven had favored acquittal; five held out for the conviction of Ossian Sweet, Henry Sweet, and Leonard Morse on a charge of manslaughter. One juror had been especially adamant. "I don't give a God damn what the facts are," he had yelled during the deliberations. "A nigger has killed a white man and I'll be burned in hell before I will ever vote to acquit a nigger who has killed a white man."[72] Perhaps he had seen the consequences of his decision in precisely those terms.

An uneasy calm settled over the city as preparations were begun for a second trial. There were no further incidents in the neighborhoods. There were no mass rallies in the streets. The black ghetto, under the urgings of John Dancy and others, busied itself raising more money for the Sweet defense. The Urban League met the rush of events with silence. The whole city, it seemed, was simply waiting.[73]

For Cecil Rowlette, however, it was a time for quiet rejoicing. He felt vindicated by the hung jury and was convinced now that had he and Mahoney alone been allowed to defend the Sweets there would have been an acquittal. He was glad too at the rumors he had heard—that the defense was now going to insist on separate trials, the strategy he had favored all along.[74]

There were changes in Darrow's colleagues among counsel for the defense. Arthur Garfield Hays pleaded the pressure of other commitments and left the case. Walter Nelson also was busy. Neither Cecil Rowlette nor Charles Mahoney were asked to stay on. Only Julian Perry, Ossian Sweet's personal attorney, was retained.[75]

Darrow found a replacement for Hays early. While the jury was deliberating he had been under pressure from Prosecutor Toms to consent to the panel's being discharged and a new trial begun. Typically, Darrow sought expert advice. On Thanksgiving day he telephoned attorney Thomas Chawke, a white man with the reputation of being the best criminal lawyer in Michigan. (Months before, Chawke had demanded $7500 of the NAACP to head the Sweet defense and had been turned down. It was not his fee which had disturbed the association most. Rather it was Chawke's renown as an attorney for the underworld. "He is without doubt a corking lawyer," Walter White had said, "but his reputation as one who gets anybody off whether guilty or not diesn't [sic] seem to be to be the most desirable thing in this particular case."[76]) Darrow, however, was under no such apprehension. When Chawke came to the telephone, Darrow quickly apologized for calling at his home, especially on the holiday, and then explained he was in need of advice. Chawke had been following events closely and had guessed at Darrow's difficulty. Get a mistrial declared as soon as you can, he said in his low voice. Then he continued dispassionately: You cannot indulge yourself in the assumption that a majority of the jurors are on your side. You have to assume that only a few are holding out for the defendants' innocence. And if this is true, there is a danger in the deliberations being prolonged, because the jurors seeking an acquittal might be tempted to make a deal. They might think that were a new trial held, all eleven defendants could be convicted, and so they would be tempted to agree to the conviction of one or two of the defendants if the majority of the jurors would concur in the release of the rest. And of course, Chawke said, this would lose the case in so far as the great issue of a man's right to protect his home is concerned.

Darrow thanked him for his advice and said that he would speak to him at a subsequent date. Four months later Darrow called Chawke from Chicago. He asked if he might come to Detroit to see him. Chawke agreed, and the next day Darrow was in the lawyer's office. Is there anything in the local situation, Darrow asked, which would prevent you from entering the case? Chawke replied there was nothing, but then added a condition. Under no circumstances would he enter the case if the eleven defendants were again tried as one. Under Michigan law every man jointly informed against for murder has the legal right to demand a separate trial; and the defense ought to demand this, Chawke said, because it avoided the risk of a compromise verdict. Also, he added, in case there is an acquittal in the trial of the first defendant, the verdict will probably be decisive in the prosecution's deciding whether or not to try the rest of the defendants. Darrow agreed.[77]

Henry Sweet, because he had admitted firing a weapon, stood alone in the second trial.[78] It was a near replica of the first. The prosecution witnesses all swore to the tranquility of the neighborhood. The defense counsel—Darrow and Chawke alternately—clawed through the fabrications to get at the truth.[79]

Chawke, towering above the witness chair, cross-examined Lieutenant Schellenberger:

Q.   Did you see an unusual number of automobiles in that district while you were there that night?

A.   (Firmly.) *I should say not.*

Q.   Were you present when Deputy Superintendent Sprott instructed Schuknecht to direct the traffic off of Garland Avenue?

A.   I was.

Q.   Did you participate in the discussion about the number of machines which were coming into that immediate neighborhood?

A.   I did not.

Q.   Do you know where the automobiles went after leaving Garland Avenue?

A.   I do not.

Q.   Do you know how many automobiles were parked just before this shooting on any of the side streets east and west of Garland Avenue?

A.   I do not.

Q.   Or where the occupants of those cars went?

A.   I do not.

Q.   You do not know whether they came back, walked back to the corner of Charlevoix and Garland, do you?

A.   I do not.

Q.   Isn't it true now, officer, that it was because there were so many machines coming into Charlevoix and Garland, that you officers determined you would divert the traffic off of Garland so as to keep them from coming up there?

A.   No, sir.

Q.   Then why did you not stop the traffic from coming up St. Clair and Bewick? [The streets to the right and left of Garland, running parallel to it.]

A.   Because it was not necessary.

Q.   *Why* wasn't it necessary?

A.   I think the streets are wider and can accommodate more cars.

Q.   (Dryly.) Tell us how many feet wider Bewick Avenue is than Garland Avenue.

A.   (Obviously embarrassed.) I couldn't tell you. I don't think there is any difference in the width at all.

Q.   How many feet wider is St. Clair than Garland?

A.   (By this time flushing a dull red.) I don't think there is any difference in the width at all.

Q.   Then, why didn't you stop the automobiles from going up St. Clair and Bewick?

A.   Why should I?

Q.   Well, you did at Garland, did you not?

A.   Yes.

Q.   Why did you do that at Garland?

A.   Because we did not want any cars in the vicinity, only what really belonged there.

Q.   Were there any persons coming into the vicinity in automobiles who did not belong in that neighborhood?

A.   Not after the traffic was diverted.

Q.   Were there before?

A.   Yes.

Q.   Who were they?

A.   I do not know.

Q.   Was traffic getting heavy?

A.   It appeared to me that people were getting curious, more so than anything else, and there was an unusual amount of traffic.

Q.   Then there *was* an unusual amount of automobile traffic there, wasn't there?

A.   There *were*.[80]

Darrow, sick with a cold, irritated at the constant evasions, cross-examined a member of the Waterworks Park Improvement Association about the meeting at the Howe school: "What did the speaker say?" (Much hedging.) "He said that they—he offered the support of the Tireman Avenue Improvement Association to the Waterworks Park Improvement Association to handle the problem that it was up against." More questions. More circumlocutions. Then, from Darrow: "Did he say they—the organization—made the Turners leave the house?" "Yes, he did." Did he talk about keeping colored people out of the neighborhood? Yes. You applauded the speech? Yes. "That is just the way you felt then and the way you feel now?" "Yes, I haven't changed." "You felt just the same as the speaker about not letting them out there?" "If by legal means we could restrict them."

The phrase infuriated Darrow.

Q.   Did the speaker talk about "legal means"?

A.   I admitted to you that this man was radical.

Q.   Answer my question. Did he talk about legal means?

A.   No.

Q.   He talked about driving them out, didn't he?

A.   Yes, he was radical—I admit that.

Q.   You say you approved of what he said and applauded it, didn't you?

A.   Part of his speech.

Q.   In what way was he radical?

A.   Well, I don't—I myself do not believe in violence.

Q.   I didn't ask you what you believed in. I said in what way was he radical? Anything more you want to say about what you mean by radical, that he advocated?

A.   No, I don't want to say any more.

Q.   You did not rise in that meeting and say, "I myself don't believe in violence," did you?

A.   No; I'd had a fine chance with 600 people there!

Q.   What? You would have caught it, yourself, wouldn't you? You wouldn't have dared to do it at that meeting.

Toms objected frantically. "Don't answer it!" And he turned to the judge. "I object to it as very, very improper." Murphy said calmly, "The objection is sustained."

Darrow kept at it.

Q.   What did you mean by saying you had a fine chance?

Toms, nervous, again interrupted. "Wait a minute. Did you get the Court's ruling?" Darrow ignored him. No word from Murphy.

Q.   What did you mean by that?

A.   You imagine I would have made myself heard with 600 people there? I wasn't on the platform.

Q.   What did you mean by saying you would have had a fine chance in that meeting where 600 people were present—to make the statement that you said?

A.   I object to violence.

Q.   Did anybody—did *anybody* in that audience of 600 people protest against advocating violence against colored people who moved into the neighborhood?

A.   I don't know.

Q.   You didn't hear any protest?

A.   No.

Q.   You only heard applause?

A.   There was—as I stated—this meeting was in the schoolyard—

Q.   You heard nobody utter any protest, and all the manifestation you heard was applause at what he said?

A.   Yes, that is all.

Toms took him at once for redirect examination. "Did he *advocate* violence?" he demanded. "I said this man was radical," the witness returned stiffly. "I know you did," persisted the prosecutor. "Did he advocate violence?" A pause, then: "Yes."[81]

John Dancy, called by Darrow as a witness for the defense, testified about his work for the Urban League, his associates, the extent of the migration, patterns of residence, the shortage of housing. Then in cross-examination Assistant Prosecutor Lester Moll put a question to him: Is it not true that when Negroes move into a neighborhood, property values decline? Dancy allowed a dramatic pause. Then he said, "No, they are enhanced." He explained: Until recently I lived on Chestnut Street, on the East Side. On either side of my house was a two-family apartment building. In each whites occupied one apartment and blacks the other. In both the blacks paid nearly double the rent for identical accommodations.[82]

Ossian Sweet repeated his depiction of the events on the night of September 9.[83]

And finally Darrow made his plea to the twelve white men of the jury, sketching the recent history of their city and asking them the question, "Who are you to judge?" "Imagine yourselves colored, gentlemen," he said.

Imagine yourselves back in the Sweet house on that fatal night. That is the only right way to treat this case, and the court will tell you so. Would you move there? Where would you move? Dancy says there were six or seven thousand colored people here sixteen years ago. And seventy-one thousand [81,000] five years ago. Gentlemen, why are they here? They came here as you came here, under the laws of trade and business, under the instincts to live; both the white and the colored, just the same. . . . Your factories were open for them. Mr. Ford hired them. The automobile companies hired them. Everybody hired them. They were all willing to give them work, weren't they? Everyone of them. You and I are willing to give them work, too. We are willing to have them in our houses to take care of the children and do the rough work that we shun ourselves. . . . We invited them; pretty nearly all the colored population has come to Detroit in the last fifteen years; most of them, anyhow. They have always had a corner on the meanest jobs. The city must grow, or you couldn't brag about it. The colored people must live somewhere. Everybody is willing to have them live somewhere else. The people at the corner of Garland and Charlevoix would be willing to have them go to some other section. They would be willing to have them buy a place up next to Mrs. Dodge's house; but most of them haven't got money enough to do that; none that I know of.

He spoke for hours. Twice he almost concluded, but then as if by some instinct realizing that a fragment was going uncovered, a point in a juror's mind unfilled, he went on. And then it was nearly done. "I know the Negro race has a long road to go," he said.

I believe the life of the Negro race has been a life of tragedy, of injustice, of oppression. The law has made him equal, but man has not. And, after all, the last analysis is, what has man done?—and not what has the law done? . . . I know before him there is suffering, sorrow, tribulation and death among the blacks, and perhaps the whites. I am sorry. I would do what I could to avert it. I would advice patience; I would advise toleration; I would advise understanding; I would advise all of those things which are necessary for men who live together.[84]

The twelve men agreed, and Henry Sweet was acquitted.[85]

NOTES

1. *Detroit Free Press,* April 10, 1925; *Detroit Independent,* April 17, 1925.

2. *Detroit Free Press,* June 24, 1925; *Detroit Times,* June 24, 1925; tape-recorded interview of Cecil L. Rowlette by Alex Baskin, Detroit, Michigan, August 1, 1960, MHC. For biographical information on Cecil Rowlette, see above, chap. 3.

3. Turner and Moses, *Colored Detroit,* p. 24; Dancy, *Sand against*

the Wind, pp. 145-46; *Detroit Free Press,* June 24, 1925, p. 1; *Detroit Times,* June 24, 1925, p. 1.

4. Marcet Haldeman-Julius, *Clarence Darrow's Two Great Trials* (Girard, Kans.: Haldeman-Julius Co., 1927), pp. 38-39.

5. *Detroit Free Press,* July 8 and 9, 1925.

6. Ibid., July 9, 1925; Haldeman-Julius, *Clarence Darrow's Two Great Trials,* p. 39.

7. *Detroit Free Press,* July 9, 1925.

8. Ibid., July 10, 1925.

9. Ibid.

10. Ibid., July 11, 1925; statement of John W. Fletcher (typed carbon), Darrow MSS, Box 18, File 246, LC.

11. Statement of John W. Fletcher, Darrow MSS, LC; Haldeman-Julius, *Clarence Darrow's Two Great Trials,* p. 39.

12. *Detroit Free Press,* July 12, 1925.

13. Haldeman-Julius, *Clarence Darrow's Two Great Trials,* pp. 31, 38, 68; Walter White to James Weldon Johnson, September 16, 1925, NAACP Legal Files, "Cases Supported—Sweet Case," Box D-85, LC; *Detroit City Directory, 1925-26;* Dancy, *Sand against the Wind,* pp. 22-23.

14. *Detroit Free Press,* July 12, 1925, pp. 1, 4.

15. Haldeman—Julius, *Clarence Darrow's Two Great Trials,* p. 39; White to Johnson, September 16, 1925, NAACP Legal Files, LC.

16. Haldeman-Julius, *Clarence Darrow's Two Great Trials,* pp. 28-29, 33-36; Arthur Garfield Hays, *Let Freedom Ring* (New York: Horace Liveright, 1928), p. 219; handwritten statement of Gladys Sweet to the NAACP [September 1925], NAACP Legal Files, "Sweet Case," Box D-86, LC; White to Johnson, September 16, 1925, NAACP Legal Files, LC; *Detroit City Directory, 1925-26.*

17. Haldeman-Julius, *Clarence Darrow's Two Great Trials,* pp. 28-30, 35.

18. Ibid.; Hays, *Let Freedom Ring,* p. 219; Turner and Moses, *Colored Detroit,* p. 119.

19. Haldeman-Julius, "The Defendants in the Sweet Murder Case," pp. 31, 32, 38, 39; handwritten statement of Gladys Sweet, NAACP Legal Files, LC; White to Johnson, September 16, 1925, ibid.; *Detroit Free Press,* November 19, 1925; *Detroit City Directory, 1925-26.*

20. Haldeman-Julius, "The Defendants in the Sweet Murder Case," pp. 27, 30-31; Dancy, *Sand against the Wind,* pp. 23-24; Recorder's Court File No. 60317-60318, Recorder's Court, Detroit, Michigan; *Detroit City Directory, 1925-26;* Turner and Moses, *Colored Detroit,* p. 74.

21. Interview of Cecil L. Rowlette, MHC.

22. Haldeman-Julius, *Clarence Darrow's Two Great Trials,* pp. 32, 56; Recorder's Court File No. 60317-60318; *Detroit News,* September 10 and November 9, 1925; Michigan v. Ossian Sweet, Henry Sweet, Leonard Morse, et al. (No. 60317, Recorder's Court, beginning November 5, 1925), opening statement of Robert M. Toms, prosecuting attorney, November 5, 1925, transcript, BHC.

23. Haldeman-Julius, *Clarence Darrow's Two Great Trials,* pp. 32-33.

24. Ibid., pp. 33, 34, 40-41; "Statement of Dr. O. H. Sweet made Saturday, Sept. 12 [1925] to Francis M. Dent and W. Hayes McKinney at Wayne County Jail," NAACP Legal Files, "Sweet Case," Box D-85, LC; handwritten statement of Gladys Sweet, NAACP Legal Files, LC; *Detroit Times,* September 10, 1925; *Detroit News,* September 10, 1925; *Detroit Free Press,* November 19, 1925.

25. Testimony of Inspector Norton M. Schuknecht, in preliminary hearing before Judge John Faust, September 16, 1925, Recorder's Court File No. 60317-60318; tape-recorded interview of Dr. Otis Sweet by Alex Baskin, Detroit, Michigan, August 1, 1960, MHC; *Detroit Times,* September 10, 1925; *Detroit News,* September 10 and November 9, 1925.

26. Haldeman-Julius, *Clarence Darrow's Two Great Trials,* pp. 41-42; J. G. Knight, "Detroit Has Fine New Police Headquarters," *American City* 27 (July 1922): 32; *Detroit Times,* September 10, 1925; *Detroit Free Press,* November 21, 1925; *Detroit News,* September 13, 1925; Recorder's Court File No. 60317-60318; Argument of Clarence Darrow in Michigan v. Sweet et al., commencing November 24, 1925, transcript, BHC.

27. *Detroit Times,* September 13, 1925, pp. 1, 2.

28. *Detroit Free Press,* September 16, 1925, pp. 1, 3; on the Mayor's committee, also see White to Johnson, September 16, 1925, NAACP Legal Files, LC. On Tracy McGregor and the work of the McGregor Institute, see *The Detroiter,* February 20, 1928; Dancy, *Sand against the Wind,* pp. 95-96; Washington, "Dependency," in "The Negro in Detroit" (1920), DPL; *Detroit Free Press,* October 8, 1905.

29. Interview of William C. Osby by Alex Baskin, Detroit, Michigan, July 27, 1960, MHC; tape-recorded interview of Charles Mahoney by Alex Baskin, Detroit, Michigan, August 1960, ibid.; interview of Cecil L. Rowlette, ibid.

30. Transcript of preliminary hearing before Judge John Faust, Septem-

ber 16-18, 1925, Recorder's Court File No. 60317-60318; *Detroit City Directory, 1925-26.*

31. Petition of October 10, 1925, signed by Rowlette, Perry, and Mahoney, in Recorder's Court File No. 60317-60318; see also documents pertaining to bail in ibid.; interview of Cecil L. Rowlette, MHC.

Frank Murphy was a liberal in the tradition of the Catholic Church's lay left wing. He believed that politics should be an extension of ethics and that temporal law ideally ought to conform to divine law. In 1925 his political career was barely under way. He had won a seat on the Recorder's Court bench two years earlier against the opposition of the Detroit Citizens League but with the endorsement of the Detroit Bar Association and public support by prominent individuals like Fred Butzel. Earlier, he had practiced law in Detroit, had also been assistant U.S. district attorney for eastern Michigan (1919-21), and had been an unsuccessful Democratic candidate for Congress (1920). At the time of the Sweet trial he was thirty-three years old.

The Frank Murphy Papers, MHC, are the major source for personal and official correspondence, documents, clippings, etc. Also see Richard D. Lunt, *The High Ministry of Government: The Political Career of Frank Murphy* (Detroit: Wayne State University Press, 1965).

32. "The Battles of Washington and Detroit," *Crisis* 30 (December 1925): 68-69, 71.

33. Walter White, *A Man Called White* (New York: The Viking Press, 1948), pp. 75-77; *Sixteenth Annual Report of the N.A.A.C.P. for the Year 1925*, pp. 12-14; Walter White, speech at the seventeenth birthday dinner of the NAACP, April 18, 1927, typed transcript of proceedings, pp. 27-30, Darrow MSS, Box 3, File 222, LC.

34. Appropriated from Ray Ginger, *Six Days of Forever? Tennessee v. John Thomas Scopes* (New York: Signet Books, 1960), p. 47; for Darrow on blacks, see "The Problem of the Negro," *International Socialist Review* 2 (November 1901): 321-35; for Darrow speaking in Detroit on crime, see *Detroit News,* November 3, 1924.

35. Ginger, *Six Days or Forever?* p. 48; Ray Ginger, "Clarence Seward Darrow, 1857-1938," *The Antioch Review,* Spring 1953, pp. 53-54.

36. Ginger, "Clarence Seward Darrow," p. 54; see Darrow's idyllic boyhood memoirs, *Farmington* (Chicago: A. C. McClurg and Co., 1904).

37. Ginger, "Clarence Seward Darrow," pp. 54, 55.

38. Clarence Darrow, *Crime: Its Cause and Treatment* (New York: Thomas Y. Crowell Co., 1922), pp. 274-75.

39. Statement of William Pickens, field secretary of the NAACP, enclosed in Pickens to Irving Stone, February 24, 1941, Darrow MSS, Box 17, File 243, LC; "The Battles of Washington and Detroit," pp. 68-69, 71; Clarence Darrow to Walter White, October 22, 1925, NAACP Legal Files, "Sweet Case," Box D-86, LC.

40. "The Sweet Case," *Crisis* 31 (February 1926): 185; "Arthur Garfield Hays," in *Current Biography, 1942,* ed. Maxine Block (New York: The H. W.Wilson Co., 1942), pp. 354-57.

41. *Sixteenth Annual Report of the N.A.A.C.P. for the Year 1925,* p. 13; "The Sweet Case," p. 185; NAACP memorandum, "Disbursements of First Sweet Trial," undated, NAACP Legal Files, "Sweet Case," Box D-86, LC.

A fourth white attorney, Herbert J. Friedman, came with Darrow from Chicago and served without fee, though the NAACP, as a gesture of appreciation, contributed $300 toward his personal expenses. Walter White, Memorandum on Expenses in Case of Dr. Ossian H. Sweet et al., November 30, 1925, ibid.

42. Interview of Cecil L. Rowlette, MHC; White, *A Man Called White,* p. 76; "The Sweet Case," p. 185. There was considerable and lengthy disagreement as to how much money was in fact due Rowlette, Mahoney, and Perry. The NAACP national office contended that their fee was to be $1500 each or whatever portion thereof could be raised locally by the Detroit branch, and that under no circumstances would the national office be responsible for any part of the payment. Memorandum of Walter White to James Weldon Johnson, February 1, 1926, NAACP Legal Files, "Sweet Case," Box D-86, LC. When the Detroit branch disbursed $1100 per man, the national office thought that was sufficient. "It is my opinion," said Walter White, "that $1100 having been paid to these men more than discharges whatever obligations, legal, moral or otherwise, to them. They have been amply paid—in fact much overpaid for their time and services." Ibid. But Rowlette, Mahoney, and Perry demanded the full $1500. They contended there was no reason why the national office should guarantee the fees of the white attorneys irrespective of local funds and not their own, and they further claimed that money raised in Detroit could easily have covered their salaries had not most of it been taken by the national office and earmarked for the white counsel. Moses L. Walker, vice-president of the Detroit branch NAACP, to James Weldon Johnson, February 16, 1926; Robert W. Bagnall to Johnson, February 18, 1926, both in ibid. When payment from New York was still not forthcoming, Rowlette threatened a public disclosure. Bagnall to Johnson, February

18, 1926, ibid. Soon thereafter the national office acquiesced and mailed checks for $400 to each of the black attorneys to close the matter. Walter White to Oscar W. Baker, March 5, 1926, ibid.

43. Interview of Cecil L. Rowlette, MHC.

44. Letters from Cecil L. Rowlette and J. W. Perry (one letter for each of the defendants) to the Honorable Frank Murphy, October 3, 1925, Recorder's Court File No. 60317-60318; *Sixteenth Annual Report of the N.A.A.C.P. for the Year 1925,* p. 13; interview of Cecil L. Rowlette, MHC; interview of Charles Mahoney, ibid.

45. Argument of Clarence Darrow in Michigan v. Sweet et al., commencing November 24, 1925, transcript, BHC; Argument of Arthur Garfield Hays, ibid. See Hays, *Let Freedom Ring,* pp. 195-233.

46. Walter White to Clarence Darrow, March 9, 1926, NAACP Legal Files, "Sweet Case," Box D-86, LC; "Memorandum of Long Distance Telephone Conversation Between Moses L. Walker of Detroit and Walter White, 9:00 P.M. Wednesday, October 7, 1925," dated October 8, 1925, ibid.; Mary White Ovington, *The Walls Came Tumbling Down* (New York: Harcourt, Brace and Co., 1947), p. 200; Haldeman-Julius, *Clarence Darrow's Two Great Trials,* pp. 48-49.

47. Interview of Cecil L. Rowlette, MHC.

48. *Detroit Times,* October 26, 27, and 28, 1925, November 3, 1925; *Detroit News,* November 2 and 3, 1925; *Detroit Free Press,* November 2, 1925. For Bowles' presence at a Detroit branch UNIA meeting again, in 1927, see *Negro World,* April 30, 1927; for UNIA-Klan ententes nationally, see Cronon, *Black Moses,* pp. 103, 188-90, 195, 222, 224.

49. Jackson, *The Ku Klux Klan in the City,* p. 141.

50. *Detroit Free Press,* October 31, 1925.

51. Ibid., November 1, 1925; ibid., November 2, 1925, p. 1; *Detroit Times,* November 2 and 3, 1925.

52. *Detroit Times,* October 30 and 31, 1925, November 4, 1925.

53. Hays, *Let Freedom Ring,* p. 198.

54. Ibid., p. 199; Haldeman-Julius, *Clarence Darrow's Two Great Trials,* p. 34.

55. See the *Detroit Free Press, Detroit News,* and *Detroit Times,* October 31, 1925, through November 5, 1925.

56. Opening statement of Robert M. Toms in Michigan v. Sweet et al., November 5, 1924, transcript, BHC.

57. Hays, *Let Freedom Ring,* pp. 203-08; testimony of Inspector Norton Schuknecht in Michigan v. Sweet et al., November 5, 1925, transcript, BHC; testimony of Lieutenant Paul Schellenberger, ibid.

58. Hays, *Let Freedom Ring,* pp. 208-09.

59. Ibid., p. 211.

60. *Detroit Free Press,* November 11, 1925.

61. Arthur Garfield Hays, *City Lawyer: The Autobiography of a Law Practice* (New York: Simon and Schuster, 1942), pp. xi-xii.

62. Tape-recorded interview of Judge Robert M. Toms by Alex Baskin, Detroit, Michigan, November 28, 1959, MHC.

63. *Detroit Free Press,* November 18, 1925.

64. *Detroit Times,* November 9, 1925; also Dancy, *Sand against the Wind,* p. 17.

65. *Detroit Free Press,* November 15 and 17, 1925.

66. *Detroit Free Press,* November 19, 1925, pp. 1, 8; Hays, *Let Freedom Ring,* pp. 225-26; Haldeman-Julius, *Clarence Darrow's Two Great Trials,* p. 15.

67. Argument of Clarence Darrow in Michigan v. Sweet et al., commencing November 24, 1925, transcript, BHC.

68. Interview of Robert M. Toms, MHC.

69. Text of Robert M. Toms' address, *Detroit Free Press,* November 26, 1925, p. 2.

70. Interview of Cecil L. Rowlette, MHC.

71. Judge Frank Murphy, Charge of the Court, November 25, 1925, from the files of Hilmer Gellein, court reporter; copy in author's possession, courtesy of Mr. Gellein.

72. *Detroit Times,* November 27 and 28, 1925; *Detroit Free Press,* November 27 and 28, 1925; Hays, *Let Freedom Ring,* pp. 231-32; White, *A Man Called White,* p. 78.

73. Memoranda of the City Wide Committee for Sweet Defense Fund, John C. Dancy, treasurer, Detroit Urban League Papers, Box 1, MHC; Dancy, *Sand against the Wind,* p. 25; tape-recorded interview of John C. Dancy by Alex Baskin, Detroit, Michigan, July 27, 1960, MHC; interview of Robert M. Toms, MHC.

The local fund-raising effort was not without its intramural squabbling. See especially Walter White to James Weldon Johnson, November 13, 1925, and Walter White to Moses Walker, December 12, 1925, NAACP Legal Files, "Sweet Case," Box D-86, LC.

74. Interview of Cecil L. Rowlette, MHC.

75. "Detroit Mob Violence Case," *Crisis* 32 (May 1926): 23; *Detroit News,* March 23, 1926; telegram of Arthur Garfield Hays to Clarence Darrow, March 22, 1926 (copy), NAACP Legal Files, "Sweet Case," Box D-86, LC.

"Confidentially," wrote Walter White to friend and associate Ira W. Jayne, "You know that the colored lawyers were of very little actual service in the first trial and would be of less service in the coming trial. However, we felt that there should be at least one colored lawyer in the case if for nothing more than effect. We felt that in engaging Mr. Perry to do nothing more really than to occupy a chair, $500 to $1,000 would be a liberal fee." Walter White to Ira W. Jayne, April 9, 1926, ibid. Jayne, a white man, was judge for the third judicial circuit of Michigan, which included Detroit and Wayne County, and was a member of the NAACP National Board of Directors representing Detroit.

76. White to Moses L. Walker, September 19, 1925, ibid., Box D-85, LC.

77. Tape-recorded interview of Thomas F. Chawke by Alex Baskin, Detroit, Michigan, August 4, 1960, MHC. Chawke received $7500 for participating in the second trial, though out of this he was to pay certain expenses for investigation of the jury panel. Thomas F. Chawke to Walter White, April 6, 1926, and James Weldon Johnson to Thomas F. Chawke, April 8, 1926, NAACP Legal Files, "Sweet Case," Box D-86, LC. The NAACP was upset that Chawke should be paid more as associate counsel than Darrow was receiving to head the defense, and put the matter to Darrow before making the final arrangements. Darrow replied that Chawke could not be had for less than $7500 and that for the services he would provide he was worth it, though Darrow did add that the man's personal interest in the case probably did not come up to his own. James Weldon Johnson to Darrow, April 3, 1926, and Darrow to Johnson, April 5, 1926, ibid.

78. Interview of Robert M. Toms, MHC.

79. There is no official transcript of the proceedings in the case of Michigan v. Henry Sweet, probably because there was no appeal. The NAACP may have had a transcript made for its own records, but it does not appear in the NAACP Legal Files. The trial, then, has to be reconstructed from other sources—particularly the Detroit press of April 20, 1926, through May 14, 1926, and the writing of Marcet Haldeman-Julius (*Clarence Darrow's Two Great Trials*), which includes some transcription of cross-examination. Copies of the opening and closing arguments of both the prosecution and defense, and a copy of Judge Frank Murphy's charge to the jury, are in the Burton Historical Collection.

80. Quoted in Haldeman-Julius, *Clarence Darrow's Two Great Trials*, pp. 60-61.

81. Quoted in ibid., pp. 65-66.

82. Interview of John C. Dancy by Alex Baskin, MHC; Dancy, *Sand against the Wind*, p. 27.

83. *Detroit Times*, May 7, 1926; *Detroit News*, May 8, 1926; *Detroit Free Press*, May 8, 1926.

84. *Argument of Clarence Darrow in the Case of Henry Sweet*, (New York: The National Association for the Advancement of Colored People, 1927), pp. 18, 36.

85. *Detroit Free Press*, May 14, 1926; *Detroit Times*, May 14, 1926. All charges against the others would be officially dropped by Prosecuting Attorney Robert M. Toms on July 12, 1927. Recorder's Court File No. 60317-60318; *Detroit News*, July 21, 1927; *Detroit Free Press*, July 22, 1927.

chapter
SIX

Epilogue

Detroit had changed greatly in the fifteen years from 1910 to 1925. People had been drawn to the city to work at its industry; they contributed to the city's growth; and they were sustained in return. A population of 465,766 in 1910 grew to nearly three times that (1,242,044) by 1925.[1]

Because of the sudden surge of numbers, Detroit progressives recognized the need for a sophisticated system of social control, based on the premise that the talented had a responsibility to lead and that their leadership must be in the service of the economic machine. From this rationale came the Ford English School and the Americanization Committee of the Detroit Board of Commerce.

But the problem of control was intensified by the consideration of race, as more and more of the newcomers were black, carried northward by the Great Migration. So the structure developed to fit the need, and in a short time, efficiency and organization in the interest of profit and social control produced the Urban League to educate blacks to the institutional expectations of northern life; delimitation of factory jobs by race to minimize nonproductive black-white rivalry; residential restriction, sanctioned by the courts, another thrust at racial disharmony; and a successful campaign to prohibit alcoholic beverages, which was itself intimately tied to the complete reorganization of Detroit city government.

There were few places of refuge for the black man in Detroit. One was to Garveyism and the UNIA, but the federal govenment would soon destroy that. Another was to the churches, and many joined; but the hand of the white man was sometimes even there. A few blacks would come to find meaning in the prophet of Islam.[2] Others turned to the local branch of the NAACP.[3]

The Detroit branch NAACP was founded in 1912. Within seven years it had 1053 members.[4] Membership in the branches was open to both races, but the executive offices were almost always in black hands (unlike the executive board of the national office, which was biracial). The branches served several functions. They provided local vigilance. They called attention to strivings and deeds of the national office. And they occasionally provided the parent body with capable administrative personnel, such as Robert Bagnall, who left Detroit for New York in 1921 to become director of branches.[5]

After Bagnall left, the Detroit branch was in constant difficulty. There were bitter factional disputes among the executive officers, with the result that for a time little real work was done.[6] More serious than this intramural bickering was the national office's suspicion that W. Hayes McKinney, Bagnall's successor as Detroit branch president, was embezzling NAACP funds.[7] There was the further allegation that the Detroit branch was appropriating money that belonged to the national office under the terms of the NAACP constitution and was using the money to enrich itself.[8] The parent body was livid. "The Board means business," wrote Bagnall to Fred H. Williams, new president of the Detroit branch, having succeeded McKinney, who stepped down, "and not only will it take legal action, but it will probably withdraw the charter of the branch, and announce to the Detroit public why it had to do so."[9]

The turmoil subsided when Judge Ira W. Jayne stepped in. Jayne, magistrate for the third judicial circuit in Michigan, was the only white man associated with the Detroit branch executive board and was also a member of the NAACP National Board of Directors representing Detroit. He now assumed the role of broker for NAACP monies. He would solicit funds from his social and professional acquaintances and would send the donations directly to New York. The national office would credit Detroit with the contribution and send a formal receipt to the donor. In this way the bulk of Detroit branch contributions would no longer have to go through the hands of its branch officers, and the money now flowed smoothly.[10]

The sources of supply Jayne tapped are familiar: Chester M. Culver, Roy Chapin, Mrs. Horace Dodge, Dodge Brothers Manufacturing Company, Fisher Body Corporation (which was, as stated, among the most restrictive of the Detroit automobile companies in its hiring practices), General Motors Corporation, J. L. Hudson Company, Fred Butzel, James Couzens, Edsel Ford, Mr. and Mrs. Tracy McGregor, Julian Krolik, Henry G. Stevens, and so on.[11] Jayne was sufficiently successful in his fund-raising efforts that he became circumspect. "I do not feel that I ought to press contributions from white people much more at this time," he wrote to New York in March 1924, "as it is well over $1,000 and is entirely out of proportion to the contribution made by the colored people and might be a just cause of criticism."[12] Meanwhile, Bagnall was berating Fred Williams because black subscriptions in Detroit for the entire year of 1924 amounted to only $69.80.[13] Again, the national office decided to reorganize the branch.[14]

In 1925, now under the leadership of the Reverend Robert L. Bradby, pastor of the Second Baptist Church,[15] the Detroit branch finally began to pursue some substantive issues.[16] A public swimming pool, to which some blacks had been denied entrance, was opened.[17] The Detroit Board of Education received an injunction issued by Judge Jayne enjoining it from further discrimination against some black school children in the sale of tickets to school-sponsored outings.[18] Three high school seniors from Highland Park denied the privilege of accompanying their class on a trip to the nation's capital were accorded the courtesies of the class after a court suit was brought against the Highland Park Board of Education.[19] A black construction worker who, on the job, had fired on and wounded three white men, including his foreman, in self-defense, was acquitted by an all-white jury, the case won by Cecil Rowlette, Julian Perry, and W. Hayes McKinney.[20]

And there had been, all the while, education for the ghetto in the form of Detroit branch bulletins periodically disseminated. "See that your windows are clean and hung with clean neat curtains." "When persons are sitting on your front porch see that they appear neat and clean." "If you have roomers do not permit them to put their feet on the porch railing or on your window sills." "If you have a place of business do not permit the grounds outside your door and in front of your show windows to be used as a Rest Room." "When we are grouped on corners, in stores, or any public place, let us not be boisterous in our manner; let us cultivate refinement. Let us stand erect on our feet and talk to those concerned and not to all in the block."[21]

With this achievement the Detroit branch NAACP stood, until the Sweet trials catapulted it into a greater prominence.

One problem in Detroit's immediate postwar period—housing—touched all others. For years it had been neglected, but now as the city's population and its racial components grew, the market need became apparent, and real-estate men hurriedly tried to build houses for the population increase. There was a frenzied air to the construction and a great question overriding the whole effort: could enough homes be thrown up fast enough to avoid a confrontation between the races for the limited housing then available?

So the ancient racial hatreds and the exigencies of the current situation carried Detroit into the frightful summer of 1925. By the time the summer was over, there had been death in the streets. Yet what had the Sweet incident, with the agony of the subsequent trial, actually proved? Did a studied reflection follow the catharsis? Was there self-examination? Or were attitudes and policies essentially unaltered?

The answer, brutally, is that it proved nothing at all. No man ever lived more in vain than Ossian Sweet. There are two ways to demonstrate this: in the effect of events on himself and his family; and, more broadly, in their impact, or lack thereof, on Detroit. For Ossian Sweet personally there was a horrible irony. He was a man who had followed all the rules. He had worked his way from difficult beginnings, studied to be a physician, established a successful practice, married and had a family. He had accepted his responsibilities as a citizen in a city particularly interested in educating its members to those responsibilities. Yet the reality of Detroit in 1925 was that black men who moved into white neighborhoods did so at considerable peril, and black men who were educated and responsible were no different from black men who were not. Ossian Sweet, never an innocent in matters of race, decided to confront that peril, and he suffered for it.

Nothing went right for him afterwards. His wife contracted tuberculosis—from the damp Detroit jail, some said—and she died a year after the second trial. His baby daughter also succumbed. His brother Henry Sweet finished his studies, passed the Michigan bar, and was practicing law in Detroit when he too developed tuberculosis and died in 1940. Ossian Sweet, who lived for more than twenty years in the house on Garland, became lonely and haunted.[22] At the age of sixty-four he took his own life in his office at 1700 Chene. He had shot himself behind the right ear with a .32 caliber revolver.[23]

For Detroit as a whole, problems persisted, and patterns and methods remained much the same. The city's population continued to grow— 1,600,000 people in 1940, of whom 150,000 were blacks; 1,850,000 people in 1950, of whom 300,000 were blacks; a seething urban sprawl by 1960 and bigger still in 1970, with 480,000 blacks (1960) increasing to 660,000 (1970).[24] And housing remained the critical problem. In 1943, a year in the path of a second Great Migration, there was an urgent shortage of dwelling space, especially for black people still circumscribed by clearly defined residential boundaries.[25] In that year too there was a bloody race riot.

The apparent connection between housing shortages and racial conflagration held in 1967. The key indicator here is Federal Housing Administration rental vacancy rates. Every spring the FHA makes a survey of the rental housing projects on which it holds insurance. The figures usually run only a little higher than the vacancy rate for the real-estate market as a whole and can therefore be considered an index.

In 1964 the vacancy rate for the jurisdiction of the Detroit insuring office was 6.2 percent, reflecting a fair balance between supply and demand. In 1965 the FHA rental vacancy rate dropped almost in half, to 3.7 percent, which was well below the national average. This sharp decline did not parallel the national trend, which showed an increase between 1964 and 1965 from 6.3 percent to 6.5 percent. In 1966 the situation became critical. The vacancy rate in Detroit dropped further, to 1.4 percent, compared to the national rate of 5.7 percent. New housing starts in Detroit were also down, thereby putting an inordinate pressure on the existing housing supply. In 1967 the FHA rental vacancy rate dropped to 1.0 percent, compared to the national aveareage of 5.6 percent. Of the fifty-three insuring offices in the United States, the Detroit office, along with the Grand Rapids office, had the next-to-lowest vacancy rate.[26]

If racial conflagration sparked by housing shortages was one persistent theme in Detroit after 1926, another was racial antagonism in once all-white neighborhoods. In the autumn following the second Sweet trial, Ossian Sweet's attorney Julian Perry moved his family into a new home on South Marlborough, near Grosse Pointe Park. The house was attacked with stench bombs; the Perry fled.[27]

In January and February 1928 a black who had moved into a house on Maybury Grand was met with threats, gunshots, and violence to the property. Police stood by passively.[28]

In April 1928 a black man bought a house on Scotten. Soon a sign was nailed to the wall: "Nigger do not move in the building or we will blow it up."[29]

In August 1928 residents of the 4000 block of Twenty-Eighth Street, near Tireman, petitioned the mayor in objection to several black families, including twelve children, who were occupying a single eight-room house at number 4037. They complained of noise and profanity and that some of the black people were urinating out the window.[30]

Another development with roots in the past was the invasion by whites of residential territory once all black. As the city grew outward, white middle-class families began to settle near the black subdivision on Eight Mile Road. By 1940 the blacks were surrounded. They could not get loans through the FHA because they did not live in strict segregation. Nor would the FHA approve mortgages on white people's homes in racially mixed areas. So in 1941 a white real-estate developer built a concrete wall six feet high, a foot thick, and a half-mile long to separate the racial settlements. The FHA then approved the white families' loans.[31]

Control of housing through restrictive covenants continued in Detroit as elsewhere until 1948, when the United States Supreme Court declared the practice unconstitutional. One of the cases heard by the high court (McGhee v. Sipes) came out of Detroit. The plaintiff, Orsel McGhee, a Detroit black, had purchased a house on Seebaldt Street, within two blocks of a densely populated black area. But the house was on the white side of Tireman Avenue, which in 1945 served as the dividing line between the white and black sections.[32]

The leadership of the Detroit Urban League was derivative. Henry G. Stevens was succeeded as chairman of the Urban League board by a professional realtor, Kenneth L. Moore. Moore served until he became suspicious of Communist sympathies in a black Urban League spokesman from New York. He resigned and was followed by Mrs. George M. Black, a niece of Henry Stevens', a prominent socialite, and president of the Detroit Junior League. Three more white people then sat as chairmen before Dr. Remus G. Robinson, a surgeon, became in 1950 the first black to hold the position.[33] Francis Kornegay, a man who had spent seventeen years in National Urban League affairs, succeeded John Dancy as director in 1960.[34]

Careers continued on the course one might have predicted. James Couzens became a United States senator. Robert Toms was elected judge of the circuit court. Lester Moll too became a judge. Forrester B. Washington was appointed director of the Atlanta University School of Social Work. Charles Mahoney would be commissioner of labor under four Michigan governors and in 1954 a United States delegate to the United Nations. Walter White succeeded James Weldon Johnson as principal officer of the NAACP. Charles Bowles was elected judge of Recorder's Court in 1926 and finally mayor in 1929. He was recalled less than eight months after his inauguration—programs of economy in government were not popular in 1930—and was replaced by Frank Murphy, who went on to be governor-general of the Philippine Islands, governor of Michigan, United States attorney general under Franklin Roosevelt, and associate justice of the United States Supreme Court.

Henry Ford would maintain his eminence and his power to his death, though for years Ford Motor Company profits dwindled. Clarence Darrow, Arthur Garfield Hays, and Thomas Chawke practiced their professions. Otis Sweet practiced his. Henry Glover Stevens continued his philanthropies and civic duties until his death in 1934. Fred Butzel also remained active in community affairs, becoming chairman of the executive committee of the Jewish Welfare Federation and president of the Detroit Community Union in addition to his work on the Urban League board. John Dancy never left Detroit. He remained at the Urban League for forty-two years, finally retiring in 1960 at age seventy-two.

The laborious fact-finding by importantly conceived, ceremoniously commissioned civic authority continued. In the spring of 1926, as a direct result of the preceding year's racial violence, Mayor John Smith created a committee to study conditions among black people in Detroit. The committee was chaired by the Reverend Reinhold Niebuhr and included in its membership Fred Butzel, W. Hayes McKinney, Donald Marshall, and the presidents of the Detroit Board of Commerce, the Detroit Bar Association, and the Detroit Citizens League. The Detroit Community Fund appropriated $10,000 to finance the study. Research was directed by Forrester B. Washington. In four months the survey staff compiled an impressive amount of data. ("Our office was practically their headquarters," said Dancy.) It treated population, industry, thrift and business, housing, health, recreation, education, crime, religion, community organization, and welfare. The study was called *The Negro in Detroit*. One hundred copies were printed; most have disappeared.[35]

Facts were there to be pondered. The survey had spent much of its energy examining the assertion that blacks depress property values. If the charge is true in Detroit, the researchers decided, a large part of the blame must be placed on banks. They have witnessed a retreat of white people from certain areas of the city and have contracted credit to the black people arriving in the wake. Expectations are thus fulfilled, new prophecies reinforced.[36] The survey studied a residential area on Harding Avenue, a white neighborhood that was for some time an agonized recipient of black arrivals. The representative block chosen for the survey—between Canfield and Warren, not far from Ossian Sweet's house on Garland—was tense with hatred in 1926. But the researchers could find no evidence that any white person who had sold his house to a black and fled, whether he had sold early or late, had received from the black purchaser less money than he might have been offered by the market under more normal circumstances. Frequently, the black buyer was willing to pay more.[37]

Depressed value, then, to whom? To black people? Given a shortage of housing, amplified for blacks by explicit race restrictions, the value of a house suddenly available outside the ghetto can soar. To white people? If unable to abide black neighbors, their property is indeed depreciated, but that assessment is visceral not economic, and would probably not be reflected in the marketplace.[38]

Nor should blacks be blamed for a decline in property values already underway before their entry.[39] In a society structured largely around residential segregation, any significant movement of blacks into an area is probably reflective of rather then responsible for deteriorating conditions. White Americans frequently romanticize the "old neighborhood," but their energies have always been directed toward the new and the untouched. Neighborhoods grow old and are discarded, and they are then traditionally taken by the only people for whom they still have any real value.

The facts were there, but the complexities were crushing, and the facts gathered dust. "The Negro problem presents one different in every respect from that of any other racial group," reported the Americanization Committee in 1919, "for in Detroit it is impossible for a Negro man or woman to secure decent quarters for self or family. His presence as a resident is not tolerated in many sections of the city. He is compelled to live in the slum districts."[40] It was structured exclusion. The black man was different because he was segregated. He was segregated because he was different. And only for black men were the restrictions given the full force of law.

On the first day of the new year 1915, the *Detroit News* ran an editorial called "A New Year's Wish for Detroit," in which the Spirit of Progress asked a citizen what he would wish for the city. The citizen replied:

> I wish it to be a good place to live in; supremely that—a good place to live in. . . .
> I wish all plagues stopped at their sources: the plague of preventable disease; the plague of unnecessary hardness; the plague of inhuman greed that lives off others; the plague of indifference to a brother's welfare; the plague of thinking we are not one family within this great and many-chambered house we call Detroit. . . .
> I wish it to be a city where life holds the first place, and the means of life are made secondary.[41]

In the next eleven years something harsher than the citizen of 1915 would have liked occurred in Detroit. The city took on in its social and political forms all of the qualities of its awesome economic base. It became machined, business-like, efficient. This was the legacy of the progressive period, and that legacy carried its price. Were the citizen of 1915 to look into the future he would find a city still worshipping the Spirit of Progress but with the plague of hardness deep into many things.

NOTES

1. Detroit Bureau of Governmental Research, *The Negro in Detroit,* sect. 2, *Population,* p. 5.

2. Sometime during the summer of 1930 a strange man, a peddler, appeared in the Detroit black ghetto. Some thought he was a Palestinian Arab, others a Jamaican black. His name was W.D. Fard. He called himself a prophet, saying he was on a mission for the one true God "whose right and proper name is Allah." He took up residence in Detroit's ghetto, and tried to teach the people there "a knowledge of self" by introducing them to the Quran, the Islamic holy book; by helping them relive, if only in fantasy, the glorious history of Black Afro-Asia; and by speaking to the glorious possibilities of the black man in a world he avowed was only temporarily dominated by the "blue-eyed devils." Within four years Fard had some 8000 followers in Detroit. It was the beginning of what came to be known as the Black Muslim church in America. See C. Eric Lincoln, *The Black Muslims in America* (Boston: Beacon Press, 1961), pp. 10-17; also Erdmann Doane Beynon, "The Voodoo Cult among Negro Migrants in Detroit," *The American Journal of Sociology* 43 (May 1938): 894-907.

3. The following account of the Detroit branch NAACP is based largely on the correspondence, memoranda, press releases, membership lists, and clippings in the NAACP Branch Files, "Detroit, Michigan," LC. Additional source material is located in the NAACP Legal Files, "Sweet Case," LC. Another source for the post-1926 period is the Moses L. Walker Papers, MHC. Walker was a longtime officer (including president) of the Detroit branch NAACP.

4. See "The Story of the Branches for 1918," *Crisis* 17 (April 1919): 284, for a list of NAACP branches with their date of founding and membership as of March 1919.

5. For additional information on the branches, see Kellogg, *NAACP,* vol. 1, pp. 117-37.

6. Maud S. Henderson, secretary, Detroit branch NAACP, to Robert W. Bagnall, March 5, 1923; Bagnall to Henderson, March 12, 1923. Both in NAACP Branch Files, "Detroit, Michigan," Box G-95, LC.

7. Robert W. Bagnall to Lillian E. Johnson, secretary, Detroit branch NAACP, March 10, 1922; Bagnall to W. Hayes McKinney, June 8, 1922; Lillian E. Johnson to Bagnall, August 5, 1922; Bagnall to Lillian E. Johnson, August 18, 1922; William Pickens, field secretary, NAACP, to James Weldon Johnson, January 16, 1924. Ibid.

8. Telegram of James Weldon Johnson to Hon. Ira W. Jayne, Detroit, Michigan, December 31, 1923; telegram of James Weldon Johnson to W.

Hayes McKinney, December 31, 1923; Addie W. Hunton, field secretary, NAACP, "Report on Detroit for Judge Jayne" [January 1924] ; William Pickens to Bagnall, January 14, 1924; telegram of Bagnall to Pickens, Detroit, Michigan, January 14, 1924; Pickens to James Weldon Johnson, January 16, 1924; James Weldon Johnson to Maud S. Henderson, January 16, 1924. Ibid.

9. Bagnall to Williams, January 18, 1924, ibid.

10. Jayne to James Weldon Johnson, December 28, 1923; Addie W. Hunton to Jayne, December 31, 1923; Jayne to the NAACP, New York, with contribution checks enclosed, February 18, 1924, February 19, 1924, February 9, 1925, February 16, 1925, February 19, 1925, February 25, 1925; also Jayne to James Weldon Johnson, June 15, 1925, May 7, 1928, May 12, 1928. Ibid.

11. "Contributors List from Detroit" [1924], ibid.; "Detroit Contributors," 1924, 1925, NAACP Legal Files, "Sweet Case," Box D-85, LC.

12. Jayne to NAACP, New York, March 24, 1924, NAACP Branch Files, "Detroit, Michigan," Box G-95, LC.

13. Bagnall to Williams, December 23, 1924, ibid. Also see Bagnall to Williams, February 6, 1925, ibid.

14. Bagnall to Williams, December 23, 1924; "Memo. from Mr. Bagnall to Mr. Johnson," December 22, 1924. Ibid.

15. "Detroit N.A.A.C.P. Reorganized; Rev. Robert L. Bradby, New President" (News release dated March 6, 1925), ibid.; *Detroit Independent*, May 30, 1925.

16. Particularly vigilant was the branch's Junior Division, a group of 556 young men and women (nominally under age twenty-one) directed by Mrs. Buelah Young. They were the first to call attention to the discriminations involving the public swimming pool, the Detroit Board of Education, and the Highland Park class trip discussed in the text. The juniors clearly found the lethargy of the seniors exasperating. "We did not think it wise to become affiliated with an organization [the senior branch in Detroit] that has no program to offer those of us over twenty-one years of age," wrote five members of the juniors' executive committee to Bagnall in August 1925. "We have paid our one dollar memberships, but why stay in a stagnant pool when there is so much work and so many problems facing us in Detroit that must be solved?" William M. Jones, president, and four others to Robert W. Bagnall, August 4, 1925; also reply of Robert W. Bagnall to Miss James [sic] Frances Green, executive secretary, August 8, 1925. Both in NAACP Branch Files, "Detroit Michigan," Box G-95, LC.

The juniors were an embarrassment to the branch's new president,

Robert L. Bradby. Their estrangement was apparent to everyone, and Detroit was once again providing an organizational headache for the New York office. Bradby suspected the juniors were going to seek their own charter from the parent body. The young people may have been flirting with this idea, but no direct request was ever made. A separate charter would not have been granted, in any case.

See Buelah Young to Bagnall, July 10, 1925; Bagnall to Young, July 21, 1925, July 29, 1925; Robert L. Bradby to James Weldon Johnson, July 27, 1925; Bagnall to Bradby, July 28, 1925; Bradby to Bagnall, August 5, 1925; Bagnall to Bradby, August 7, 1925; also "Suggestions for Work for Former Juniors Who Have Been Transferred to the Branch" [August 1925]. All in ibid. Also, on the Detroit branch Junior Division, see "Boys and Girls of Detroit," *Crisis* 28 (October 1924): 272-74.

17. *Detroit Independent,* April 3 and May 30, 1925.

18. *Detroit Independent,* June 19, 1925.

19. *Detroit Independent,* May 30, 1925; "Detroit N.A.A.C.P. Wins Three Cases for Colored People" (News release dated June 5, 1925). NAACP Branch Files, "Detroit, Michigan," Box G-95, LC.

20. "Statement of Facts," in Michigan v. Lee Sullivan [May ? 1925]. NAACP Branch Files, "Detroit, Michigan," Box G-95, LC; "Detroit N.A.A.C.P. Wins Three Cases for Colored People," ibid.; *Detroit Independent,* May 30, 1925.

21. Bulletin No. 2, Detroit Branch, NAACP, April 22, 1921. NAACP Branch Files, "Detroit, Michigan," Box G-95, LC; Also see Bulletin No. 1, September 13, 1920. Ibid.

22. Interview of Otis Sweet, MHC; White, *A Man Called White,* p. 79; *Detroit News,* January 21, 1940; *Michigan Chronicle,* August 25, 1945; *Detroit City Directories,* 1928-29, 1957.

23. *Detroit Free Press,* March 20, 1960; *Detroit City Directory, 1957;* Detroit telephone directories, 1959, 1960.

24. U.S. Department of Commerce, Bureau of the Census, *Sixteenth Census of the United States, 1940, Population,* vol. 2, *Characteristics of the Population,* pt. 3 (Washington, D.C.: Government Printing Office, 1943), p. 889; U.S. Department of Commerce, Bureau of the Census, *U.S. Census of Population, 1950,* vol. 3, *Census Tract Statistics,* chap. 17, "Detroit, Michigan" (Washington, D.C.: Government Printing Office, 1952), p. 7; U.S. Department of Commerce, Bureau of the Census, *U.S. Census of Population, 1960,* vol. 1, *Characteristics of the Population,* pt. 24, "Michigan" (Washington, D.C.: Government Printing Office, 1963), pp. 76, 77, 79; U.S. Department of Commerce, Bu-

reau of the Census, *Census of Population, 1970. General Social and Economic Characteristics. Final Report PC (1)–C 24 Michigan* (Washington, D.C: Government Printing Office, 1972), pp. 24-237, 24-371. Proliferation of urban populations and the consequent changes in statistical definitions of "city" make it difficult to show decennial increases for a place over an extended period. In 1960 and 1970 the United States Censuses of Population considered Detroit in three ways—as part of a massive "standard metropolitan statistical area" of 3,762,360 persons (1960) and 4,119,923 persons (1970); as part of a somewhat smaller "urbanized area"; and as a considerably smaller "urban place." The designation "urban place" most nearly corresponds to all earlier U.S. census definitions; therefore, the figures for the 1960 and 1970 Detroit black population are taken from this designation.

25. Robert C. Weaver, *The Negro Ghetto* (New York: Harcourt, Brace and Co., 1948), pp. 114-16 and map, p. 101.

26. Metropolitan Federal Savings and Loan Association of Detroit, *The Quarterly Indicator on Savings and Housing*, vol. 4 (October 1967).

27. *Detroit Times*, clipping ca. autumn 1926, in scrapbook, "Henry Sweet" reading room file, BHC; *The Owl* (Detroit), January 21, 1927.

28. W. Hayes McKinney to Honorable John C. Lodge, mayor of the City of Detroit, and Honorable William P. Rutledge, police commissioner, January 13, 1928; McKinney to Lodge and Rutledge, February 9, 1928. Mayor's Office Papers, 1928, Box 2, "Inter-racial Commission" folder, BHC.

29. Wm. D. McDaniel, president, The West Side Improvement Association, to Mayor John Lodge, April 26, 1928, ibid.

30. Petition to Honorable John C. Lodge, mayor of the City of Detroit, signed by twenty-five residents of the neighborhood [August 1928], ibid. The action taken by the city was to dispatch an investigator to see if overcrowding in the dwelling was sufficiently severe to warrant evicting the tenants. The inspector found the second floor of the two-story house empty, and eight people on the first floor indicated they were planning to vacate within a month. [Illegible name], chief sanitary engineer, Department of Health, City of Detroit, to Ralph E. Quinn, secretary, office of the Mayor, August 16, 1928, ibid.

31. Black, "Restrictive Covenants," pp. 41, 48; Lester Velie, "Housing: Detroit's Time Bomb," *Collier's* 118 (November 23, 1946): 14.

32. Shelley v. Kraemer, McGhee v. Sipes, 334 U.S. 1 (1948); Dancy, *Sand against the Wind*, p. 215.

33. Dancy, *Sand against the Wind*, pp. 96-98, 243-44; list of Detroit

Urban League board chairmen, from the files of Mrs. Theresa M. Moss, Detroit Urban League, Detroit, Michigan.

34. Interview with Mr. Francis A. Kornegay, Detroit, Michigan, April 13, 1967.

35. In addition to the study itself, which has been frequently cited herein, see the following: *Report of the Mayor's Committee on Race Relations* (Detroit, 1926); Bruno Lasker, "The Negro in Detroit: Review of the Report of the Mayor's Committee on Race Relations," *Survey* 58 (April 15, 1927): 72-73; Report of the Director to the Urban League Board, September 16, 1926, Detroit Urban League Papers, Box 1, MHC; Detroit Urban League Board, Minutes, January 27, 1927, ibid., Box 2; John C.Dancy to the Rev. Rheinold [*sic*] Niebuhr, January 31, 1927, ibid.; John C.Dancy to W. C. Donnell, April 1, 1930, ibid.; Arna Bontemps and Jack Conroy, *They Seek a City* (Garden City, N.Y.: The Country Life Press, 1945), p. 230; Dancy, *Sand against the Wind,* pp. 218-20.

36. Detroit Bureau of Governmental Research, *The Negro in Detroit,* sect. 4, *Thrift and Business,* p. 5.

37. Ibid., sect. 5, *Housing,* pp. 46-58, especially pp. 51-53.

38. The most comprehensive study yet made of price trends in house sales in middle-class, home-owning neighborhoods undergoing nonwhite entry, compared with price trends in comparable neighborhoods without nonwhite entry, is Luigi Laurenti, *Property Values and Race: Studies in Seven Cities* (Berkeley and Los Angeles: University of California Press, 1961). On the basis of this research, Laurenti reached two broad conclusions:

> *First,* price changes which can be connected with the fact of nonwhite entry are not uniform, as often alleged, but diverse. Depending on circumstances, racial change in a neighborhood may be depressing or it may be stimulating to real estate prices and in varying degrees. *Second,* considering all of the evidence, the odds are about four to one that house prices in a neighborhood entered by nonwhites will keep up with or exceed prices in a comparable all-white area. These conclusions are chiefly based on observations of real estate markets in a period of generally rising prices. This period, moreover, was characterized by unusually strong demand for housing, particularly by nonwhites who had been making relatively large gains in personal income. These conditions seem likely to continue into the foreseeable future. [Pp. 52-53.]

For a much less comprehensive but nevertheless useful study of Detroit property values, see Richard Marks, "The Impact of Negro Population Movement on Property Values in a Selected Area in Detroit" (Report written for the City of Detroit, Mayor's Interracial Committee, January 16, 1950). Copy in the Municipal Reference Library, City-County Building, Detroit, Michigan.

Laurenti's conclusions would seem to hold for Russel Woods, the residential area northwest of downtown Detroit, which began experiencing nonwhite entry in the mid-1950s. See Mayer, "Russel Woods: Change without Conflict," pp. 202-09.

39. See Detroit Bureau of Governmental Research, *The Negro in Detroit*, sect. 5, *Housing*, p. 32.

40. *The Detroiter*, December 15, 1919, pp. 1-2.

41. "A New Year's Wish for Detroit," *Detroit News*, January 1, 1915, p. 4.

Index

ABOUT THE AUTHOR

David Allan Levine was professor of history at Wayne State
University from 1968 to 1974. He obtained his B.A. in
American civilization at Brandeis University in 1963, his M.A.
in history at the University of Chicago in 1965, and his Ph.D.
at the University of Chicago in 1970.

$13.50

DETROIT PUBLIC LIBRARY

The number of books that may be
drawn at one time by the card holder
is governed by the reasonable needs of
the reader and the material on hand.
Books for junior readers are subject
to special rules.